Brit at the Ballpark

Brit at the Ballpark

An Englishman's Baseball Tour of All 50 States

PETER TAYLOR

McFarland & Company, Inc., Publishers
Jefferson, North Carolina, and London

LIBRARY OF CONGRESS CATALOGUING-IN-PUBLICATION DATA

Taylor, Peter (Peter A.)
    Brit at the ballpark : an englishman's baseball tour of all 50
states / Peter Taylor.
        p.   cm.
    Includes bibliographical references and index.

    ISBN 978-0-7864-6460-9
    softcover : 50# alkaline paper ∞

    1. Baseball fields — United States — Guidebook.   2. Stadiums —
United States — Guidebooks.   3. Baseball — United States.
4. Minor league baseball — United States.   5. Taylor, Peter (Peter
A.) — Travel.   I. Title.
GV879.5.T39   2011
796.357'640973 — dc23   2011025430

BRITISH LIBRARY CATALOGUING DATA ARE AVAILABLE

© 2011 Peter Taylor. All rights reserved

Front cover design by David Landis (Shake It Loose Graphics)

Manufactured in the United States of America

McFarland & Company, Inc., Publishers
    Box 611, Jefferson, North Carolina 28640
    www.mcfarlandpub.com

To all those who made the journey possible; those who gave me gifts and encouragement beforehand, who provided me with contacts, hospitality or food and drink, gave me tickets, offered me an upgrade on my car; those whom I met along the way, and who shared a smile and showed an interest; those who diagnosed my eye problem, operated on me and nursed me back to health.

Thank you those who travelled with me, for a few miles or for many, and shared the experience. Thank you those who stayed at home and held the fort, and who made sure I had a brand new granddaughter waiting for me.

The names are too many to list, but you know who you are.

But most of all this is for my darling wife Sally; my inspiration, my determination, my base camp, my angel of mercy, my chauffeuse, my mascot, the love of my life. Thanks Sal! I couldn't, and wouldn't, have done it without you. This is for you.

Table of Contents

Table of Contents

Preface

Why would a reasonably sane, 56-year-old Englishman give up his home, family and work for seven months to travel the length and breadth of the United States?

It all started one evening in 2002 or 2003. I didn't note the exact date as it didn't seem significant at the time. My wife and I were enjoying a meal in our local Indian restaurant. "What would you do if you could start over again?" she asked me. I came up with the tactically adroit answer of meeting her ten years earlier, and was scoffed at. "No, I mean in job terms," she clarified.

I had enjoyed an 18-year teaching career, and was now working for the Office for National Statistics; a good, enjoyable job, but not exactly a vocation. My wife, Sally, is a wonderfully supportive woman, whose opinion of me is much higher than my own, and she could see me cruising lazily towards retirement.

"I would be a sports journalist," I ventured.

"So why don't you?" she demanded.

"Why don't I what?"

"Why don't you become a sports journalist?"

"Because nobody would take me on."

"How do you know if you've never tried?" she persisted.

"Okay," I conceded, "Even if I could find an editor of a local paper crazy enough to take me on as a cub reporter, he would want me to go out and write about Banbury Town vs. Daventry United. If I was a decent sports journalist, by the time I'm this age I would want to be at the Bernabeu writing about Real Madrid vs. Barcelona."

She went quiet, but it was just a pause. "So if you could write about anything to do with sport, what would it be?" she asked.

I didn't even have to think, as it was something I had surmised on previous occasions. I had begun to fall in love with baseball some five years earlier, when Channel 5 started to broadcast live games throughout the summer. Not only was I attracted to the game, I was fascinated by the devotion of those that love the game, and by the genuine respect that is paid to the game's heroes, both past and present.

1

"I would travel around the United States, visit each of the 30 major league ballparks, and write about my experiences."

"So why don't you?" was the inevitable enquiry. I came up with the obvious, but nonetheless appropriate, responses: job, family, elderly mother, mortgage. Each one was swatted aside by a woman now truly on her game and, weakened by lamb dupiaza, brinjal bhaji and a couple of pints of Kingfisher, I began to concede that it might just be an excellent thing to do.

We had last visited the States in October 2001. My cousin lives in Virginia Beach with her husband, and we had been invited to the wedding of their daughter. Being October, baseball was in its post–season phase, so there was no chance of seeing a game. We had, however, walked admiringly around the outside of the ballparks in Pittsburgh and Boston, and had also paid a visit to the marvellous Baseball Hall of Fame in Cooperstown, New York. So at the time my plan was in its conception, I had not even seen a professional baseball game live.

Over the next couple of years, the plan was lovingly nurtured, mainly in my head. My first thought was that, if I limited my trip to major league ballparks, there would be an awful lot of the States that I would miss. New Orleans, just as an example, does not have a major league team. So I came up with the idea of seeing a baseball game in every state that does not have a major league team. If I visit every state, I'll see the whole country!

I made a tentative enquiry to my employer, and met no resistance. Christmas and birthdays saw a regular supply of books about ballparks, road trips, and baseball trivia come my way. By 2004, when we next visited the States for the wedding of my cousin's other offspring, I had a fairly firm plan, and was able to talk reasonably convincingly about it. I also saw my first professional ballgame!

When my interest in the game had begun to develop, I had decided that I could not be a real fan unless I supported a team. But which one? I have always been a severe critic of people who support teams just because they are the best. But, not living in the States, I was unable to apply either of my normal criteria of inheritance or locality. One day, whilst watching one of my favourite films, *Blues Brothers*, I watched the scene where Elmore gives the police his address. It turns out to be Wrigley Field, home of the Chicago Cubs. That was it, I was a Cubs fan!

The more I discovered about the Cubs, the more convinced I became that I'd made the right decision. The lovable losers, the curse of the Billy Goat, the ivy-covered outfield wall at Wrigley. This was the team for me — long years of failure that must one day end.

So our 2004 trip began in Chicago, and we managed to secure three tickets (our younger daughter, Nina, was travelling with us) for the Cubs vs. the Mets at Wrigley Field. The Cubs won, and Matt Clement threw 14 strikeouts! It was all I had hoped for and more. The die was cast.

The year 2006 was earmarked for the trip, until my other daughter, Anya, decided that was when she was getting married. So 2007 it was, and preparations began in earnest. In theory it was easy; decide upon which way around the continent I wanted to go, work out which towns and cities had baseball clubs, and we're away. Fill in the gaps with sites of baseball trivia, and a splendid itinerary presents itself.

In August 2005, I was offered a promotion at work, initially on a temporary basis. By now I was so committed to the trip that I double-checked with my new boss that the trip could still go ahead before accepting the job on a permanent basis. He was totally supportive, even making the job permanent before I left, so that I could still have it when I returned.

Early in 2007, the clubs published their fixture lists, and then the fun began. Because of the distances involved, baseball teams do not play alternate home and away series, as is the norm in many sports. They have home stands and road trips. So my hypothetical itinerary may have, for example, a visit to Florida during the third week of April, when the schedule sees the Marlins on the road for the whole of that week. Add to that the need to be in Alaska on June 21st, and San Francisco on July 10th, for two special games, when my plans had me in San Francisco first! So the original, logical route had to alter, and eventually contained lots of U-turns, doglegs and other such inanities due to the whims of the schedule.

Next came the clubs; when I had worked out exactly which games I would attend — there were 65 of them — I wrote to each of the clubs, asking for free tickets. Most ignored me completely, but those that did reply were, in the main, extremely generous. Perhaps 12 clubs promised me free tickets; one club in Oregon offered me two tickets in exchange for a copy of my book; a club in Connecticut thought what I was doing was applaudable, and offered to give me tickets in the owner's seats, to introduce me to the crowd, and let me throw out the first pitch.

My own beloved Cubs, however, pointed out that they sell out every home game, all 81 of them, and wondered why they needed to give tickets away. I suppose you can't fault their logic.

By this time support had started to pour in from family and friends. My dear friend and neighbour, Greg, is American by birth, and has a large family and many friends still living there. Similarly I have a long-standing friend living in Pittsburgh, Steve, who also opened up a large network of family and friends whose hospitality was mine to abuse. My Christmas present from Greg was a computer programme which would show me the way around the entire continent.

Plane tickets were relatively easy to book; a day trip to London was needed to obtain a visa from the U.S. embassy. The fact that it was for six months, and my trip was scheduled to last seven was, I was told, not a problem, and I could sort it out with the Immigration Department on my arrival.

I had weighed up the pros and cons of buying a car against renting one, and decided on the latter. An exploratory e-mail to one company was answered by an enthusiastic phone call: "If anyone wants one of my cars for seven months, I'm very interested! How do you fancy a double upgrade?" So I was to be billed for an economy model, but receive something more salubrious.

My friends and family were amazingly supportive, throwing advice, gifts and even money in my direction. A friend from school days sent me a survival pack: a miniature of Scotch, a sachet of HP sauce, a packet of pork scratchings, and a $50 bill to have a few beers and send him a couple of postcards.

By the last week of March the phone calls of support were coming in thick and fast. A farewell dinner with my family produced fine speeches, and a wallet of photographs so that I could keep them with me.

Finally, on Sunday, April 1, April Fools' Day, the time had come!

Virginia
Monday April 2–Thursday April 5

The promise that my need for an extended stay would not be a problem proves unfounded. The immigration people at JFK can do nothing to help me, but take so long to tell me this that I miss my connection. So the first night of my trip, scheduled to be spent in my cousin's comfortable home, is transferred to a seedy airport motel.

Monday morning, my 6:30 shuttle waits in the cold and foggy car park. The other passengers are a Puerto Rican and his wife, off to see his mother in the old country. He's wearing a Yankees jacket, thus giving an early impetus to the baseball content of my journey.

I am writing this book for an audience, some of whom know little or nothing about baseball. Rather than explaining the game in detail at the beginning, I intend to explain things as we go along. The Yankees are one of the two New York teams, and have been the dominant team of the last century. Their emblem is franchised worldwide, and is even worn by people who have no idea what it means. They are to American baseball what Manchester United is to English football.

My fellow passenger learns all about my trip, and my own affiliation with the Cubs. I assure him that the last page of my book is already written, with the Cubs beating the Yankees in Game 7 of the World Series. He smiles politely and wishes me luck.

Check-in and security comes and goes and, just when I think it's time for a cup of coffee, the flight is called. Still in transatlantic mind-set, I go through boarding, and suddenly trip over what turns out to be the plane taking me to Norfolk. It has "made by Airfix" on the side, and propellers! I'm not put off by the propellers, so much as the ground crew putting the big key in the side to wind them up.

Needs must, however, and this 34-seater plane takes off to show me that, above the New York fog, it's a lovely, sunny day. Soon we descend into a beautiful Virginia coastline and Norfolk airport, where I'm met by my cousin Pam and her friend Liz but, sadly, not by my luggage.

We decide to get my hire car, and I know I'm going to confuse someone. I have booked a 212-day hire, when the normal limit is 45. The assistant is a prime target for confusion. She photocopies my UK driving licence, because she can, and stares blankly at the papers until her colleague does some prompting. I eventually succeed in my mission, only to be told to bring the car back on May 25!

No, make that October!!

Overcoming these setbacks, we proceed to the car park, where I find out why I got such a good deal on the car. It has no gearstick, only two pedals, and the steering wheel on the wrong side. I have never before driven a left-hand drive, nor an automatic. My car rental company has given me an upgrade because of the length of my contract, so I'm paying for a basic model, but driving a Jeep Compass. Liz offers to join me for the ride back, an offer I accept with alacrity. She is happy to explain the basic workings of an automatic, and I am happy to be taught. We make it back to Pam's house in one piece, my left hand and left foot occasionally drifting through space, trying to find something to do.

By Tuesday my luggage has arrived, so I spend the morning trying to solve the puzzle of the extra month which I need to complete my project, but which the Immigration Department at JFK refused to give me. A little explanation would not go amiss here.

Baseball has a six month-long season, April to September, and each team plays 162 games. At the end of September eight teams have qualified for the playoffs, and they then play what is effectively a knockout tournament, ending in the World Series. So if I return home at the end of September I will miss the culmination of the season.

After hours of searching websites and listening to automated phone messages, I actually get to speak to a very pleasant lady who tells me exactly what I have to do—download a form, fill it in (or, if you're American, fill it out!), and send it off. She neglects to mention, as I discover when reading the instructions to said form, that I have to enclose $200! My initial visa cost me $130. $130 for the first six months, $200 for the seventh — you do the maths!

Although I will return to Virginia Beach to sleep, Wednesday marks the real beginning of my itinerary. It is an itinerary littered with seemingly trivial landmarks in the worlds of sport and music and, to the casual observer, makes me seem a complete anorak.

This is not actually the case. I am embarking on a seven-month journey across a continent, and I want to ensure that I see a true picture, not just the well-trodden paths of the tourist. My theory, which may or may not turn out to be true, is that the way to do this is to head for places, and that the stories and experiences will occur during the journey.

Today, therefore, I drive to Portsmouth to visit the Virginia Sports Hall of Fame. Because of its colonial heritage, many of the place names in Virginia are English-related — except the geography doesn't quite add up — I don't usually drive through Norfolk on my way to Portsmouth.

The Hall of Fame is a modern building, with matchstick-men statues of sports people decorating the sides. The content is pretty good, lots of interactive stuff for kids, lots of memorabilia and tributes to Virginia's sporting sons and daughters. Two things quickly become apparent. Virginia has no major league team in any sport, so is desperate to find links where it can. The Washington Redskins are therefore Virginia's sporting heroes, because their training headquarters are in northern Virginia. This also leads to a great emphasis on college and high school sport. Those who represent their state university are sporting heroes, whereas in Britain they are famous only in their own college bars.

Secondly, those in a secondary role are also liable to be given the status of heroes, particularly coaches. Also broadcasters—those who commentated *(made the call)* on great sporting moments are revered as much as the actual participants. Whereas in Britain "They think it's all over" is just a cheesy quiz programme, in the U.S. Kenneth Wolstenholme would be in the Hall of Fame.

I must admit to not recognising many of the stars in the Virginia Hall of Fame. Arthur Ashe is probably the most famous, plus golfers Sam Snead and Curtis Strange. I also recognise Mia Hamm, the female soccer star, and Sean Casey who, as a baseball fan, I know as a veteran slugger with the Detroit Tigers. I spurn the chance of a NASCAR simulator, and set out in search of my first American breakfast.

George Bernard Shaw once wrote that America and England are two countries divided by a common language. This is nowhere more true than in the two areas of sport and food. I have tried to use both versions wherever possible, but it's getting more difficult. It's even worse than learning a foreign language, because they use the same word or phrase to mean something different. So (English version first) football is soccer, American football is football, hockey is field hockey, ice hockey is hockey, athletics is track and field, but baseball is always baseball.

On Thursday, I make my farewells and hit the road. The weather is sunny and chilly. Virginia is a state of lakes and pine forests, and has a roadside shrub, which I later discover is a redbud, that is a striking pink/purple at this time of year.

Before leaving home, I got on the Major League Baseball website, and purchased every type of T-shirt they had in my size that was reduced to a giveaway price, so that I would have some gear for my travels. Today I am supporting Japan in the 2006 World Classic. Guess what? We won!

Having reached Salem and located my motel I set off for the game, the first of my trip. The stadium is located at the foot of

> ... the *Blue Ridge Mountains of Virginia,*
> *on the trail of the lonesome pine.*

Excitement has got the better of me, and I am ridiculously early. The stadium is modern and concrete, surrounded by huge car parks, so there are no time delays to excuse my early arrival.

I wander around, staring at the scenery and taking photographs until the ticket office opens. My complementary ticket is waiting for me as arranged, so eventually I go in, examine every square foot of the stadium, sample the snacks and beer, and wait.

It is a bright, sunny evening, with a wind chill factor of minus 3000. The fashion accessory de rigueur is a blanket. Being the first game of the season, Opening Day they call it, there are a few pre-game festivities. The teams are paraded before the crowd, and the National Anthem is sung.

Everything in American sport is sponsored. My favourite pre-game announcement is *Tonight's injury report is sponsored by the Roanoke Orthopaedic Center. There are no injuries.* I wonder how much they had to pay to sponsor that.

Between innings some mascots occasionally drive a truck around the field, and fire hot dogs into the crowd from a hydraulic gun in the shape of a giant hot dog, or some young ladies climb on the dugout and lead the crowd in a rendition of "YMCA." And, of course, in the middle of the seventh inning, we all sing "Take Me Out to the Ball Game."

American readers will have to excuse me for a moment, but for the benefit of my English audience, I feel obliged to explain a little about baseball itself. Today, the basics—baseball is played by two teams of 25, nine of whom can be on the field at any one time. Combatants wear a uniform similar to a baby-grow, with the trousers, if the traditional approach is adopted, tucked into the socks. It's a bit like rounders, but with attitude. Each batter tries to hit the ball and get to first base, or further. Any batter who gets all the way round scores a run. If three batters are out, it's the end of the inning. There are nine innings for each team.

Tonight's game is very watchable, if you can forget that you are freezing to death. The home team, the Salem Avalanche, takes an early lead, but in the middle of the game the away team, or road team, the Frederick Keys, has two good innings and goes ahead 4–1. That looks like it, but in the bottom of the eighth the Avalanche has a purple patch, and ties the game at 4–4.

In American sport, draws are unheard of. If the score stays tied after nine innings, they keep on playing until they achieve a result. So the possibility of extra innings looms. A call is made to the local hospital, which puts a hypothermia unit on stand-by. Fortunately for the continuation of this project, the Keys score in the ninth, and hold on for a 5–4 win. The stadium announcer informs us that the firework display has been cancelled due to high winds, and those of us who have stuck it out to the end, about a quarter of the original 3,000 crowd, head for our car heaters.

As I get back to my room and crawl into my bed, I notice that the feeling is beginning to return to my feet. So there's hope for the rest of the tour, as

April 5, 2007, start of the big adventure — Salem Avalanche, in the Blue Ridge Mountains of Virginia. Welcome to summer sport, temperature in the 30s, wind chill minus 3000!

long as I can get far enough south tomorrow to avoid the snow that is forecast! Don't you just love summer sport?

North Carolina
Friday April 6

Southeast to North Carolina — the sun eventually breaks through an insipid sky and we have sunshine and a beautiful day. I only go the wrong way once, but spend much of the journey thinking I'm going the wrong way, which is almost as bad. I think I may have to splash out on a satellite navigation system before much longer.

I eventually reach Durham, spend an inordinately long time finding my hotel, which is very cleverly concealed, check in and head into town for game 2 of my tour. Compared to last night, this is a whole new ballgame, literally and metaphorically. Baseball does not have promotion and relegation, and each of the 30 major league teams stays in the major leagues season upon season. Almost all of the minor league teams are affiliated to one of the major league outfits, and there are three levels, single-A, double-A, and triple-A. Salem was a single-A affiliate of the Houston Astros, while the Durham Bulls are a triple-A affiliate of the Tampa Bay Devil Rays. The two steps up are reflected in the stadium, the crowd, and the standard of play. These are players one step away from the major leagues.

The stadium is in the town centre, and impresses. As I approach, I notice a red brick pavement with plaques embedded therein, paying tribute to important groups and individuals in the club's history — Negro league teams, famous players, and even one to the fans themselves.

If you have ever seen the film *Bull Durham*, this is the club on which it was based, and where it was filmed. The stadium has a large bull on top of the scoreboard which snorts when the Bulls score a home run. The club has been going over a hundred years, and was originally the Durham Tobacconists, after the local industry. Durham Bull was a popular tobacco brand.

We are almost at a major league level with the concessions, which is how they refer to the food stands. Last night two stands, tonight 20-odd. My philosophy with ballpark snacks will be to experiment with caution. A hot dog and a Budweiser beer (oxymoron) can be obtained anywhere, so I want to look for something a little different, and perhaps unique to the locality. I find a small stand at the end, belonging to a local company, and selling bratwurst, and a local brew called "El Toro" (Spanish for bull — geddit?). This turns out to be an amber beer with a rounded flavour, and the bratwurst a hot dog with decent sausage. I enjoy my snack, and try not to be too smug with my admirable choice.

The game has a lot happening — unfortunately for the Bulls, none of it happens during their times at bat. The away team, the Syracuse Chiefs, dominates. After three innings it leads 6–0. In the sixth inning 12 batters come to the plate — how can that happen? You will remember that three outs end the inning. If all nine batters have a turn, and there are still not three outs, they start again! Nine runs are scored, and the Chiefs lead, 15–0.

The home crowd is also faced with the unedifying spectacle of its pitcher walking in a run. I'll try to explain. I'll explain balls and strikes when I have a day or two to spare but, basically, a good pitch is a strike and a bad pitch is a ball. Three strikes and you're out, we all know that. But four balls give the batter a walk to first base. If there is already a batter at first he moves to second, and so on. So if there are batters on all the bases (bases loaded), the batter on third base comes in to score. It's one of the worst things a pitcher can do.

The Bulls fail to trouble the scorer, let alone the Bull, so I will never get to see it snort. The final score is 16–0. So far I have witnessed two away wins. I may be outstaying my welcome.

Apart from the game, we are treated to the national anthem sung by a barber shop chorus, Lucy the Wonder Dog, the mascot Wool E. Bull, joined for this Good Friday special by the Easter Bunny, and a genuine old-fashioned organist. I have decided that all the clubs will be judged by the presence of an

The Durham Bull, which snorts whenever the Bulls hit a home run. For my visit, he remained silent, as the home team slumped to a 16–0 loss.

organist, and whether "Take Me Out to the Ball Game" is sung in the seventh inning. Durham passes both tests.

The evening is cool but no worse. I arrive back at the hotel to find that Cleveland's game has been postponed due to snow. What will tomorrow bring?

ESPN, the Sports Channel, also informs me that, back home, despite Fullham scoring first, Everton goes on to record its winningest victory! My computer knows winningest isn't a real word, so why don't they?

South Carolina

Saturday April 7

I pack up the car in Durham under a bright sky, with the temperature a chilly 42 degrees. Without the aid, yet, of satellite navigation, I come straight from motel to motel in two and a half hours.

I realise that, for the first time in days, I actually have a few hours without having to drive or go to a ballgame, so I make a note of all the jobs I can do when I get on line this afternoon. Returning to my room I find that this is the first place I've stayed in without broadband, so the jobs will have to remain undone until tomorrow.

This does, however, provide some thinking space. Over the last couple of days I have found myself thinking a lot whilst driving of my wife and daughters, and how lucky I am to have their complete support in this venture. I sit down and write to them, expressing my gratitude and telling them how wonderful they are.

Despite being further south, the temperature is still only 48 degrees, and the TV is predicting chilly weather. Texas is 29 degrees! If I can get past tonight's game without freezing to death, I have no more until Tuesday in Atlanta. I determine to borrow the blanket from my bed.

I leave for the ballpark wearing my jacket, plus one that Pam's husband Graham lent me, and carrying the blanket off my bed. I make my first major error of the tour, and forget my camera. If there is ever a good time to forget a camera this is it, as the stadium is a concrete lump on the edge of town with no character. The Charlotte Knights are a triple-A affiliate of the Chicago White Sox, and are playing the Pawtucket Red Sox. The Knights mascot is a dragon — good to see them on the same side for once.

Pedants' corner — those of you who have been paying attention will know that I am trying to see a game in every state, and this one is in South Carolina. Please don't write to the Guinness Book of Records, pointing out that Charlotte is in North Carolina. It is, but the ballpark is in Fort Mill, which is just over the border.

Tonight I decide to have a Carolina Blonde — we're talking beer here — a locally brewed lager, and a barbecue chicken sandwich. Barbecue sandwich is well-cooked meat, pork or chicken, shredded and mixed with barbecue sauce, and slapped into a roll. It turns out to be tasty.

The anthem is sung by Jamie Lee Ward, fresh from "American Idol." When she gets to the line about "bombs bursting in air," two huge fireworks explode above the scoreboard. Ms. Ward has her back to the scoreboard and, from the look on her face, was not forewarned.

The game is tight, and is 3–3 after nine, so we go to extra innings, despite the dropping temperatures. I am pleased for all my various coverings— what state I would be in without them I dread to think. The programme notes inform us that the Pawtucket Red Sox took part in the longest ever game, which went to 32 innings. Fortunately, tonight they score in the tenth to win, 4–3, and the curse of the home team remains intact.

In tonight's game we had a player caught stealing. Stealing bases is an integral part of the game, and is a way for a runner to advance his position and put pressure on the pitcher at the same time. It's most common between first and second base. The runner on first will edge away from the base towards second, and the pitcher has to watch him as well as concentrate on throwing his pitch. If the runner decides to go, and the batter misses the pitch, the catcher will throw to second base to try and run him out. The second baseman has to collect the ball and tag the runner, before the runner touches the base, and that's just what happened tonight.

When I return to my car the temperature has dropped to a spring-like and tourist friendly 35 degrees. I'm heading south — Georgia on my mind.

Georgia
Sunday April 8 – Wednesday April 11

For the sake of completeness, I spend the first few minutes of Sunday returning to last night's ballpark, with my camera this time, so that everyone will be able to see just how nondescript it is.

I then set off south on I-85, in search of warmer temperatures. My biggest fear before starting this trip was that I would not be able to cope with the heat, a fear that has yet to be tested. Crossing the border into Georgia, I turn off in search of Demorest. This proves a little more difficult than anticipated, as it is not well signposted and, being Georgia and being Sunday, there are no pedestrians to ask. Eventually I find Demorest and Piedmont College, which contains the Johnny Mize Sports Center and Museum.

Mize, "the Big Cat," was a first baseman with the Cardinals, Giants and Yankees, since elected to the Hall of Fame. He was born here in Demorest. Unfortunately, I am not able to get in to the museum — it's still Georgia and it's still Sunday — but I'm not too disappointed as it's a lovely spot to visit. The Americans are much better than us at honouring their sporting heroes, and the fact that this centre exists in the place of his birth attests to this.

The college is built in the middle of a lovely forest, and behind the museum the landscape falls away into a baseball park, surrounded by trees. After the hectic schedule of the last few days, it's so relaxing just to be here and mooch around in beautiful surroundings.

I check in at a motel in Lavonia, which is little more than a junction on the interstate. I first make sure that they have an internet connection. Checking my e-mails, I am amazed at the amount of support there is out there, not just from friends, but from friends of friends. My friend and neighbour, Greg, is at present in New Hampshire, spending Easter with his family. He e-mails to say that one of his brothers is a representative of a national company, and has e-mailed his entire network of colleagues, telling them about my trip. Many of them are already replying to offer me support and accommodation. I doubt if I will be able to take up all the offers, but the mere fact that they are coming in is very humbling.

Monday starts with a short drive to the Ty Cobb Museum, in Royston, another fine example of respectful treatment of sporting heroes. Cobb was one of the finest players to grace the game of baseball, yet the history books have him respected and reviled in equal measures.

A museum in the town of his birth, largely paid for by money donated by Cobb and his estate to the local community, is obviously going to concentrate on the plus points, and there are many. Today's lesson in baseball trivia will concern batting average, a statistic by which players are often judged. Batting average involves dividing the number of times a player successfully hits the ball by his number of at-bats. Thus, if you hit successfully two out of every ten times, your average is .200. A season's average of .300 is excellent, .400 is unbelievable, and has not been achieved for nearly 70 years. Cobb had a lifetime average of .367, which is still the highest career average in the history of the game. He was an original electee, in 1936, to the Hall of Fame, achieving a higher vote than Babe Ruth.

The other side of his character recalls him sharpening his spikes before games, so that fielders might think twice before getting in his way when he slid into a base. He once leapt into the stands to beat up a handicapped fan who was heckling him. But in this part of Georgia, "the Peach," as he was known, is revered, and the museum, although small, is a heartfelt tribute to a great player.

Returning to the interstate, I find that Exit 111 promises me fine shopping, so I find a Walmart to check out satellite navigation systems. The cheapest is $300, twice as much as I expected, so I invest $7.50 in a Janis Joplin CD, which will make being lost much more tolerable.

I pop for a quick rest, which I assume is the American term for what one does in a rest room, and discover the highlight of the tour so far — a toilet which flushes when you rise from the seat. What an excellent invention, unless, of course, you leave your newspaper on the floor and have to lean forward to reach it!

On to Atlanta, and my first experience of a crowded six-lane highway. The ballpark is visible from the highway, and the hotel is practically next door, so who needs satellite navigation? This is a real hotel, not one where you park your car outside your room, and I'm here for two nights, which is a little bit of a luxury. I spend the first couple of hours sorting out laundry, as it's now nine days since I left home. It's a job I would take for granted at home, but in my present situation dealing with the intricacies of a hotel laundry single-handed leaves me feeling ridiculously smug!

I spend the early evening walking around Turner Field, which is the home of the Atlanta Braves, whom I will be watching tomorrow. It is named after Ted Turner, media magnate and husband of Jane Fonda. I'm not sure if they're still together or divorced, and briefly consider looking it up so that my report is accurate but, quite frankly ... bovvered???

It is a wonderfully spacious stadium, surrounded by open plazas with statues of previous Braves greats. One of the more attractive features is a row of giant baseballs, mounted on plinths, each decorated with a different colourful design. At one end of the stadium is a giant Coca-Cola bottle, its unique shape covered with baseball-related designs, a reminder that Atlanta is the world headquarters of this huge organisation.

The address of the stadium is 755 Hank Aaron Drive, which is slightly odd as there is only one building in Hank Aaron Drive. Hank Aaron is one of the greatest names in baseball, and for the last 30-odd years has held the record for the most career home runs. His total — 755 — how obliging of him to hit exactly the same number as the stadium's address?!

I dine at the Bullpen BBQ and Grill, opposite the stadium. On a point of vocabulary, the bullpen is the part of a ballpark where the pitchers warm up. The place is a classic sports bar, with a television screen in your eyeline whichever way you look, and the choice of several different sports on offer. It is covered with excellent memorabilia, but fails to make good on the microbrews which its menu, thoughtfully placed in my hotel room, promises.

On Tuesday morning I head into Atlanta on a bus, giving myself a day off from driving. My last visit to this city was 35 years ago, and not too much remains in my memory. I wander around the centre, which is full of elegant skyscrapers, becoming vaguely aware of a sensation I thought I might have experienced previously, but which has been strangely absent — too warm! I find a Starbuck's and sit outside, drinking iced coffee and writing postcards.

Aware that, if things continue as at present, there is a danger of not fitting into the plane seat at the end of October, I opt for a salad lunch. I forget my previously acquired knowledge of American food sizes — small means large, medium means huge, and large means three weeks' supply — and opt for a large tub. This consists of enough lettuce to feed several warrens, which is put into a large bowl, and to which I am invited to choose add-ins. I do just that, and am surprised when the server, after adding a pint of Caesar dressing, puts it back into the original tub, which had been full previously. It's obviously sleight of hand, but he manages it, and I spend the next 30 minutes devouring this concoction. I never knew you could feel bloated after salad.

Finding the bus back, I realise that it is full of vending staff, security staff and parking staff for Turner Field, so I don't have to ask when to get off. I return to my room and put on the Sports Channel, thinking the Cubs might be showing — instead I find Manchester United demolishing Roma!

Off to Turner Field, for the Atlanta Braves against the Washington Nationals. I get there early, so I can walk around and not miss anything. Once through the main gates, I am able to observe even more of this beautiful stadium than I could last night. There are several large numerals, each about three feet tall, standing around one of the plazas. These are the retired uniform numbers; in American sport there is a tradition that the outstanding servants of a club have their numbers retired, which means that no other player ever wears that number. There is a lot going on — drum bands, dancers— and once I get underneath the stands there are loads of displays about the club's history, and some very attractive and modern murals.

The entire stadium, on three levels, is surrounded by concessions, but there is not a great deal of choice. The local brew is called Tomahawk (Braves— geddit?), and I order one. I am foolishly thrilled to be asked for ID by a woman less than half my age! The beer is good but the food is dull and disappointing. Most places have at least one thing that is just theirs, but not Atlanta.

The game is enjoyable, and my curse of the home team is well and truly purged, as the Braves win, 8–0, with two homers, one of them a three-run shot. A homer, or home run, occurs when the batter hits the ball far enough, usually into the crowd, to enable him to circle the bases and get home. Any other player already on a base scores also.

The spectators are lively and do as they are instructed by the scoreboard. Many of them carry foam tomahawks, which they wave up and down when called upon by the scoreboard to do so, and the PA plays the tune that was always played in 1950s westerns when the Indians approached. Representatives of the indigenous population have constantly pointed out to Mr. Turner and his club that they feel this to be demeaning to their culture, but have been so far ignored.

Hey — it's only a game! Hmmmm!

On Wednesday I leave behind a grey, drizzly Atlanta and head south. I leave the interstate at Macon, a music legend, mentioned in many songs. It has a particularly strong link with the Allman Brothers, who did most of their recording here and who, in the case of two of them, died here in motorcycle accidents. Incredibly, they died in separate accidents, just over a year apart, at the same road junction.

After a morning at the Georgia Music Hall of Fame, the music memorabilia books insist on a visit to the H&H restaurant, much beloved of the Allman Brothers and, as I skipped breakfast, off I go. It's an unassuming little place, which would be really easy to miss— just a small sign tells you what it is. Inside I find brick walls, lino on the floor and plastic tablecloths, and a simple menu, one piece of A5 card, laminated. The menu is broken down into days of the week, and for each day the formula is the same —four meats, pick one; seven vegetables, pick three; iced tea or lemonade, both homemade, and off you go. I go for pork chops, with rice and gravy, okra with tomatoes, and collards (kind of a chopped cabbage). I think I have discovered soul food! What's more, there is a grave danger that I might begin to like iced tea.

Loins suitably girded, I return to the Georgia Sports Hall of Fame, next door to its musical equivalent. After last night's request for ID, I am delighted to find that the fact that I am over 55 means I am a senior, which qualifies me for a discount in some hotels and both of today's museums.

As with other similar institutions, there are a lot of names I don't recognize, but Georgia does have major league sports. I am drawn to an exhibit about Greg Maddux, long-time pitcher with the Atlanta Braves, who recently returned for a couple of seasons with the Cubs.

At the motel the internet connection is not working; this makes me feel strangely cut off from home, and the day before my 28th wedding anniversary too. I take a little drive around the area, and find the road junction where the two fatal accidents occurred. I was expecting a busy crossroads, but it's just the intersection of two suburban streets. I return to my room to write. Shortly after I arrive, my TV suddenly goes quiet, and broadcasts a severe thunderstorm warning for this area for the next 45 minutes. "A Rainy Night in Georgia," as Ray Charles sang.

Florida

Thursday April 12–Thursday April 19

Thursday is my 28th wedding anniversary, and it feels odd to be spending it like this. I stop for breakfast and my waitress is a very pleasant woman in her early fifties, named Sally. Coincidentally my wife just happens to be a very pleasant woman in her early fifties, named Sally. Someone else has been reading the script.

These next few days are free in terms of my baseball itinerary, so I have decided to head south and see the Florida Keys. Pam and Graham are holidaying in Treasure Island, which is on Tampa Bay, so that seems an obvious place to break my journey, and that's where I'm headed.

I find my hosts on the beach, with temperatures well into the eighties—quite a change from Macon. They are accompanied by their daughter Katie, as well as cousin Phil and his wife Carol, whom I met back in Virginia Beach. My arrival is greeted by a mist descending over the entire beach, making me very popular, so we return to their nearby condo, which is short for condominium. This is not a contraceptive factory, but a holiday apartment, this particular one towards the top of a tall building which offers sea views.

After a wash and change, we set out for Sloppy Joe's, a beachside restaurant and bar. From the excellent menu I select grouper, largely because I haven't had it before, and new experiences are largely what this trip is about. So I am lucky enough to spend my anniversary at a good restaurant in good company — all that's lacking is my wife.

My hosts and their guests apparently have a habit of reading my diary over breakfast. I think they should get out more. However, as I have had no access to the net for the past couple of days, I am forced to produce my computer and have my work read out loud to the assembled company. It is not as embarrassing as I would have thought, but I do feel the need to explain certain parts, which leads me to think that my writing is lacking something.

Onward to the Florida Keys; I drive on I-75 all the way south, and it then veers east and goes through the Everglades. This stretch is known as Alligator Alley, and so I stop at one of the rest places to see if one of the eponymous creatures will put in an appearance. Sure enough, there they are, four of them, together with some moorhens (the American one is larger than the British — nothing new there) and a green heron.

My original plan was to spend the night somewhere around Miami, but nowhere appropriate presents itself. So I keep going onto the Keys, which are a long string of islands, linked together by Highway 1. I pause briefly in the first town, Key Largo, in the hope of bumping into Humphrey Bogart and Lauren Bacall. They are nowhere to be seen, so I have the bright idea of phoning the place where I'm booked for tomorrow, to see if they can accommodate me tonight. Eventually I'm here, the Lime Tree Bay Resort, south of Islamorada. They remember my phone call, and my room is free tonight, so I'm sorted.

My room is about 30 feet from the ocean, there are pelicans, there are lizards, and it's around 90 degrees. That means I've experienced a 60-degree change in temperature driving south in the last week. The ocean is visible on both sides of the highway, the Straits of Florida to one side and the Gulf of Mexico to the other, and it's a beautiful evening.

The similarities between English and American culture, and the common language (sometimes, at least), have made the journey to date fairly comfortable. Today I have seen alligators, lizards and pelicans, and am sitting in 90 degrees of heat, ocean on both sides. I think my journey is well and truly under way.

On Saturday I drive along the remainder of Highway 1, which is quite spectacular. Key West is right at the end of the line, the southernmost point of the United States. Although I consider myself fairly familiar with the geography of this country, there are occasions when the odd fact will jump up and bite me. For example, when I am in Key West, I am closer to Cuba than I am to Miami. The latter is 129 miles to the north of me, whilst the former is but 94 miles south, across the Straits of Florida.

Inevitably, the drive back to the hotel is along the same highway. I have been invited to dinner, so I stop on the way home and collect a hand-crafted Key Lime pie. The key lime is indigenous to this area, and is much smaller than the common version, so, when in Rome...

I also visit my first liquor store. American licensing laws are state laws, as opposed to federal laws, so attitudes differ vastly. In some states you can pick up booze in supermarkets, elsewhere you have to find the official stores. The place I visit is inelegant, but very well stocked. I purchase a bottle of rose for tonight's gathering, and a bottle of bourbon to keep in the boot, or should I say trunk, of my car. The latter costs $15 — I'm surprised there are any sober Floridians left.

My dinner date is with Pam and Graham's son, Marcus, and his wife, Jenny. They are here for a short vacation, along with Jenny's parents, sister, brother-in-law and nephew. I know all these people from Marcus and Jenny's wedding, and am welcomed warmly.

I enjoy the company very much and, as I leave, it dawns on me that the next time I am due to meet someone I know is May 18, five weeks from now. The drive back to the hotel is relatively short, and I spend a few moments just gazing out over the water, ensuring that I remember this beautiful spot.

On Sunday morning, I decide on a different route for my return journey across Florida, and seek out Highway 41. This takes me on a 90-mile drive through the Everglades and Indian reservations but, as I find out almost to my cost, not past any gas stations!

The radio is broadcasting storm warnings, and the air, as I leave the car, feels as if I am walking into a bathroom after someone has just showered. I have the air conditioning directed to the windscreen, which is steaming up on the outside!

I reach my hotel, which is only a couple of miles from the holiday condo I visited three days ago. It's a comfortable, slightly old-fashioned, family-run place and, more to the point, it has internet. Before leaving for my trip, I contacted a few TV and radio stations in places I am intending to visit. There were no replies, but today I have an e-mail from Randy Bell, who is a radio reporter in Jackson, Mississippi. He wants to interview me while I'm at the Mississippi Braves game a week from now — a first small step on the road to international stardom.

After dinner, I return to my room for a live baseball broadcast from Dodger Stadium, Los Angeles. It is an important day for baseball — Jackie Robinson Day. Sixty years ago, Jackie became the first black man, in the face of great opposition, to play major league baseball. Previously, black players had only been permitted to play in the Negro Leagues.

I recently wrote about clubs retiring the uniform number of great players. Robinson's number, 42, was retired by the commissioner ten years ago, which means no player in any club gets that number in the future. To honour Robinson, several players have asked permission to wear the number today, and a trend has developed. The Dodgers, for whom he played, all wear number 42!

The tributes are fulsome, but some commentators point out that the number of black Americans playing the sport professionally is dropping, and that there is still plenty of work to be done before the path that Robinson was the first to tread reaches its end.

In the Monday morning sunshine, St. Petersburg becomes vaguely Mediterranean in nature, so I decide to explore some of its delights. But the point of my being here is more major league baseball so, after playing the tourist, I set off for Tropicana Field, to see the Tampa Bay Devil Rays against the Baltimore Orioles. In case you haven't yet worked it out, major league ballparks are either named after a benefactor, as in Turner Field, or after a corporate sponsor, as is tonight's case. Honourable exceptions, such as Yankee Stadium, are few and far between.

Tropicana Field is a dome, as in it has a roof, so the weather is irrelevant. From the outside, it has no character at all, so the atmosphere approaching the game is non-existent. Inside is just like a regular stadium, with loads of concessions and interesting features. I sprint past the rows of Bud and Miller stalls, and come to a place that sells cocktails, with a few interesting beer pumps at the end of the counter. I select a Blue Moon, Belgian style wheat beer, and proceed.

The main feature is the Ted Williams' Hitters Hall of Fame. Williams is generally acknowledged as the greatest pure hitter of all time. He was the last man to hit .400, nearly 70 years ago. He rejoiced in such wonderful nicknames as Teddy Ballgame, and the Splendid Splinter. The museum concentrates on hitters, as opposed to other aspects of the game, and is inhabited by people wallowing in nostalgia. This is a major part of baseball, as parents and grandparents pass on memories of their youth to the kids. Taking your kid to the game seems more important in baseball than any other sport I know.

In search of decent food, I approach a seafood stall, and go for a grouper sandwich. Ciabatta bread, with a fried fillet of grouper, which is a thick white fish, and all the trimmings you require. Excellent! My faith restored, I return to the good beer stall for a Home Run Red, and I'm ready for the game.

The Devil Rays are a relatively new team, and are celebrating their tenth year of existence. In baseball, there are only two ways for a new club to start up. The league can decide to expand, and award expansion franchises where it deems fit, or a franchise can just move, as happened last year when the Montreal Expos became the Washington Nationals overnight. The Devil Rays are the former, so have a relatively thin fan base — the stadium is two-thirds empty.

Because it is not exclusively a baseball stadium, some of the normal features are missing, like the bullpen. This means that opposing pitchers warm up in front of third base, where I'm sitting. This provides a wonderful opportunity for the fans in the area to hurl abuse at the pitchers as they prepare to perform. This is very entertaining, and gets better as the beer goes down.

One of the things I haven't yet written much about is the entertainment at a ball game. Many ball parks have an organist, or the modern equivalent of one — tonight's has a series of keyboards and sound effects for all eventualities.

The crowd is remarkably obedient, and makes whatever noise the organist requests. I am particularly amused by the reaction to the away manager visiting the mound, which is the place where the pitcher stands. This occurs when the pitcher is not doing well. If the pitcher is allowed to continue, the PA plays "Carry On My Wayward Son" by Kansas; if he is lifted, we hear Ray Charles' "Hit the Road, Jack."

The game is bizarre. The Orioles start appallingly, at one point committing three errors on one play — this is so rare that when I return to the hotel later it has made the highlights programme. By the end of the fifth the Devil Rays lead, 7–1. At this point their starting pitcher begins to tire, and concedes a few runs. The relieving pitchers are not up to the job — final result, 9–7 to the Orioles — a bit of a turnaround to say the least.

Tuesday morning sees me retracing my steps yet again, over the Skyway, and down I-75 to Miami. At least, that's the plan. When I reach Fort Myers the traffic grinds to a halt, so I pull off and soon find myself heading east on I-80. Even with a stop for lunch, I find myself in Miami by 2:30. It is huge, hot and busy. The hotel is a beach resort — pool, beach and sea on one side, hugely busy dual carriageway on the other. Having said that, it is quite luxurious, and my room has a balcony with a view of the sea.

When evening arrives, I go in search of dinner. The other side of the main road has a local precinct, with a restaurant for each of the minorities that Miami hosts, Cuban, Mexican and Russian. I opt for Mexican, and am not disappointed. As I am eating early, the place is empty, so I grab an outside table, and receive the full attention of the manager. I receive an excellent starter and main course, and also the manager's life story. He also learns some of mine, and the setting sun enlightens a pleasing hour of drink and discussion.

Wednesday I have an early swim, repack my suitcase, e-mail a week's worth of pictures home, and phone Houston to confirm my free tickets for their game. The hotel has an excellent broadband connection, and the wire is just long enough for me to sit on my balcony and gaze at the sea whilst accessing my e-mails. It is slowly beginning to dawn on me that events at home are not standing still while I'm away. The internet is instantaneous, so news both happy and sad is reported to me as soon as it happens. My physical isolation makes me even more determined to be a part of it, so I regularly send off cards and e-mails of congratulation or commiseration.

So off to the game — Florida Marlins vs. New York Mets. In this country they always put the away team first, so I should really say the Mets at the Marlins. Dolphin Stadium is an exception to both the rules mentioned previously, as it gets its name from the football team which also uses it. Again, it's an out-of-town concrete mass, with not a lot of character. The range of concessions is poor, and I have to go a long way to find a Yeungling's lager. The food is even worse — the two stalls with something particular to this area are both closed, so I settle for the foot-long dog, which is exactly what is says on the tin, except that the roll is not, so a great deal of overhang is involved.

Despite the anonymity of the place, there is an obvious camaraderie amongst the people. As I take my seat, a steward, in a very pleasant fashion, says, "Not that one, sir, that's George's seat." I look confused, check the seat number, and offer the steward my ticket. "Oh," he says, with some surprise, "George can't be coming tonight!"

The pre-game show involves a moving tribute to Jackie Robinson, a moment of silence for the victims of the Virginia shootings, and a really quite decent rendition of the national anthem in four-part harmony by the cast of "Wonderful Town," which one can only assume is playing in Miami at the moment.

We also have cheerleaders. Other baseball teams have had fresh-faced young ladies in T-shirts and shorts, encouraging the crowd to cheer, but these are the genuine article, spandex, gyrations and all.

The Marlins pitcher is the famous Dontrelle Willis—the D-train—who has won all three of his starts this season. On this occasion the train doesn't leave the station, and the Mets get four hits in the first which, coupled with two errors by the defence, give the Mets a 4–0 lead. This sets the tone for the whole game—the Marlins don't get a hit until the seventh, and the game finishes 9–2.

With Miami being a holiday resort, there are as many Mets fans as home fans, and they are much louder, relishing their victory with some powerful New York catcalls. I enjoy the company of my two neighbours, Marlins fans, who heckle the Mets, and in particular the shortstop Jose Reyes each time he comes to bat.

"Reyes, you're useless!" Reyes hits a double. "Reyes, I wouldn't have you on my team!" Reyes hits a triple. "Reyes, you suck!" Reyes hits a home run, at which point my neighbour spots my grin and gives a sheepish smile, knowing that Reyes has the edge on him for tonight at least.

He and his friend consume much beer, become more and more impressed with my knowledge of the game, and keep asking me very simple trivia questions to illustrate the depth of said knowledge. I know I'm still very much in the shallow end.

Knowing I have 760 miles ahead of me to my next destination, I determine to put 500 of them behind me on Thursday. I impress myself by being on the road by 7:15, and plough onwards, first through 70 miles of urban sprawl from Miami, on to 300 miles of boredom on the Florida Turnpike and I-75, and finally the wooded splendour of I-10 in northwest Florida.

During the early afternoon I pull off the interstate for gas. There is an old guy sitting on the porch of the gas station. He asks in which direction I am travelling and, when I tell him, asks if he can have a ride to a town about 20 miles down the road, as his car has broken down and he needs to get home. It's not out of my way, so I agree. He is excellent company, and we exchange stories of families and children. He has seven, and they all live in this area, which is why he moved down here.

It turns out that this guy went to school with Pete Rose. Rose was a star of the Cincinnati Reds team from the 70s, whose undying effort won him the nickname of Charlie Hustle. He still holds the record for the most hits in a career. Sadly, after his playing days were finished, and he was managing, he was found to have bet on games in which he was involved, and was banned for life. This also precludes him from membership of the Hall of Fame, which otherwise he would long since have graced.

And here I am chatting to an old school friend of his, who informs me that Pete married his childhood sweetheart, a girl named Rose, who thus became Rose Rose!

I drop him at a gas station close to his home. As he gets out of the car, he explains that he is $35 short of the cost of his car repair; if I lend him the money and give him my address, he will post it on to me. I decline and drive away, slightly disappointed that such a friendly encounter should end like that, not for the first time on this trip. As I continue along the interstate, the guy plays on my mind; I wonder why he has to ask me for money if he has seven kids living around here.

Reaching my hotel I receive a discount, and am also presented with an extra hour, as I have just changed time zones. So 5:30 becomes 4:30, and bedtime is even further away. But there are 526 miles behind me, and I have surpassed my previous highest mileage in a day by quite some distance.

The hotel is very new, and the discount has given me a really good deal. I also have broadband, so spend an hour or so catching up on things. With the earlier encounter on my mind, I look up Pete Rose on the web — he was, it appears, married twice, on neither occasion to a girl named Rose. So presumably the seven kids were a lie as well.

Having earlier waxed lyrical about the way baseball treats its heroes, I think they have this one very wrong. Rose put together a career amongst the very best in baseball, and his actions after it was finished cannot diminish that. Similarly with Joe Jackson, "Shoeless Joe," star of the 1919 Chicago White Sox team, eight members of which were banished for throwing the World Series. Although Jackson may well have been given money, he batted .375 for the series, and played error-free defence (fielding). So how exactly did he throw anything?

For those of you familiar with the film *Field of Dreams*, Joe Jackson was the character played by Ray Liotta, the first "ghost" to emerge from the corn.

He should be in the Hall, and so should Pete Rose.

Alabama

Friday April 20

After eight days in Florida, the state-hopping now begins in earnest. If it's Friday, it must be Alabama. Today's mileage is comparatively short, so it's not long before I'm at my Birmingham hotel. It has a nice pool which, sadly, is not open for use, because it's not yet summer. In the American tourist trade, summer does not start until Memorial Day, which is at the end of May. So anything even slightly summery, such as opening a swimming pool, is apparently forbidden until then. So I rest up until it's time to leave for tonight's game.

Responses to my daily e-mails are many and varied, and reading them at the end of a day's drive is always a time of excitement. Today I learn from Graham that he has obtained me tickets for the two major league teams in Chicago, and they will be posted to my hotel in Memphis.

A short drive out of town takes me to Hoover Metropolitan Stadium, for the Birmingham Barons against the Montgomery Biscuits. I don't know who thought up that name. The stadium is another edge-of-town concrete bowl, but it is welcoming and comfortable. I have to see a security guard and acquire a wristband to buy beer — he declines to ask for my ID with a wry grin. The bratwurst is served with sauerkraut and melted cheese, which is different.

The team is a double-A affiliate of the Chicago White Sox, and the game is one of the most interesting to date. Defence dominates, and the visitors scratch out two runs, one in the first and one in the fifth. The Barons have only one hit, until the eighth, when they score two runs, the first on a balk by the pitcher.

The balk rule makes explaining offside in football simple, and I don't fully understand it. Checking the rules of the game doesn't help much, so I'll try a simplified version. Basically it is to do with the pitcher deceiving the runners when trying to throw them out as they edge off their base. If he has begun his pitching action when he attempts to do this, he cannot throw to a base unless he steps toward that base. If he fails to do so, a balk is called, and the runners are each awarded a base. In this evening's example, one of the runners is on third base, so a run scores.

That levels the score at 2–2. In the ninth, the Barons bunt and sacrifice their way to the winning run. More jargon that needs explaining! A bunt is when the batter changes his grip on the bat, and just kills the speed of the ball, dropping it down in front of him. If he is really quick, he may reach first base before the fielding side realises what's happening. More often than not, though, he has no intention of reaching base, and sacrifices himself in order to advance the other runners.

So now you know all about the balk, the bunt and the sacrifice. There's still an awful lot of jargon to go, but at least we're making inroads into America's game.

Mississippi
Saturday April 21–Monday April 23

I'm sure that Birmingham, Alabama, deserves more than 17 hours of my time, but that's all it gets. There are times in this schedule when I can relax, and times when I have to move. This is the latter, so on to Mississippi.

Each time I leave a motel I am almost paranoid with checking that I have left nothing behind. So, when I stop for breakfast, it comes as a major disappointment to realise that my Panama hat is missing, probably left under my seat at last night's game. This is a setback in three ways; first, it was a great hat, and actually fitted me; second, my hair is so sparse that my head needs protection; third, I was contacted yesterday by a journalist who wants to interview me at tomorrow's game, and told him he would recognise me by my Panama.

I come across a baseball cap that was given me at yesterday's game, to celebrate 20 years existence for the Birmingham Barons. Now, as I have a large head, baseball caps never fit me; but this one proves the exception. So the emergency is over, but I still need to make myself recognisable for tomorrow.

First stop Saturday is Jackson, where I visit the Mississippi Sports Hall of Fame, which is another fine exhibit of sports memorabilia. It even includes an exhibit on stickball, which apparently was the majority sport in the area before Europe colonised it. Again, I don't recognise many of the names, the most notable being Ralph Boston, the Olympic long jumper whose record stood for decades, and Jerry Rice, Brett Favre and Walter Payton, names I recognise from the world of American football.

The baseball exhibits don't provide many recognisable names, with the exception of Cool Papa Bell, about whom I have read. He was a star of the pre-integration Negro Leagues, and was supposed to be one of the fastest people to ever play the game. Although the phrase has been borrowed many times since, Bell was the first about whom it was said that he could turn out his bedroom light and be in bed before the room got dark.

Sunday breakfast features a pleasant conversation with my waitress (sorry, server!), who is interested to learn of my trip. When told of my wife's support for my venture, she replies "That's a guuuuurrrrrrrrrrd wuuuuuuur-rrrrrrrrrrman." Yeah, tell me something I don't know!

Today's game is a novelty, being my first daytime game, starting at 1:05. The ballpark, again in a huge lot on the edge of town, is a new brick structure, a pleasant change from the usual concrete lump, and pleasing on the eye. It goes under the corporate name of Trustmark Park. The Mississippi Braves are affiliated to the Atlanta Braves, and the stadium was built in a deal with them, to bring professional baseball to the town.

I have arranged to meet Randy Bell, news director of several local radio stations, for an interview. Despite my lack of distinctive headgear, we eventually find each other, and end up spending almost the whole game together. He is good company, and asks some fairly straightforward questions, basically encouraging me to talk about what exactly it is that I'm doing.

Spending the game talking to someone adds a new dimension, as it becomes a shared experience, but ceases to be the centre of attention. I decide to pass on trying to score, which is what I usually do when watching the game alone. The game passes in a straightforward fashion, ending 2–1 to the home team, all the scoring resulting from solo home runs. One of these is scored by the home team catcher, who glories in the name of Saltalamacchia. My companion assures me that this is the longest name in the professional game, and that the lettering on his shirt had to be reduced in size to enable it to fit.

Starting driving each morning is the time which requires the greatest concentration, as I have to convince my brain afresh that driving on the right is a sensible thing to do. So I always make a point of getting the journey under way, and getting clear of any nasty traffic, before I turn on the radio.

Having gone through such a routine on Monday morning, I hit the radio button, leaving it tuned to whatever station it was on previously. Within seconds, literally, I hear someone opining on the differences between baseball and other sports. Nothing extraordinary there, you might think, except that it is my own voice I can hear. I almost drive off the road. Without trying, I have managed to tune in to the interview I did yesterday with Randy Bell. What an amazing piece of timing.

The interview is well put together, incorporating all aspects of my trip. I even get to talk over Elvis singing, "That's All Right, Mama."

I have no more baseball scheduled until Thursday, and have decided that, as a music lover, I can't visit Mississippi without paying my dues. So I head for Clarksdale, where I visit the Delta Blues Museum, and pause for reflection at the intersection of highways 49 and 61, which is marked by a road sign topped with crossed guitars, visible in all the tourist material. This is the "crossroads" of blues legend, where Robert Johnson improved his guitar technique by selling his soul to the devil.

I move on to Tupelo, birthplace of a certain Mr. Presley. After finding the motel, I discover that there is yet again no broadband. The receptionist informs me, however, that the hotel next door has broadband, and that my room faces in that direction. She even knows the password.

So, after settling in, I find myself sitting on a kerb next to my car, picking up my e-mails. It doesn't work in the car, or in my room, or anywhere else in the car park. It's worth the effort, as there is an e-mail from my wife, sent to me before I did the interview, informing me that she had checked out Randy Bell on his website. Apparently he has witnessed two state executions!

Tennessee

Tuesday April 24 – Thursday April 26

Tuesday begins sitting on the kerb in the car park again. I have installed Skype on my computer so that I can talk to the folks at home for free. I use headphones for this purpose, so to any passing observer I am sitting on the ground in a car park talking to myself!

After a visit to Elvis Presley's birthplace, and breakfast near the hardware shop where he acquired his first guitar, I set off on the 100-mile drive to Memphis. I find my hotel quite easily. It's along Union Avenue, which also contains the Sun Studios, where Elvis made his first recordings.

Another spooky coincidence occurs; they seem to be becoming a habit lately. A couple of hours after checking in, I suddenly remember that Graham has arranged for my White Sox and Cubs tickets to be delivered to this hotel. So I run down to reception, and ask one of the receptionists if a package has arrived for me. The other receptionist, who is on the phone, says, "Are you 711?— I'm just phoning your room to tell you there's a package for you!"

Tickets safely stowed, I set off in search of refreshments, and decide to head for Beale Street, the musical epicentre of Memphis. I stop for a beer outside a club, and sit writing cards and listening to the music. Following complaints from home that there are no photos of myself, I decide to enlist the help of a couple of locals. They turn out to be locals only in the vicinity of Hertfordshire, but very helpful nonetheless.

I have 40 hours before baseball, and I'm in Memphis, so I overdose on music trivia. Wednesday sees me wearing myself out at the Rock and Soul Museum, followed by Sun Studios, and from there to the Stax Museum. By 4:30 I am back at the hotel, feet aching, head swimming with all the musical detail it contains.

Thursday starts with the obligatory visit to Graceland. This is Memphis, and I'm a tourist! It has to be done! I have regarded this visit with a combination of awe and apprehension, dreading the possible tackiness and the encounter with the over-devoted fan. But I find a multimillion dollar operation that runs, as you might expect, like clockwork. I collect my ticket, I am put into a queue for a shuttle bus, I am photographed in front of a backdrop, I am given a headset, and I am bussed to the house, which is actually on the other side of the highway. A guide tells me how to start my headset, and I am more or less left to my own devices. The headset directs me around the house, and is like an MP3 player, so that I can opt into various bits of commentary by entering a number, I can pause it if the person in front of me is acting the snail, and I can repeat bits if necessary.

After a break, I set off to say goodbye to Memphis. I decide to leave early for the ballgame, and have a look at the Mississippi. The riverfront is very relaxing, as is the part of downtown which I haven't yet seen. The ballpark, Autozone Park, is the nicest I have yet visited. Smack in the middle of downtown, it nestles amidst shops and office buildings, a lovely modern park in red brick.

Tonight's guest is Johnny Bench, catcher with the famous Cincinnati team of the 70s, "the Big Red Machine," and he catches the first pitch, as opposed to throwing it. The game is between the Memphis Redbirds and the Iowa Cubs, the triple-A affiliates of the St. Louis Cardinals and the Chicago Cubs, so I recognize the names of some of the players who have had stints in the majors, and the standard of play is high. At a major league level, the Cubs and the Cardinals have a rivalry dating back over 100 years.

One of the things that everyone tries to do at a ballgame is catch a foul ball; that is, a ball sliced or hooked outside the field of play, usually behind the batter. In the first inning the hitter fouls one, and it flies straight to a guy in the front row, who makes a nice catch. Two pitches later, the batter fouls one into the upper deck, no one catches it, it hits the back wall and rebounds out again, dropping to ground level, where it is caught by exactly the same guy. And later on in the game the same guy catches a third one. Chances of that??

The Cubs win, 7–4, so the home crowd is disappointed, but I'm not. My walk back to my car affords me one last glimpse of Beale Street. Tomorrow I'll be on the road again, but my time in Memphis has been special. It's a city I have come to love in a very short time, and I hope to one day return.

Illinois
Friday April 27–Friday May 4

At 7:30 on Friday morning, I get into my car in Memphis. At 7:30 on Friday evening, I get out of my car in Chicago. I'm here for two games, the White Sox on Sunday and the Cubs next Friday. I'm sure I'll find some other stuff to do as well, but those are the main attractions.

The drive goes well until the outskirts of Chicago; the last few miles take well over an hour. I have deliberately chosen a hotel on the north side because of its proximity to a station suitable for the baseball trips. The downside of this is that this evening's drive takes me into the city and out again as I find said hotel.

The prospect of a week in one place, relying on public transport, is very attractive. The hotel is not exactly salubrious, but it is well located, and it has a fairly safe car park. It also has broadband. Before I began the trip I had no idea how important this would be to me; now it's my lifeblood.

One of my biggest challenges on this trip is to score a ticket for the All-Star Game in San Francisco in July. Yesterday I noticed on Major League Baseball's website that they were inviting people to register for a ballot to buy such tickets, so I included this in my daily e-mail with a plea for assistance. Today I have lots of reassuring e-mails that friends across Britain, the U.S., and even in Spain have registered for the ballot to try to get me a ticket.

I am spending eight nights in Chicago, and my plan was to start here, and look around to see if anywhere was cheaper or better placed. But, having discovered that the manager is a baseball fan, I have persuaded him to give me the lowest rate he can manage, and I am pleased to report that I will be spending the rest of this week in the same room. So I have just done some really exciting things, like hang up clothes. Perhaps I'll decorate? Perhaps not!

On Saturday, after attending to my laundry, I set off in search of the L. The L (it stands for elevated) is Chicago's train system, and turns out to be efficient and simple. A $20 ticket covers me for the whole week. I set out for Wrigleyville, which is the area of North Chicago surrounding Wrigley Field, the Cubs' stadium. I discovered this area on my last visit, three years ago, and to call it unique is an understatement. Wrigley Field is the second-oldest park still functioning in the major leagues, and the community around matches it perfectly. You can find cafes and restaurants of all shades—during our last visit we dined in an Abyssinian restaurant, and lunched in a café with a Harley half-buried in concrete outside. There are book shops, clothes shops and, of course, sports bars inhabited by Cubs fans, who are amongst the most devoted and manic in sport.

After drinking in the atmosphere for a while, I spend some time in a second-hand bookshop, and treat myself to a couple of W.P. Kinsella books. Kinsella is the author of *Shoeless Joe*, the novel which was turned into the film *Field of Dreams*. His main themes tend to be baseball and the ethnic groups of the continent, particularly the indigenous Americans. I find him very readable.

I then head for Murphy's Bleachers, a famous sports bar next to the ballpark. The Cubs are playing in St. Louis, and Murphy's is showing the game. I find a seat at the bar and order a beer from the impressive blackboard, a Two Brothers Memorial Altbier. This is jet black and flavour packed. I then notice a card on the bar in front of me, with details of the draft beers, and find that this one is 7.8 percent—no wonder I'm enjoying it. Food next, and the menu informs me that burgers are what made Murphy's famous. Four weeks into an American trip and I have yet to buy a burger, so it has to be done. You can tell when a place is serious about its burgers—they ask how you want it cooked, as if it were a steak. The food is good, the beer is good and, in the fifth inning, I encounter a local tradition. When the Cubs score a run, one of the bar staff runs to the end of the bar and rings a bell.

The Cubs blow a tight game wide open with seven runs. There are high-fives and whoops all over the bar, everybody is happy, or at least merry, and the way the bell is going you would think that Quasimodo had walked in. The Cubs win, 8–1, and I head back for the L. Good beer, good food, a new book, a Cubs win and clean underwear. Does it get any better?

On Sunday I go to see the Chicago White Sox play. As a Cubs fan, this is not quite the anathema that it would be to fans of teams in the same city in England. Intra-city rivalry is not great in baseball because, by and large, teams in the same city rarely play each other.

Major League Baseball is split into two leagues, the American League and the National League, and each league is split into three divisions, East, Central and West. Now it would take Stephen Hawking with a brain extension to explain the schedule, but basically you play the teams in your division a lot, and the teams in the rest of your league not so often. Until recently, you didn't play the teams in the other league at all, other than a possibility of meeting in the end of season World Series, but in the last few years interleague play has been introduced a couple of times a year, to take commercial advantage of fixtures such as White Sox vs. Cubs and Yankees vs. Mets.

Purists are not happy with this, and the real rivalries are still the traditional ones, such as the Yankees vs. Boston Red Sox, and the Cubs vs. St Louis Cardinals.

The journey to U.S. Cellular Field —catchy name — is straightforward, but there is a diversion on the L, so it takes a little longer than expected. The stadium is quite new, totally integrated into its surroundings, and easily approached from the station.

I have been given an excellent ticket, and have a great view. But I have to present the White Sox with two black marks. Firstly, the seats are the narrowest in which I have yet sat. Now I know I'm a big lad, but compared to some of the other fans present I'm positively sylphlike, so how they manage I can't imagine. It wouldn't be so bad were it not for the fact that these fans are the keenest socialisers and consumers I have come across, so I have to get up and down from said seat so many times I lose count. This, combined with the procession of fans and vendors up and down the gangway, means I don't see an at-bat uninterrupted until the seventh inning. The game, what I can see of it, is good, with three home runs and several exciting double plays (that's when two players are out on the same play), and ends 5–2 to the visiting Angels.

The Angels, up until recently, were the Anaheim Angels, when they decided that a stronger link with Los Angeles would be more profitable. So they became the Los Angeles Angels, which annoyed the purists, and meant they compromised on the catchy Los Angeles Angels of Anaheim. Anyway, they won.

I return to Wrigleyville, with the plan of watching the Cubs game over dinner in one of the sports bars again. I check out a couple of places, but neither of them compares to yesterday's venue, so I return to Murphy's. After ordering a beer, the TV announces the sad news of the death of one of the St Louis players in a road accident, so the game is postponed.

On Monday afternoon I visit the National Italian American Sports Hall of Fame, purposely built in an area of town I now know to be called Little Italy. It figures really. This city has many different ethnic areas. The post office I used earlier was surrounded entirely by Mexican shops and restaurants—the Hall of Fame is in an area where, for many, the first language still appears to be Italian.

This particular ethnic group appears to have contributed more than its fair share to the ranks of American sporting heroes. Even those of you not enthusiastic about sport may recognize the names of Rocky Marciano and Jake

LaMotta from boxing, Mario Andretti from motor racing, Joe DiMaggio from baseball, and Dan Marino and Joe Montana from American football. This community seems extremely proud of their achievements, and the museum has been largely funded from within its ranks, including the estate of a certain Mr. Sinatra.

Some of the exhibits particularly catch my eye; there is a poster for the film *Raging Bull*, signed by De Niro himself; there is a page from a newspaper dated May 18, 1941, when Joe DiMaggio failed to hit in a baseball game. It wasn't celebrating the failure, rather the fact that he had hit in his previous 56 games, and the streak had come to an end. This particular record for hitting in consecutive games stands to this day, and has never really been threatened.

DiMaggio, "Joltin' Joe," "the Yankee Clipper," remains an icon in the game to this day. As well as his prodigious sporting feats, he also managed to marry Marilyn Monroe, which didn't harm his public profile at all.

Opposite the museum is the Piazza DiMaggio, a small park with a statue of the great man, erected in 1991, the 50th anniversary of "the Streak." The statue is dedicated to the Italian immigrants who developed the original community. A slight irony, as DiMaggio, despite making his name as a New York Yankee, was born and brought up in San Francisco.

I still haven't figured out Chicago weather. On Sunday I was far too warm returning from the game, so today I adjust my dress accordingly and freeze, due to an extremely chilly wind that arises in the afternoon.

I call at Murphy's for dinner and the Cubs on TV. Monday, apparently, is 25-cent chicken wings; as many as you like, 25 cents each. Healthily (for Murphy's) served with celery. The Cubs manage to snatch defeat from the jaws of victory, but the wings are good.

Tuesday brings the beginning of May — one month down, six to go! More catching up this morning, and then off to lunch at one of Chicago's institutions, Harry Caray's restaurant. Harry is a Chicago legend, particularly amongst Cubs fans, and his statue now stands outside Wrigley Field. To describe him as an announcer and broadcaster would be somewhat of an understatement; his status within the club was such that, the season after he died, all the players wore a patch with a caricature of his face on their uniforms.

In the middle of the seventh inning, referred to as the seventh inning stretch, he always led the crowd in the singing of "Take Me Out to the Ball Game" in a manner considered so inimitable that, following his death, the task has been taken on by a series of guest stars.

He started the restaurant himself, and it has become a haunt of stars of the game. Seating myself at the bar, I opt for a sandwich, a light lunch. Remembering that the chicken vesuvio was supposedly the great man's favourite dish, I go for the sandwich version. Delicious it is, cooked with garlic and herbs, and smothered in Swiss cheese, served on tomato ciabatta. Light it is not, coming with French fries and an excellent dipping sauce.

Before leaving, I spend a few minutes looking at the memorabilia that cover the walls. These include scraps of the infamous foul ball, "the Bartman ball," deflected by a Cubs fan out of the grasp of a fielder in the 2003 League Championship Series. If the fielder had been allowed to catch the ball, the Cubs would have been just four outs away from the World Series. Instead they went on to lose the game and the series.

The restaurant purchased the ball for $113,000, and blew it up in an attempt to change the luck of the team, which has not won a World Series since 1908. In a gesture of solidarity, they invited representatives of the Boston Red Sox and the Chicago White Sox to the ceremony, as neither had won a World Series for almost as long. In 2004 the Red Sox won, in 2005 the White Sox won, and in 2006 the champions were ... the St. Louis Cardinals, the Cubs' greatest rivals. The Cubs' curse remains.

Wednesday's first destination is the Billy Goat Tavern, another piece of Cubs folklore. The tavern was founded in 1934 by William Sianis, a Greek immigrant. In 1945 the Cubs reached the World Series, and took a 2 games to 1 lead. Sianis bought two tickets for Game 4, one for himself and one for his pet goat,

Harry Caray's, Chicago, home of chicken vesuvio and the notorious Bartman ball. Despite the ball's destruction, the Cubs still have not won the World Series in 102 years.

which he intended to parade around the park to bring the team luck. The goat was asked to leave, and Sianis was heard to say that the Cubs would never again win a World Series until the goat was allowed in.

The Cubs lost Game four, and went on to lose the 1945 World Series. They have never appeared in a World Series since, despite being one of the most successful clubs financially. Whenever they come close to winning the National League, a bizarre event will routinely occur, such as the fan interference in 2003, which I just mentioned.

On such occasions, Chicago is rife with mutterings about the Curse of the Billy Goat, on the back of which the Sianis family has built a successful chain of businesses. The original tavern is on Michigan Avenue, one of the main thoroughfares, but is quite difficult to find. The avenue is elevated above its original level, but the bar remains where is always has been, and so finds itself among the delivery entrances of the shops around and above it.

The outside is awash with neon signs, highlighting the legend, and the ethnic origins of the owner and many of the staff. It also offers lunch suggestions, such as, "Cheezborger, cheezborger, cheezborger, no pepsi ... coke!"

So in I go for a double cheeseburger — sorry, cheezborger — it appears that's the lunch *de rigueur*. It is also customary, apparently, to ask for fries, so that the guy at the counter can shout, "No fries, cheeeeeps!" and throw a packet of chips at you. Another note is required here about the differences in the gastronomic nomenclature between our two nations. What we call chips, they call fries, what we call crisps, they call chips! Anyhow, it's all good fun.

The place is a wonderfully unchanged cellar bar. The eating area has the appearance of an old café, plastic tablecloths, basic plates and cutlery, or silverware as it's known here. There is nothing fancy, but there are references to the curse everywhere. Even the toilets have "Billy" and "Nanny" on the door.

I remember that the Cubs are playing a lunchtime game, which is being shown. So I move to the bar, beneath a sign saying "Wise Guys Corner," order a beer and watch the game. The wise guys prove good company, so I stay until the end of the game. Once I am marked down as English, the conversation, as usual, turns to London, Tony Blair and the Queen. One guy even manages to move the conversation thus, from the Queen, via aristocracy, to knights of old. He then asks me, "When you were a kid, which was your favourite knight?"

I reply (and I hope at least half of you are ahead of me here), "Friday night, we always had fish and chips." He looks confused, but fortunately his mates all crack up, and the penny finally drops.

If it weren't for the demands of the baseball schedule, I would be on the road again by now. But there's no Cubs home game until Friday, which gives me a chance to take care of some business. My daughter Nina has designed a card for me, to be given to people who show an interest in what I'm doing. The issue at hand is to turn it from an e-mail attachment to an actual card, or even a few of them. So on Thursday I set off, laptop and all, in search of an appropriate establishment and, to my surprise, find one half a mile south of the hotel. My laptop won't pick up the internet there, but I realise I can get it on one of their machines, and I need not have brought my laptop after all. I am promised 200 cards by tomorrow evening. I wonder!

Like all good weeks, Friday eventually comes, and I'm off to Wrigley Field, to see the Cubs play the Washington Nationals in a day game, first pitch 1:20. I arrive at the ground at 11:30, planning to wander around for a while, but the doors are already open, so in I go. There is a free T-shirt for each of the first 10,000 fans through the gates, so I tuck it under my arm and set off in search of my seat.

I have a ticket for the bleachers, which are the uncovered part of the ground directly opposite home plate, frequented by the real fans. If you have ever seen the film or the play "Bleacher Bums," this is where it supposedly takes place. I discover that the ticket does not entitle me to a specific seat, so I find a place on the back row and settle in.

As I have written earlier, Wrigley Field is unique amongst baseball stadia. While I greatly admire some of the new ballparks, they can never compare to Wrigley, and nor should they try. Set in the middle of Wrigleyville, which I have already described, it is surrounded by four-story townhouses, several of which have built seating on the roof, which is occupied by yet more fans. Inside, the outfield wall is covered in ivy, so visiting outfielders have an entirely different set of problems when the ball is hit off the wall. Sometimes they can't even find it!

The opposition is warming up in front of us, and the more enthusiastic fans are heckling already. Two female fans enquire if the seats next to me are vacant, and as they settle in I discover they are from Manchester. Instead of learning, I have to explain certain aspects of the game to them — the student has become the teacher.

The fans' hopes are high. The Cubs have won four of their last five on the road and, returning home, have their star pitcher on the mound — Carlos Zambrano — big Z (pronounced zee, of course). Sadly, he hasn't read the script; two walks, a double, a triple and a home run put the Cubbies down 4–0 by the middle of the first. The bats are quiet for the first two innings, and the fans become restless.

In the third the Cubs start to hit, and a Derrek Lee home run, plus a double, brings it back to 4–3. The fourth sees the comeback completed, and a couple of doubles gives the Cubs the lead, 5–4. As the go-ahead run is scored, there are high-fives all around. I receive one from the guy in front who, after high-fiving all his mates, turns around and says, "Anyone else while I've got it up?" That's a phrase I must try and use more often!

We are in the right field bleachers and, during one of the many breaks in play, the fans in our section leap to their feet, gesture to our friends in the opposite bleachers, and start to chant, "Left field sucks!" The chant is returned, and more beers are drunk. Some of the fans in front of me start to get restless, and begin a Mexican wave, a common sight in many ballparks. However, the guy at the end of our row, who looks as if he was here for the last World Series in 1945, is distinctly unimpressed, and barks at them, "Sit down, this is Wrigley!"

The Cubs add an insurance run in the bottom of the eighth, and the crowd cheers each pitch as the Nationals' final batter strikes out. Cubbies win! Another unique Wrigley tradition can be witnessed; this is the only club in the country that flies a flag to inform passers-by of the result, either a W or an L. Today it's the W!

The printer has left me a message to say that my cards are ready, so I call and collect them. I am pleased with them, she is delighted with them, and keeps pointing out to me how good they are.

I look for somewhere different to eat dinner, without much luck, and am just about to turn back towards the hotel when I see a Bar and Grill — not exactly what I was looking for, but they serve a steak, so it will suffice.

It specialises in sport and music, so I drink my beer, eat my dinner, watch Tiger Woods with my left eye, basketball playoffs with my right eye, and listen to Lou Reed singing "Satellite of Love," all at the same time.

Missouri (Part One)
Saturday May 5 –Sunday May 6

Saturday is a special day. Saturday is the first day since April 12th that I haven't slept in a hotel. I explained earlier how my friend Greg, when visiting his family in the States in April, spoke about my tour with his brother, who e-mailed his national network of colleagues on my behalf. Many of them have replied offering accommodation, and this is the first chance I have had to take advantage of one of these offers.

So I drive down from Chicago to St. Louis, and as I cross the river I can see the Gateway Arch and Busch Stadium, where I will be tomorrow. In no time I arrive at my destination, a spacious house just north of the city. My hosts are Melissa and Mike Greene, a lovely couple in their 30s. They have a two-year-old son, Ryder, who, on waking from his nap, eyes me suspiciously for half an hour before deciding I should be high-fived and allowed to play with his cars.

After a relaxing afternoon watching the Kentucky Derby, Mike and I venture to Delmar, a nearby street which houses St. Louis' Walk of Fame, where the city honours its luminaries with stars in the pavement. Many of the names are new to me, but Chuck Berry is there, as are Ike and Tina Turner (separately), and Miles Davis. From the movie world we have John Goodman, Vincent Price and Shelley Winters. Sports fans will recognise tennis player Jimmy Connors, Negro League baseball player Cool Papa Bell, and broadcasting legend Harry Caray, who broadcast Cardinals games before moving to Chicago. Add to these T.S. Eliot, Charles Lindbergh and many more whose names are less familiar, and it would seem the city has a lot to shout about.

Sunday morning begins with nine holes of golf with Ryder. The course is an intricate one, taking in the most challenging aspects of the kitchen and the lounge, and finishing with a long straight hole down the porch. Ryder wins easily. He is more familiar with the course, denies me the use of either of the clubs, and kicks the ball from time to time.

Mike throws together a tasty breakfast, after which he and I set out for a lunchtime start at the ballgame. St. Louis has recently acquired a metro train system, in an attempt to overcome its appalling traffic problems. It's all shiny and new, and the automatic ticket vendor gives me my change in dollar coins, the first I have come across.

The train takes us straight to Busch Stadium. The Busch is the same as in Anheuser Busch, makers of Budweiser. For St. Louis is home, indeed, to "the king of beers." It is a beautiful stadium, two years old, brick, and in the heart of town. The Gateway Arch can be seen peeping over the roof of the stadium;

New Busch Stadium, St Louis, Gateway Arch in the background. The picture of me was taken by Mike Greene — he and his wife Melissa provided me with hospitality, despite the fact we had never met before.

for those who are unsure as to what this is, it's the one that looks like half of a McDonalds logo, and supposedly symbolises the gateway to the West.

The St. Louis Cardinals are the reigning world champions, which means they won last year's World Series, which can only be played for by American (and one Canadian) teams. Despite this, they have started the season poorly, losing several players to injury, one fatally to a car crash, and yesterday they lost, 13–0. The St. Louis fans are a devoted bunch, and the stadium is a sea of red. But even they become restless when the Cardinals go a run down in the first to the visiting Houston Astros. The Cards rally in the fourth to take a 3–1 lead, and that's how it ends— relief all round.

At the end of the game we wait for the crowd to leave, and Mike shows me around the stadium. From up on top of the third tier there are wonderful views of the city and the river Mississippi, and the immaculate playing surface is hosting a local high school game, a rare treat for the winners of a competition.

In the evening we go to eat at a Vietnamese restaurant. The portions are reasonable, the ingredients are healthy, it all tastes great, and I come away feeling neither bloated nor guilty. So to make amends we stop off on the way home at Mr. Wizard, purveyor of the local delicacy, frozen custard. The menu is ridiculously long, and I think I have ordered a concrete turtle, only to be informed by mine hosts that it is, in fact, a turtle concrete. This consists of vanilla frozen custard, with caramel and loads of pecan nuts. Ah cholesterol!

Kansas

Monday May 7

Mike and Melissa are both working people, so I start my Monday at the same time as theirs.

The weather is becoming warmer, usually a kind of watery sun of which you don't take much notice. My arms are burnt from yesterday's game, which I didn't realise until last night.

My drive to Kansas City is straightforward, so I take a couple of detours to ensure I don't arrive too early. Nearing my destination, I detour again to a shopping mall. These are always good places to stretch legs, find refreshments and kill an hour or so. Sunday is Mothers' Day here, so I purchase a small brooch so that I can get it in the post. We already celebrated British Mothers' Day before I left, so she will be getting double rations this year.

Once I have found my motel, I still have 25 miles to go for tonight's game. I am playing the borderline game again, in order to achieve my objectives. My motel is in Kansas City, Missouri, as is the stadium of the city's major league team, the Royals. The minor league team, however, plays in Kansas City, Kansas, which is my destination for this evening.

The team is called the Kansas City T-Bones, and the stadium, Community America Ballpark, is again an edge of town property. They play in the Northern League, which doesn't start until later this month, but they have a pre-season exhibition against the Fort Worth Cats. At least, that's what the website said when I booked my ticket. The opposition turns out to be the Kansas City, Kansas, Community College Blue Devils—try getting that on a shirt—and there is no information as to why the change.

As you may guess from the team's name, Kansas is beef country. There are various meat-related sponsorships to be seen, and I have to say the burger is exceptional.

The game is unremarkable. The college kids are visibly outclassed, and when the home team takes a 2–0 lead in the first it looks like a walkover. But one of the college batters hits a home run, and it remains tight until close to the end, when the T-Bones take advantage of the college substitutes to seal a 6–2 victory.

Missouri (Part Two)

Tuesday May 8–Thursday May 10

Today is one of the days that I have marked down as a highlight of this trip; a visit to the Negro Leagues Baseball Museum.

Earlier I wrote about Jackie Robinson Day, and the tributes that were paid to the man who was generally acknowledged as the first black to play major league baseball. The Negro Leagues are what preceded this, and the museum paints a vivid picture of life at this time, and the trials and tribulations, and the joys, experienced by black men trying to make a living out of playing baseball.

In the late nineteenth century, a handful of blacks actually played in major league teams, a practice that ended when certain star white players made it known that they would not play with or against black players. There followed a "gentlemen's agreement" amongst the owners not to employ blacks, and that's how things remained until 1947 and Jackie Robinson.

The interim is full of fascinating stories, both poignant and funny; black players pretending to be Cuban, and inventing their own language that they hoped their opponents would think was Spanish; an entire Negro League team bought in mid-season by a Latin American dictator, to beat the team employed by his main political rival.

Then, in 1947, Jackie Robinson was employed at great risk by white integrationist Branch Rickey. He was not the best black player around at the time, but he was the one Rickey considered could best deal with the flak that was going to come his way. Later that year a second club took the plunge, and by 1959 every major league team had at least one black player. This, of course, quickly heralded the demise of the Negro Leagues. Major league baseball has long since acknowledged the contribution of these players to the development of baseball, and many of them have retroactively been elected to the Hall of Fame.

The museum, as I have become used to with museums in this country, is comprehensive, easy to follow, modern and beautiful. The end of the route around the museum leads you into a miniature ballpark, with dimmed lighting, containing statues of the best Negro Leagues player in each position — it's so reverential it's almost like being in church.

The museum is located on the corner of Eighteenth and Vine, and it appears that this whole area is steeped in musical history. So it is no surprise that the building is shared with the American Jazz Museum. Not being a jazz fan, I plan to give it a miss, but the combined ticket is hardly more expensive than a single ticket, so I have a quick look. Again, the design is most impressive and, as well as giving a comprehensive account of the development of jazz, opportunity is there for listening to a wide selection, and to partake in a series of interactive exhibits intended to develop an appreciation of this musical form.

Negro Leagues Museum, Kansas City. The year 2007 was the 60th anniversary of Jackie Robinson changing the face of baseball, and this was a highlight of the trip.

Wednesday morning is office work. My present project is organising my brother-in-law Alan to spend some time with me later on this summer. He has decided he would like to join me in New York in August. My cousin's son Marcus is organising my New York leg for me, and doing rather well, but his guest room will only sleep one, so I am having to play middle man and get Marcus to accommodate Alan in our plans. I need a full-time secretary.

After lunch I set off for the Nelson Atkins Museum, half expecting what turns out to be the case. The painting I want to see, Andy Warhol's "Baseball," is in a section being renovated, so I'm not able to see it. I have a little look around but I'm not really a lover of classical art. I do find a moment, however, to gaze at a giant shuttlecock in the middle of the lawn outside.

I head back towards the hotel, and pause to go shopping for essentials, before returning to take care of business. This includes fielding a phone call from the Assistant Director of the Colorado Rockies, confirming my complimentary ticket, so I leave for tonight's game full of my own importance.

Kauffman Stadium, home of the Kansas City Royals, is probably the most spectacular ball park to date, with a huge frontispiece visible from the interstate as you approach. The reverse of this is the outfield scoreboard, which is framed by a ridiculously excessive, but nonetheless very attractive, water feature. As the night grows darker, the lighting in the fountains comes into its own, and becomes even more impressive.

The stadium is extensive and comfortable, and the local microbrewery, Boulevard, has as many pumps visible as the megabreweries. I reward them by sampling both their wheat beer and their Solar Ale, an excellent dark.

The game is close, and tied at two until the home team wins it with a solo home run in the eighth. There are a couple of rain showers, which push those of us in the open back under cover. When everyone moves back, I decide my new vantage point and a dry seat are preferable, so I stay where I am, and have a better view of the fireworks which accompany the game-winning homer.

On Thursday I move on to Springfield to see the Missouri Sports Hall of Fame which, once I find it, is much the same as other such museums. That should not be read as derogatory, as I have been very complimentary of such places, and this is no different — modern, comfortable and informative. It is located in Stan Musial Way; "Stan the Man" was a St. Louis Cardinals great, and I paused at his statue outside Busch Stadium on Sunday.

I particularly enjoy the exhibits depicting various areas of baseball, with lifesize models of heroes in situ; Stan Musial in the locker room and, my particular favourite, a young Harry Caray in the broadcasting booth. There is also a beautiful garden full of statues of Missouri's sporting greats.

I am booked into the Motel 6 in Springfield; I did write and ask Homer and Marge if I could stay with them, but it seems that now the kids are growing up they no longer have a spare room.

At about 6:15, the weather eventually catches up with me. I am just leaving to find some dinner as it starts to rain, and by the time I reach the other side of the car park I think it best to sit it out for a while — which turns out to be about 20 minutes. It is almost pitch black, with forked lightning, thunder, and the car park swimming with water. When it subsides to a mere downpour, I edge my way to the first restaurant that looks reasonable, which happens to be Mexican.

At this juncture a little light-hearted baseball banter occurs. You may remember me writing about the great rivalry between the Chicago Cubs and the St. Louis Cardinals, and I am very much in Cardinals territory. I am wearing my Cubs cap.

I run to the door, but still get very wet. As I enter, a family is just leaving. The woman, jokingly (I think), says to me, "You're already wet! Why don't you run to our car and get the umbrellas?"

I politely decline, but offer them the use of my Cubs cap. The husband smiles, and replies, "No thanks, I'd rather drown than wear that!"

Arkansas

Friday May 11

An early start takes me out of Springfield and down I-65 through southern Missouri. Before long I find I am driving through the Ozarks, which I soon realise is an area of outstanding natural beauty: rich forests, rocky outcrops, steep inclines and descents, and the occasional patch of morning mist. This is probably the most spectacular countryside I have yet encountered.

Arriving in Little Rock I find, once again, my hotel has no broadband, so I head into town to see if I can find any there. I am told that Starbucks is always good for broadband, so I stop for a drink. Unfortunately this one is so new, it hasn't had it fitted yet. So I arrive at the ballpark ridiculously early, and find a beautiful new stadium sitting on the north bank of the river. I leave the car and stroll through the park and over the bridge towards downtown.

Arriving back at the stadium, Dickey-Stephens Park, I notice that start time is 6:30. I was expecting 7:10, so in I go for a look around. It's a gorgeous, new, red brick ballpark, with views across the Arkansas River to the city's skyline on the opposite bank. Full marks to the architect, especially as the right field bleachers incorporate a beer garden, which stocks the locally brewed Diamond Bear Pale Ale.

Game time, and the home team, the Arkansas Travelers (that's how they spell it), jumps out to a 3–0 lead, holding on to win, 3–1. In the sixth, the announcer informs us that, since this is a doubleheader, the game will last only seven innings.

Now a doubleheader is when two games are played on the same day, usually to make up a game that has been rained off, so I assume that the first game took place earlier, and feel slightly cheated. After the seventh, as the game ends, we are informed that the second game will start in 30 minutes, so I haven't been cheated after all.

During the interval, the children in the ground are invited onto the field to run the bases, and chaos ensues. Obviously the phrase "once and once only" is not taught in local schools. Early in the second game there are a couple of thunder claps, and the group behind me, whose entire conversation has been written by Tennessee Williams, decides to leave, as they don't want to get wet. We are then treated to an impressive display of lightning over the city skyline, but no rain.

This game is the inverse of the first, with the away team, the Tulsa Drillers, taking an early lead. As the game is again only seven innings, and we didn't bother in the first game, we have a fifth-inning stretch, which could be considered a 12th-inning stretch. The announcer is obviously a big fan of the late Harry Caray, as he opens the window of the booth and leads the crowd in singing "Take Me Out to the Ball Game," without accompaniment.

The home team fights its way back into the game, and after seven innings, the score is 4–4. So we go to extra innings and the away team wins it 5–4 in the eighth. Honours even, we could all have stayed at home — the game finishes at 11:45!

Oklahoma

Saturday May 12–Sunday May 13

When I put this route together in the cold light of an English winter, it all made perfect sense, so it is a little surprising to find myself heading northwest this morning. I have been under the illusion I am heading steadily south. However, the drive does confirm that Arkansas is the most attractive state I have yet driven through.

Just before leaving Arkansas, my eye is caught by yet another eccentric billboard, "Alma — Spinach Capital of the World — visit us!" Not having a very pressing schedule, and feeling in a particularly obedient mood, I do just that.

Alma turns out to be a few scattered houses, with a main street consisting of a dozen shops and a small park, smaller than my back garden. There, in the middle of the park, is a large statue of the man responsible for the worldwide fame of Alma and spinach — Popeye! The great man stands in typical pose, a can of spinach bursting open in one hand. I have pictures to prove that my detour to Alma is well and truly justified.

Finally, to Tulsa, and the Desert Hills motel; this is a classic, independent motel of the kind seen in many movies; so much so that the lobby is full of cuttings from movies featuring the motel. It is a typical rooms around a car park arrangement, but the rooms are all set at a diagonal, best utilising the space available (so the website informs us, but geometrically I can't see it).

I'm receiving many heartening e-mails telling me that people are supporting my quest for All-Star Game tickets. Some people are even e-mailing all their contacts asking them to register, so my chances of scoring a ticket improve with each passing day.

I have now driven over 6,000 miles and probably have another 15,000 to go. At the Thai restaurant tonight I am given a fortune cookie which says, "Stop searching. Happiness will come to you!" That messes up my itinerary!

Sunday is Mothers' Day in the States. For breakfast, I walk to Tally's Café, about 300 metres from the motel. Today's special is a huge breakfast, served all day — ham, bacon, sausage, eggs, hash browns, plus pancakes and syrup, plus coffee, plus more coffee, plus some extra coffee, for $5.75. Extortionate, especially as you have to add tax!

The place is heaving, presumably because this is the thing to do locally on Mothers' Day. The café is a typical local diner, the like of which is not very evident these days, particularly when travelling. As tables are in great demand from mothers and offspring, I park myself at the counter, just like in the movies. The food arrives relatively quickly, is hot, good and plentiful. As my Mom isn't here I have to eat her share as well.

Come game time, I decide it is necessary to avail myself of sun block for the second time this trip, the first being Florida. The sky is cloudless and the temperature has reached the low 90s. The stadium is a pleasant 15-minute walk, but again has very little character. Now the Americans take Mothers' Day very seriously, and Major League Baseball has teamed up with a breast cancer charity, encouraging players to use pink bats for this day only. Many have chosen to do so, and the Tulsa Drillers have taken this one step further. They seem to be a very politically aware club — all season they have been making donations to a domestic violence charity for each home run hit.

Today they are giving pink baseball caps to women entering the ground, and the players themselves are wearing pink shirts. Now I fully applaud the sentiment, but this could be the worst sporting fashion statement since Coventry City chose chocolate brown for an away strip. Thankfully the fashion police don't work on Sundays.

The shirts fail to weave their spell, and the visiting Wichita Wranglers (surely they should have been called the Wichita Linemen) score four in the first. Tulsa chips away, getting a couple back, and it's 4–2 halfway through the seventh. Now those of you who have been paying attention will know this is the time for a pause to sing "Take Me Out to the Ball Game," which is led with great verve by a local soprano. Having finished, she announces, "And now for our state song," and launches forth into "Oklahoma" (yes, that's Ooooooooooooooooooklahoma!), from the musical of the same name. The crowd joins in, and people actually know the actions, as if it were "YMCA" or "The Birdie Song."

The game recommences, Tulsa sends 11 men to the plate in the bottom of the seventh (which makes scoring very difficult, as scorecards only have nine spaces), and takes the game, 11–4. Talk about inspiration—"Oklahoma, OK! (l-a-h-o-m-a). Yahoo!"

Texas (Part One)

Monday May 14–Tuesday May 15

On Monday morning I leave Tulsa and head for Texas. Ten hours and 520 miles later I am in Houston, with not an awful lot to write about in between.

The purpose of my visit to Houston is to see the Astros play tomorrow, and to visit a dear old friend. Karen and I first met in 1974 and, although there has been the odd card and missive, we have not seen each other since 1978. Since then she has acquired daughter Lindsay and husband Mike, so there are introductions as well as reunions.

Today is Lindsay's last day of school, so there is celebrating to be done, and we all decamp to the local steakhouse, an obvious choice in Texas, although Karen and Lindsay are both vegetarian. Lest I embarrass myself, I am given a brief explanation as to the sacred role of beef in Texan society. Sure enough, when the menu arrives, it comes with a diagram of a cow, so that I am in no doubt as to which bit I am eating—splendid steak it is too.

My e-mails continue to provide tantalising previews of the rest of my trip. Today I receive confirmation of my free tickets in Anaheim, news that my friend in Phoenix will have traditional English food waiting for me—she also has a friend in New Orleans who will show me around when I arrive there; and New York appears to be sorting itself out, so I will sleep easy tonight. Nothing like 520 miles driving and a steak meal as a sedative.

On Tuesday, Karen leaves early for a conference in Washington, and Mike for work, so my host for today is to be Lindsay, footloose and fancy free after finishing school. After a lazy morning, we set off to take the metro to the game. A lot of American cities are now developing metros—with petrol rising to the astronomical figure of $3 a gallon (do the maths, we still pay more than twice as much) there is a crisis at hand.

After a mercifully brief walk, it's 90s and humid, we come to Minute Maid Park, a fairly new stadium with a retractable roof. The former name of this stadium was Enron Field, but you may remember that the company of that name had a lot of problems a few years back, and the club wisely decided to ditch the name for something more homely — and it doesn't get more homely than orange juice.

We collect our complimentary tickets — this is one of my successful begging letters — and the club has done us proud; third base side, 30 rows back. The roof has remained closed, so the stadium is pleasantly cool.

When we arrive, the opposition is taking fielding practice. To continue your baseball education, it's time you learnt a bit of jargon. A high catch hit to the outfield is referred to as a fly ball, often abbreviated to fly. The correct vernacular verb for catching fly balls during practice in those big gloves that they wear is "to shag." Therefore, when we arrive, the opposition is in the outfield shagging flies. Insert your own joke here, preferably without mentioning pencil sharpeners.

Tonight we will watch the Houston Astros against the San Francisco Giants. The Giants have a star hitter named Barry Bonds, and it is highly likely that, within a few weeks, he will break the career home run record. This is one of the most revered records in the game, and has stood for more than 30 years since Hank Aaron, a very popular and respected player, took it from Babe Ruth, who had held it for about 50 years.

On any other occasion the fans, even the home fans, would be rooting for Bonds, wanting to see the record broken. The problem here is that Bonds is high on the list of players suspected of steroid abuse, and a fair percentage of fans don't want him to break the record for that reason. So he is mercilessly booed every time he comes to the plate.

There are some unique things about this stadium, most of them peculiarly Texan. The scoreboard, as well as showing the results of the other games being played, keeps us up to date with oil prices. At the end of each of the lines leading from home plate there stands a huge pole, as there does in all parks, called the foul pole. This enables the umpires to tell whether a ball in the air is fair or foul. In Houston these are sponsored by a local chicken restaurant, and are called "fowl poles!"

Also, up towards the roof, there is an old steam train, which runs along a 20-metre track, hooting and flashing, every time Houston scores a home run — thankfully they do so, and we get to see it perform.

The game is one of the better ones I have seen. Houston calmly takes a 3–0 lead, and appears in control of the game. In between innings, one is often treated to pictures of individual fans, who are supposed to react in a particular way according to the instructions on the scoreboard screen. One of these is the "kiss-cam," where couples framed are obliged to pucker up. On this occasion one of the gentlemen concerned has obviously pre-arranged his framing, and falls to his knees to propose. Said partner tearfully accepts.

This emotion is evidently too much for the Houston players, and by the top of the eighth they are behind, 5–3. But in the seventh inning stretch they take a leaf out of Oklahoma's book, and the bonus song is (clap, clap, clap, clap) "Deep in the Heart of Texas." This inspires a two-run homer in the bottom of the eighth to bring them level, and the game goes to extra innings. In the bottom of the tenth Houston's Carlos Lee sends us all home happy with a walk-off homer. No home runs for Bonds, and Houston celebrates.

Louisiana
Wednesday May 16–Saturday May 19

My next scheduled game is not until Saturday, so I'm off to spend a couple of days in New Orleans. But first I must pay some dues. A relatively short drive from Houston brings me to Port Arthur, in the extreme southeast of Texas. The target of my visit is the Museum of the Gulf Coast, which is dedicated to this area and its native sons and daughters.

The reason I am here is that it's the birthplace of Janis Joplin, one of my all-time musical greats, and the museum holds a copy of a film about her life. I have phoned ahead and arranged a viewing and, true to form, it is waiting for me when I arrive. I sit alone in a small cinema, for what seems like ten minutes, but is in fact an hour. I am completely absorbed, both by the video and the other exhibits.

Returning to the gift shop I run into two elderly ladies, volunteers for the museum who, being local, know the Joplin family, what's left of it, and they treat me to a home-made brownie while talking about their beloved museum. I am generally being economical regarding the purchase of souvenirs, due to restrictions of both space and budget, but Janis and the old ladies merit a book, a T-shirt, and some cards.

The next day I'm off to New Orleans, one of the cities in the U.S. that actually shaped my trip. I remember thinking that if I were only going to visit the 30 major league parks I wouldn't get to see New Orleans, and that set the ball rolling.

The only upsetting thing about the drive is that, travelling east along the south coast, you don't expect to see the sea on your left. It turns out to be Lake Pontchartrain, but I can't see the other shore, so it might as well be the sea.

The hotel really is very good, possibly my best yet, and I seem to have secured a very good deal. Not only is it a good room, but the fee includes cooked breakfast and parking. Cooked breakfast is rare in American hotels, and, in city hotels, parking is usually very expensive.

After settling in, I walk in the general direction of the city centre, in search of a bus stop, and soon realise that it is walking distance, so I keep going. New

Orleans is unlike many U.S. cities, as it has a centre, and distinct areas. In many ways it is more French than American, which figures. I walk through downtown and into the French Quarter, and it is all the films promise — narrow streets, houses with columns and balconies, and groups of street musicians. The sound of a riverboat hooter pulls me right, and I find myself on the banks of the Mississippi.

I stop at the Crescent City Brewpub and order gumbo, which is something I feel is a must in this city. This is described as a soup, but is quite thick. As Harry Hill once said, "It's a thin line between soup and stew." Anyhow, it consists of rice, with chopped smoked sausage, crabmeat and shrimps, in a thick brown spicy sauce. I follow this with a shrimp salad — in the States shrimps can be anything from the tiny ones that we get, and that I had in my gumbo, to king prawns, and these are indeed royal.

The food is excellent, the beer is excellent, but the band fails dismally to make it three out of three, so I stroll into the night in search of diversion. I soon come across the main street, full of clubs, each one offering a different kind of music. I am taken by two guys playing zydeco, so settle myself in and order a drink. It's a few minutes before I realise that I am, in fact, drinking bourbon on Bourbon Street.

On Friday I return to the city centre, in search of a post office and a riverboat. Last week the cost of postage was increased, and it seems the powers that be have updated all the lists and computers, but neglected to send out stocks of stamps in the new prices. So you are left with the choice of paying over the odds, or letting your mail back up.

I turn towards the river and walk to the dock, as I have decided to take a river cruise. This turns out to be a very relaxing way to spend a couple of hours. The boat is an authentic paddle steamer, and we are welcomed aboard by a woman playing a steam organ, powered by the steam of the engine. We also receive a full commentary from one of the crew, and see the lower ninth quarter, which suffered worst at the hands of Hurricane Katrina.

On Saturday I bid farewell to New Orleans, a place to which I would like to return. As I drive north on I-10, I also have a final hour with my favourite radio station so far, before eventually losing reception. The Ragin' Cajun is an idiosyncratic mix of birthdays, death notices, local community notices, things for sale, and some Cajun and Zydeco music. Think of a mix of Jean Metcalf and Noel Edmonds, in a thick local accent, plus decent music. I could get 30 12-inch barn door hinges this morning, but where would I put them?

On to Shreveport, and I arrive at the usual motel on the outskirts of town. I check in and am given room 113, which happens to be next to where I have parked. I open the door, and am quite surprised to be joyfully greeted by two Labradors! I quickly close the door and return to reception, to ask if I have to pay extra for this. The other customer in reception says that, when he opened his door, he found a woman sitting on the bed. I ask if he would like to swap. Sadly, it's an error and I'm moved to 119.

And so we come to the game, Shreveport Sports vs. Pensacola Pelicans, at Fair Grounds Field. Another concrete stadium on the edge of town, but this one happens to boast the best, for me, ballpark snack yet. A slow-cooked turkey leg, probably marinaded in something first, because the flesh is the colour of ham. I expect to eat it in the classic, carnivorous way, but the chef informs me I will need a fork, and she is proved right, as the flesh dislodges itself as soon as I open the foil. It is smoky, spicy, and so tender it just falls off the bone in lumps. At $6 it certainly puts your average hot dog in its place.

The game is close, and dominated by the pitchers. The home team trails 1–0, leads 2–1, is pegged back again, and wins in the bottom of the ninth on a wild pitch.

Texas (Part Two)
Sunday May 20–Thursday May 24

Sunday is a free day on my schedule, so I decide on a slight detour, and return to Houston to spend more time with my old friend Karen. I think a 30-year separation deserves more than one evening of her company, and what's a couple of hundred miles between friends?

On Monday I awake with a cold, not a full blown thing, but one of those irritating ones which dry up your throat, make your brain feel too big, and tire you out. If I were at home, I would just take it easy, and consume warm rum, but my schedule puts both of those options out of bounds. So I buy some tablets and lots of orange juice, and keep going. The tablets, so it says, are non-drowsy, but the cold isn't, so I need a few more stops than usual.

Arlington is just west of Dallas, and turns out to be a designer-built entertainment complex, containing two theme parks as well as the ballpark. This isn't as bad as it might sound, and in terms of accommodation and transport makes a lot of sense. When I check in I am given a voucher and informed that the trolleybus will stop at the back of the hotel and take me to the game.

So at the appointed hour I mount said trolleybus, even though I could probably walk in 20 minutes. The park is another of the modern red brick constructions, and is very attractive, with lots of grass and open space. There is also an excellent Legends Museum, with the usual collection of memorabilia, but two particularly notable sections. There is a room dedicated to the 25 greatest plays of all time, with video footage of many of them. Displayed around the walls of the museum are various quotes— and one thing in which baseball players have the edge over other sportspeople is being quotable. Two in particular impress me:

"You gotta be a man to play baseball for a living. But you gotta have a lot of little boy in you."— Roy Campanella, one of the game's greatest catchers in both the Negro Leagues and Major Leagues.

"Baseball has done more to move America in the right direction than all the professional patriots with their billions of cheap words."— Monte Irvin, left fielder and hitter, also in both the Negro Leagues and Major Leagues.

I try to travel light to ballgames—a small shoulder bag and my scorepad— so there inevitably comes a moment when I run out of hands. This usually arrives about 20 minutes before the first pitch, when I go to my seat, pad under arm, bag over shoulder, snack in one hand, drink in the other hand, needing to put things down, lower my seat—I'm sure you've all been there.

Tonight, just as my buttock is about to touch the seat, the first drops of rain fall. So I pick everything up and retire to the tunnel, along with a few other sensible people. The sport then becomes seeing how long other people will sit and get rained on before admitting that us early movers have done the sensible thing after all. There are some very wet people on show.

The ballpark staff immediately takes appropriate action. The infield is covered before I am. When the rain stops, and it has been pretty hard, there is an announcement that the game will start at 7:30, 25 minutes late. In the States, it is not uncommon, when arriving at a stadium, for a steward to escort you to your seat, and wipe it down for you. Tonight, the stewards are armed with huge rolls of absorbent paper, which is doled out to us as we return to our seats. The game, as promised, starts at 7:30.

The game features the Texas Rangers, whose previous owners include George W. Bush, against the Minnesota Twins. Both teams begin hitting well, and after four innings Texas leads, 4–2. In the bottom of the fifth, Texas scores two more, and the pitcher is substituted. His replacement is a disaster, and we are treated to one of the most exciting sights in the game—a grand slam. This means that the batting team has a runner on each of the bases when the batter hits a home run. It scores four runs, the most that can be scored with a single hit.

Each home run, and there are three in all, is greeted by fireworks, so it turns out to be quite a spectacular evening. Texas goes on to win, 14–4, and the crowd is ecstatic. That's the biggest major league score I've witnessed to date, but this is Texas.

I would find it hard to justify visiting the Dallas area without paying a visit to the Kennedy Museum. I can remember the assassination quite vividly. I was just turned 13, and recall the news coming through early evening. The TV companies stopped broadcasting as a mark of respect, so I went to listen to Radio Luxembourg, only to find they had done the same thing.

The museum is surprising in some ways. I was expecting it to stand out and be the centre of attention, but it's tucked away, and not particularly well signposted. The atmosphere inside is respectful, and even the party of primary school kids eventually quietens down and works out what it's all about. There are no big surprises, I have seen all the footage before, countless times, and the shock of the nation, and the world, was overwhelming. But what I had forgotten was how good he was. The first part of the museum shows his campaign trail, and the presidency, and his ease with public speaking, and the witty and clever repartee, is good to see.

I wander around for a while afterwards, see the low-key memorial, stand on the grassy knoll, and then head off. I have no particular destination, but plan just to head west, and break the journey somewhere. I decide to break my journey in Abilene, because it features in countless Westerns and songs.

The receptionist spots my accent, and asks where I am from. When I admit to being English, she goes all dewy eyed, and says how cool it must be to live there, while she's stuck in a dump like Abilene. This completely contradicts my own feelings, as I have been aware of the name of Abilene since my childhood, and find it redolent of the old West.

On Wednesday all I really do is move 200 miles west along I-20. As I drive, the trees become smaller and sparser, the horizon seems further away, the soil becomes very red and then sandy coloured. I guess I must be in the desert, or at least moving in that direction.

This evening the weather is hot enough for me to swim in the hotel pool, which is open despite the date, after which I am curious enough to drive into Monahans to see if anything is there. There is nothing much, but it is the closest to a classic small American town that I have yet seen. If you remember the movie "The Last Picture Show," it could have been shot in Monahans—railroad line, wide streets, low houses.

As nothing else is happening today, it might be appropriate to give you your next baseball lesson, a review of the season so far. I think I mentioned that baseball is split into two leagues, the American League and the National League, and that the winners of each league play at the end of the season for the World Series. But how do they decide who has won each league, because I told you earlier that each league has three divisions—East, Central and West.

At the end of the season each of the division winners goes to the post-season, where they are joined by the wild card. The wild card is the runner-up with the best record over the season. This happens in each league. They then play knock-out series in each league; Divisional Series reduce the teams from four to two, Championship Series produce a winner for each league, and these two teams play in the World Series.

If the season ended today, the teams going through would be the Boston Red Sox, Cleveland Indians, Los Angeles Angels and Detroit Tigers from the American League, and the New York Mets, Milwaukee Brewers, Los Angeles Dodgers and Atlanta Braves from the National League.

Bearing in mind that we are less than a third of the way through a 162-game season, there is plenty of time for this to change. But you may have observed that the best-known team in baseball, the New York Yankees, is noticeable by its absence. This is due to two main reasons: an outrageous run of injuries to the pitching staff, and the outstanding form of their divisional rivals, the Red Sox, who are already ten games clear.

This has led to talk that the Yankees might sack their manager, Joe Torre, one of the most respected men in the game. The Yankees have also paid an enormous amount of money to bring Roger Clemens, one of the greatest pitchers of recent years, out of retirement. This is such a big story that tonight the TV was showing Clemens pitching in a minor league game as part of his preparation.

This is keeping Barry Bonds and his home run record off the screens just at the moment, aided by the fact that he is going through a slump. As soon as he starts hitting again, the controversy will reappear.

No more baseball until Sunday, so I fill in the gaps with more musical exploration. First up is Wink, population 909. Despite its size, it is apparently a city. It has city limits at least. It is also the place where Roy Orbison grew up, and boasts a museum to his memory.

From there I hit the road to Lubbock which takes me, for a short while, over the border into New Mexico, and through some of the strangest landscape I have seen. The terrain is scrubby and sandy, and the fields are full of those machines that look like huge nodding birds. Add to this the huge spherical storage tanks, and "The War of the Worlds" comes to mind.

In the midst of all this stands a unique sculpture. You first catch sight of it from the highway — a pair of cowboys driving cattle along the skyline. On closer examination these creations are about 15 feet tall, and made of sheet metal!

Arriving in Lubbock, the home of Buddy Holly, I relax in my room reading a brochure I picked up in the lobby. It turns out that the statue of Buddy Holly and the Walk of Fame are just a couple of blocks from my motel, so I set off and inspect them.

From there I walk on to the centre of town, where an excellent meal is found at a brew pub. The barman immediately becomes a great friend and I succeed, without prompting, in ordering his favourite meal from the menu. He is very jealous of what I am doing, so I ask him why he doesn't do the same thing. I often ask this of people, and they never seem to have an answer.

New Mexico
Friday May 25 to Wednesday June 13

If you're paying any attention at all to the dates, you may be wondering why New Mexico justifies 20 days. Read on, and all will be revealed!

Friday is all about Buddy Holly — the day the music died? The statue and

Walk of Fame I did last night, this morning I visit the Buddy Holly Center, a building dedicated to his life and music. It is easy to find, especially with the huge pair of dark-rimmed spectacles by the sign outside. It is as tasteful as you would expect, with great emphasis placed on the early days in and around Lubbock, and reminiscences from the people who played with him during his formative years.

I then drive across town to visit his grave, a simple affair, with his parents laid to rest next to him. The name on all the graves, incidentally, is spelt Holley. It seems the "e" was only dropped professionally. The notice in the cemetery says that the custom is to leave a plectrum on the grave, so that the music will live on. I have just bought six plectrums at the gift shop in the museum, so I think about leaving one of them, but decide that the music will live on better if I send them to people I know who play guitar.

The short journey from Lubbock to Clovis is the journey that Buddy Holly and the Crickets took to make their first recordings, at the studio of Norman Petty. Norman died in the 1980s, followed by his wife in the early 90s. At this point the studio was left in the Pettys' estate, with the instructions that it should not be destroyed, to the mercies of two of his advisers. One of these is Kenneth Broad, and I have arranged to meet him on Saturday morning for a tour of the studio.

The studio is staffed entirely by volunteers, and is a study in devotion and reverence. The other visitor and I see the studio and the attached apartment, and are taken into town and shown around the Lyceum Theatre, which was used by Norman for recording activities which were too big for the studio. From there we go past the Foxy Drive-In, where the artists would dine, to Clovis Cemetery to see the Pettys' grave, and return to the studio for farewells. This is a morning which has produced more than I could have expected.

The drive to Albuquerque this afternoon is just over 200 miles, yet produces some amazing contrasts in scenery. I manage to avoid the weather, besides being able to see storms on either side of me, as the scenery changes from the flatlands around Clovis, in gradual stages to the Rockies, on whose southern tip Albuquerque stands.

On arrival, I realise I need clean laundry, and am directed to the local laundromat. So in the bright early evening sunlight, I am able to complete my chores, whilst staring out of the window at spectacular mountain views. I am also able to contemplate a small red blob which has appeared in the corner of my left eye this afternoon.

I am in Albuquerque for a game on Sunday evening, so that gives me a good few hours to kill. The hotel has a small swimming pool which I make use of, and then I have a job to do. The blob in my left eye is growing larger and beginning to affect my vision, but it's Sunday, and tomorrow is Memorial Day, so medical help would be hard to obtain. I find an open pharmacy and acquire some eye wash. The pharmacist advises that, as it's just one eye, it's more likely an infection than an allergy, so I will have to wait.

After a couple of hours' rest I set off for tonight's game. You may have noticed that some teams have names which reflect some aspect of their location. Hence tonight's visitors are the Nashville Sounds, and the home team, somewhat more bizarrely, is the Albuquerque Isotopes.

The park is pleasant, with a backdrop of the Rockies, locally brewed beer, and more turkey legs (though not as good as Shreveport). The game also is good. The home team takes an early lead, the Sounds equalise in the fourth, and go ahead 3–1 in the fifth. In the sixth the Sounds catcher slams a solo home run, after which the home team pulls it back to 4–3. But they have not learnt their lesson. The next time the Sounds catcher comes up, he does it again, with two runners on this time. It ends 9–7 to Nashville.

When I awake on Monday, the minor eye irritation is now blocking the sight of my entire left eye, so I ask at reception where I might find some emergency medical aid, this being the American equivalent of a Bank Holiday. I have enough foresight to make use of the hotel computer and print off a copy of my medical insurance.

The emergency hospital turns out to be on the other side of the road junction from the hotel, so I only have a short walk. Sure enough, the first question I am asked refers to how I will be paying for my treatment but, that apart, I have no complaints. The woman who takes me from reception to the consulting room insists on giving me a lecture on Albuquerque chili — apparently if it's too hot you should drink milk, not water!

The doctor has a quick look, and tells me that it looks like a detached retina, but that he would like me to be seen by a consultant, whom he has on call. So I walk back to the hotel, climb in my car, and drive a couple of stops down the interstate to another facility, which does not prove particularly easy to find.

The consultant confirms the first doctor's suspicion, and calls in a senior colleague, the retinal expert. He informs me that he is prepared to operate on me tomorrow, and that I must decide whether to take him up on his offer or return home. How I manage to drive back to the hotel, my eyes full of a mixture of dilating drops and tears, I don't know. But I make it, and collapse on my bed, feeling as low as can be.

Having almost decided to fly home, I eventually get hold of my wife, Sally, who gives me a verbal slap and tells me I must have the operation as soon as possible, as travelling home would be dangerous. She promises to join me as soon as she can, so I call the hospital and book the surgery.

They tell me two things upon which I must act. Firstly, I will need to be accompanied tomorrow; secondly, I must starve after midnight. So I go through the phone book until I find a nursing agency, and rent myself a companion. Then I head downtown to find some food and top up my cash, as tomorrow threatens to be quite expensive. I stumble into a bar to grab something to eat, but I am in such a state of shock that the fact that the waitresses all wear school uniform with knee socks and very short skirts is sadly wasted on me.

I return to the hotel, wondering how long it will continue to be my home, and have further conversations with my incredibly supportive family, still wondering what sort of demon decided to curse my trip thus.

On a positive note, I had an interesting conversation earlier with one of the doctors regarding last night's game. Although there is an obvious link to local industry, it seems that the name of the Albuquerque Isotopes was chosen by the local public in a poll, and the main reason given for the choice was that there was once a baseball team featured in "The Simpsons" called ... the Albuquerque Isotopes!!

Tuesday starts with my opening my e-mails, still on quite an emotional low, and being incredibly lifted by the outpourings of support from friends and family. I am so grateful to receive all these messages. The solitude of the last couple of days has been the hardest part, so having all these people rooting for me is very important to me. I had secured free tickets for the Colorado Rockies, and was due to be there in a couple of days, so have had to write and cancel. Even my contact there, whom I have never met, replies with a very supportive e-mail.

At the appointed hour, my companion arrives. We drive to the hospital, and I check in. I am asked what relationship my companion has to me, and my reply, "rent-a-pal," causes some amusement. Eventually I am shown into a room with beds, and asked to undress and don a gown. The nurse in attendance is an absolute sweetheart and, as I start to become emotional, reassures me that the process will be painless. I try to explain that I have no fear of the process but that, were I at home, I would have a wife and two daughters in close attendance, and these are just tears of loneliness. She offers me the bedside phone to call home, but I decline, explaining that that would make me an even bigger mess.

There is only one thing in the whole process I could criticise. When I sign the consent form I am adamant that they should alter it to read "left eye," as that is the one out of which I can see nothing. Fortunately it is just a typo.

The operation itself is quite bizarre. The anaesthetic is very strong, but local, so I am conscious for the proceedings. My right eye is covered, so all I can see is through the eye on which they are operating — vague shapes poking things into my eye. If you've ever seen one of those old sci-fi films where someone has been abducted by aliens, who operate on his brain, it is not too far removed from that.

I don't know if they then give me something stronger, as my next memory is of my rent-a-pal appearing, to claim the body, and the two of us slowly decamp to a neighbouring restaurant for a very welcome meal.

Now I'm back in the motel room which I'm learning to call home, complete with a nicely developing headache. I have some fairly strong painkillers, which I am to use at my discretion. It appears the operation has been a success. I still have a huge patch over my left eye, and need to return to outpatients in the morning to see how things are, but the surgeon seems optimistic, so it's fingers crossed.

Wednesday starts with a visit to the surgeon, accompanied by rent-a-pal mark 2. The news, as might be expected, is both good and bad. The operation, it appears, has been a success. The negative side is that I am confined to barracks in Albuquerque for the next two weeks.

I have tablets and drops to administer, and I have been allocated a strangely shaped pillow with a hole in the middle, as I am to spend the majority of the time lying flat on my face, and am not allowed up for more than 30 minutes at a time. This has prompted some of my nearest and dearest to suggest that the book now be entitled "20 Things To Do in Albuquerque Lying Flat on your Face." At the moment I have not got further than two.

The rest of Wednesday is spent in the company of Lissie from Phoenix, who has flown over just to keep me company for the day. We met through our parents, who are friendly back home, and I was to have stayed with her and her husband when in Phoenix. Irritatingly, this part of the trip, along with Southern California, has now been blown out of the water. If I get the all clear in two weeks, the earliest part of my schedule I might catch up with would be Oakland on June 17.

Lissie has wisely brought along a book. Lying prone and face down is not the best position for conversation, and I think that there is something in my medication to help me sleep; understandably, as this is quite an easy thing to do in this position. Her husband has business contacts in Albuquerque, so she calls one of them for a lift, and does some food shopping for me before returning to Phoenix.

I continue to be amazed by the support and sympathy I am receiving from my readers, particularly as regards the decision to stick it out. Messages range from the sincere and concerned on the one hand, to the advice, on the other hand, to get myself a pirate hat and keep going. The die is now cast because, even if I change my mind, I can't fly until the gas bubble dissipates from my eye. But the good wishes are overwhelming—I even receive a call from Ken Broad, the guy who showed me around the studios last week, who has discovered my plight whilst looking at my website.

Sally appears to have achieved the unachievable, and got a passport issued quickly. Her target is to board a plane on Friday morning, so I can but wait.

Thursday is a blur. If you lie face down a lot you tend to fall asleep a lot. The good news is that Sally has managed to get a flight, and arrives Friday evening. That might increase my list to three.

I am existing on cold meat and cheese sandwiches, from the stock that Lissie kindly provided for me, plus a daily visit to the diner, where I have discovered the breakfasts are more palatable than the dinners. The good wishes continue to pour in, ranging from the sincere to the hilarious, via the downright cynical. As I am only allowed to be upright for 30 minutes at a time, the computer is my lifeline, even more so than the TV, which has to be viewed from some pretty peculiar angles.

During my allotted vertical time, I get busy cancelling the next two weeks of my trip. The most frustrating thing is that, after Colorado, there was not another motel on the agenda for the whole fortnight. Denver was to have been followed by the Arizona Diamondbacks in Phoenix, where I was to stay with Lissie; the Angels and the Dodgers in Los Angeles, where my projected host was the son of my next door neighbour; and the Padres in San Diego, where Debbie, a friend of a friend, whom I have yet to meet, had promised me a beach-side residence and margueritas on the sand, plus a visit to the Hotel del Coronado — that's the big white hotel where *Some Like It Hot*, one of my favourite films, was shot.

Friday is dull. I don't even get to the door of my room. When I awake I receive the news that Sally is on her way, so I find a programme on the computer that enables me to track her flight. It's amazing what you will do for entertainment when times are hard. After a five-hour change-over in Minneapolis, which is pretty dull viewing, the little cross that is my wife starts to move again and at ten minutes to twelve, after 24 hours of travelling, she appears at the door of my motel room. Two months is the longest we have ever been apart, so this reunion is marked with a particularly firm handshake.

Saturday morning is devoted to sorting out business, so we now have Sal's name on the car insurance and tomorrow we'll be moving to a new location. How I shall miss my home of the last eight days, the downtown Econo Lodge, with stunning views of I-25, with noises to match — especially since Sally insists on having the window open because she doesn't like the air conditioning.

The highlight of the morning is our 50-yard walk to Winston's Diner. This has been my main source of food over the last few days but it is Sal's first experience of a classic American diner. I choose staple American fare while Sal opts for Mexican eggs and pinto beans. Now you might realise why I am encouraging her to have the air con on.

Sal's final act of mercy to date has been to confiscate my laptop, in fact she is typing this piece as I dictate. This might help explain why there are fewer long words than usual (He'd better watch out, I can easily get the next flight back — Ed.)

A few hours before Sally arrived I received an e-mail from a young woman I have never met, a baseball fanatic who wants to leave her husband and run away with me. Before I could consider this objectively Sal had arrived. I feel a readers' poll coming up. (One vote in favour — Ed.)

Sunday is a day of great activity, moving the one-eyed man and his angel of mercy to new accommodation. The move itself is relatively straightforward. The problem proves to be finding things to do between the 12:00 check-out time of the Econo Lodge and the 3:00 check-in time of the Suburban Extended Stay Hotel.

Lunch seems a good idea, and we are progressing along Central Avenue when my one good eye falls upon the Frontier Restaurant. My one good brain cell remembers that this has been recommended by several people, so in we go.

My present drug regime has killed my appetite, so actually finding something appealing with a queue building up behind me is quite a trial. I end up settling for steak and salad, which turns out to be very nicely presented, but I still have to force it down.

This leaves us only 2½ hours to kill. We can go anywhere we want as long as it involves me lying face down. As we are opposite the University complex, we set off in search of grass and shade, and find some outside the University theatre, Popejoy Hall Center for the Arts. We pull into the car park, and enquire of a passing local if we can stay there for a couple of hours. He somehow guesses we are English, and immediately turns into the perfect host.

He turns out to be an American of Norwegian descent, who has always wanted to marry an English girl so he can spend half of his year in England and half in the States. Sensing an opportunity here, we show Joel, for that is his name, a picture of our younger daughter, watch his eyes light up, and fully expect to announce an engagement any day. He is fascinated by the tale of my journey, and immediately offers us hospitality. We take his phone number and promise to make contact.

At the appointed hour we move into the new hotel which is not unpleasant, and has flowers and trees instead of the I-25. Having settled in, Sal sets off in search of the local Walmart to stock us with provisions. After what seems like an eternity she returns, having taken half an hour to get there and three minutes to get back.

Each day, as I write the heading to my journal, the word "Albuquerque" appears yet again. I look at it carefully, making sure that all those "qs" and "us" are in the right place, and wonder how much time I would have saved if I had had my operation in Iowa.

Monday is a day of great import. Today I am allowed, my diary reminds me, to remove my eye patch. Only two days remain to my next hospital appointment, so I am getting ever so slightly excited. The hospital has provided me with a large pair of wraparound style dark glasses, so large that they fit over my regular glasses. I must look like a B-list celebrity, desperate to be recognised whilst wanting to give the opposite impression.

The young woman who wants to run away with me turns out to be a writer, a client of my cousin's daughter-in-law, who is in publishing. The writer, Crystal, shares my love of baseball, and has a background in sports journalism.

I write to Jenny (the publisher) and her husband Marcus, to ask for advice as to whether I should leave my wife for this woman. Marcus prevaricates, as he has never actually met the woman, and Jenny, fearful of losing her seat at our annual Christmas fondue, votes against. So it appears my marriage is safe for the present.

On to Tuesday, and the good news is that I'm writing this myself. No disrespect to my lady wife, but it feels good to be able to do some of the simple things for myself again. I would probably have died of depression and boredom by now if she had not arrived to rescue me, but a little self-sufficiency is good for the soul. Even if I'm going to have to do it in installments, as my 30 minutes of being upright has just ended, and I have to go and face my mattress for another little while.

Something positive appears to be happening in the eye department. Whilst lying face down, I have noticed a circular shape in my bad eye, which I assume is the gas bubble holding the retina in place. I have now realised that I can see through this bubble, and my close-up vision is pretty near perfect.

More positive news arrives, in the shape of two of our number being successful in the ballot for All-Star Game tickets. As one of them is my daughter I am able, with her consent of course, to hack into her e-mail and apply. The application is successful, and I now have tickets for all stages of the All-Star festivities. In fact, since they made me buy a complete set, I now have duplicates for the first three parts, which I had already managed to acquire prior to the ballot.

On Wednesday I awake early, prepared to face my day of reckoning. Not only is this the day for visiting my eye surgeon, it also involves Sally coming face to face with an Interstate for the first time since 2004. If the latter is not successful, the former will lose all relevance.

Thankfully, the latter is successful, and we pull up outside the offices of Eye Associates of New Mexico with 20 minutes to spare. As these offices back onto the Econo Lodge, home of my heart for those eight wonderful days of mattress watching, I am able to take a moment to reflect, and gaze lovingly at my favourite stretch of I-25.

We proceed to the waiting room. After a relatively short wait, we are beckoned by a lady in purple pyjamas who, rather thoughtfully, has a biro which matches her pyjamas perfectly. I wonder if she has sets at home? She probes, pokes, measures, dilates and notes, and we are dispatched back to the waiting room, which turns out to be very appropriately named. As I have to sit staring at the floor for the majority of the time, it is Sal who does most of the exploring. She starts by picking up a card from a rack on the wall, which contains the c.v. of my eye surgeon. Now there have been some rather disparaging remarks in these columns, and the responses I have received, along the lines of, "Of all the places this could have happened, why somewhere like Albuquerque?" Well, I should retract them all. This guy appears to have won everything short of the Nobel Prize (and I would have thought that a mention in these columns would make him a hot favourite for next year), and I just happen to be in a motel next to his surgery when my retina falls out. How lucky is that?

Eventually my name is called, and we wander through to the consulting room. Dr. Reidy comes in, looks deep into my eyes, and says, "You look lovely."

I thank him and ask what he's doing after work, and then we both realise that my wife is watching, and return to a professional basis. To cut a long story short, it appears that the operation has been a success, my long days of mattress watching have paid off and, subject to another check-up next Wednesday, I should be free to continue my travels.

Back to the hotel to book in for another week; I am now allowed to read, watch TV, and lie on my left-hand side. I spend the rest of the day counting my blessings, and get to 28 before I fall asleep — on my left-hand side. Make that 29.

After lunch on Thursday, the phone rings, and it turns out to be Joel. If you don't know who Joel is, turn back a couple of pages. Feeling sorry for two visitors to his city finding themselves in our situation, he invites us to his house for the afternoon.

You may recall that on Sunday I offered this gentleman my daughter. I feel we can learn a lot from Eastern culture, and if arranged marriage is good enough for them, count me in. So this is quite an important visit for me. He is 37, has a job, his own house, a black leather recliner in front of a wide screen TV, and all the sport channels on satellite. When we arrive he's watching cricket! I mail my daughter a plane ticket.

Our host is still insistent that we go and stay in his house, and Sal finds it difficult to understand my reluctance. The truth is that I am still taking the evil drugs, and while I continue to burp, fall asleep and cry a lot, I don't see myself as a very good house guest.

Friday morning just passes in a blur of TV sport and naps, and then we receive a call from Joel. We drive over to his house, where we meet his charming mother Jettie. Once again we are regaled with offers to stay there during our time in Albuquerque. Maybe after the weekend we will reconsider.

Back at the hotel I decide to tempt fate, and look at where my trip goes from here. On Thursday evening I should have been in San Diego, watching the Padres play the Los Angeles Dodgers. I check the scores— the Dodgers were leading 5–1 coming into the bottom of the ninth, and the home team scored five to win the game. That was not a good game to miss!

The games I will have missed are all major league: Colorado, Anaheim, San Diego, Phoenix and Los Angeles. There was also a trip to Hawaii, which can probably be fitted in at the end of the summer. I might be able to fit in Colorado in July after Las Vegas, but Southern California and Arizona will have to go on the back burner, so Sal and I are already talking about a trip next year to finish the project. If all goes according to plan, we will hit the road again on June 14 and head for Oakland. It's just over 1,000 miles, but we have three days to do it, so it should be manageable.

Saturday is another fun-filled, action-packed day here out West — at least until I wake up. I should, of course, be in Phoenix for the interleague game, where the Red Sox come from behind to defeat the Diamondbacks 4–3 in the tenth. Another thrilling climax missed!

Sunday brings more good news on the bubble front; not only is the bubble in my eye gradually becoming smaller, it's beginning to break down. Little bubbles are going out to make a life for themselves, but usually come back and reattach to the main bubble, making it look like the bubble has appendages.

In the evening I watch baseball on TV, a game I am particularly keen to watch as my Chicago Cubs are playing. In the first inning, the Cubs starting pitcher hits one of the opposing batters with the ball. This is not an uncommon occurrence, and gives the batter free passage to first base. If the umpire senses intent, he will sometimes issue a warning that future miscreants will be punished. On this occasion he simply ejects the pitcher, a decision which mystifies players, fans, commentators and all. The effect on the game is dramatic, as a starting pitcher will usually go at least five or six innings before the manager turns to his bench. This leaves the Cubs relieving pitchers to fill over eight innings. They almost manage it, and take a 4–2 lead into the eighth before things go pear-shaped and they lose, 5–4 — a tough loss to take.

Monday is moving day. We say goodbye to the Suburban Extended Stay and move to Joel's house. As soon as we arrive, Sal is ushered away by Joel's mom, while I am led to Joel's car. He is hungry, so we have to go eat. I am taken to a place called Charley's Backdoor, which is probably the darkest restaurant I have ever been to, but the food is great — chicken and green chili enchilladas, served with sopas. Now sopas are concoctions of soft wheat, about the size and shape of a Shredded Wheat, but hollow. The idea is to bite off one corner and pour honey inside. It's an interesting idea, although I'm not sure about honey and chili.

Back at the ranch we crash for a couple of hours — I think my fatigue is contagious — and then Joel prepares for a barbecue. He has invited a couple of friends, James and Sally, to meet us. Having assured us at the weekend that, when it rains in New Mexico, it rains very hard for about 30 minutes, we proceed to watch as it rains steadily for about six hours — good to know that we share the same traditions when it comes to barbecues.

By Tuesday, the bubble in my eye is down to a mere pin prick, so I am hoping for a clean bill of health when I see the doctor. Tomorrow sees me take the last of this marvellous medicine and return to what passes as normal in my life, drinking beer and staying awake all day. Sal decides that Joel needs a humming-bird feeder for his garden, so a short stroll to the local store provides this. On our return, we are introduced to Joel's ten-year-old son Lucas, and then Joel's mom arrives. We have arranged to treat everyone to dinner as a thank you for the hospitality we have received, and have planned seafood at the Red Lobster.

The meal is splendid, and enjoyed by all. If you have never seen a hungry ten-year-old attack a pound of crab legs, it truly is an awesome sight. The only slightly odd thing is that, as I attempt to pay the bill, it is spirited away by Joel's mom, and our attempt to repay the hospitality ends up as yet more hospitality.

Wednesday is an exciting day for me, the rest of which pales into insignificance compared to the visit to the doctor. Unfortunately it's not until four o'clock, so there is a day to kill first.

After the inevitable morning nap, we decide on an early lunch and a visit to the Botanical Gardens, which are supposed to be a must-see in Albuquerque. It's a very impressive place, and some of the landscapes in the desert section are like something out of science fiction. There is also a lake, frequented by the most stunning, bright scarlet dragonflies, different kinds of hummingbirds, and some excellent statues.

I would like to have spent longer, but four o'clock beckons, and we drive to the surgery. Again there is a lot of waiting involved, which I don't really mind. But the worst part comes when I'm seen by the purple lady, who announces that the pressure in my bad eye is high, and that the doctor will want to speak to me about that. The next part of the waiting process is excruciating, and I sit and imagine just how much longer this pressure business will keep me here. But it turns out that all is well; Dr. Reidy is his usual charming self, and signs me off with a flourish.

The drive home is exhilarating. We stop at Borders, to buy gifts and thank you cards, and at a liquor store to buy beer. The first one certainly tastes good, my first for 16 days!! We have a splendid, eat up what's left dinner, with Joel and his friend Jeff, who apparently lives in Albuquerque because this is where his friend's bus broke down. And then I get on line and order tickets for Sunday's game in Oakland, which is where we are headed next.

It's amazing how life's small pleasures become so important when they are taken away from you. My last act of the day is to go to bed and lie on my back — an act which has been denied to me since the operation. It feels ridiculously good!

California (Part One)
Thursday June 14–Sunday June 17

After gifts, cards and fond farewells, we are at last ready to leave Albuquerque — a day I was beginning to think would never arrive. The sight in my right eye has been completely unaffected by the goings on next door, so my vision is pretty good. Sal, however, has decreed that I should not drive for the first day at least, so my job is to navigate. It is a comparatively simple job. I find I-40 quite easily, mutter "Go west for 600 miles," and fall into a stupor.

The scenery leaving Albuquerque is quite breathtaking. Somebody, in their infinite wisdom, has stuck these huge lumps of red, sandy rock everywhere.

Now I don't know the difference between a mesa, a bluff and a butte, but I'm willing to bet there are more than a few of each. The only surprising thing is that the Lone Ranger and Tonto don't appear from around one of them, pursued by a gang of baddies.

When we cross the border into Arizona, all the character suddenly leaves the landscape, and the terrain is flat in every direction, for as far as the eye can see. Then, very gradually, the dark shapes start to appear on the horizon and, slowly but surely, the Rockies come into view.

The rest of the afternoon is a glorious drive through the foothills of the Rockies, on occasion up to an altitude of 7,000 feet. We put a good 450 miles on the clock before stopping at 7:00 at the Rodeway Hotel, Kingman. We have completely ignored the fact, of course, that when we passed from New Mexico to Arizona we gained another hour, so it is only 6:00. The midday sun is not, it seems, the height of folly — when we arrive at the hotel the temperature is up to 99 degrees.

Friday we renew our long acquaintance with I-40 and continue to head west, through the stunning Arizona landscape, which starts to level out as we reach the border with California. I am surprised to find that there is actually a border control — California must have declared independence. A guard asks if we are carrying apples, oranges, plants or pets. I find that British humour usually does not elicit a positive response in such situations, so we answer curtly and honestly. He neglects to ask about the ham sandwich we are carrying, nor does he mention cocaine or illegal aliens. So neither do we.

After having crossed the border, the landscape takes a dramatic change, it has to be said for the worse. Sal and I both make a comparison with the moon. It really is quite desolate, but in a spectacular kind of way. We stop for breakfast in Barstow, and this is where we part company with I-40. I think, all told, I have done something like 800 miles on this road, so it's time I went. At this point I take my first turn at driving since the operation, and manage an hour and a half.

We stop in Fresno, decide to splash out on a decent hotel, and find one with effective air conditioning and a pool. Bear in mind that even this level of hotel is still considerably cheaper than a Travelodge at home. We wait an hour or so to swim before risking the heat. I give up after a couple of lengths and return to the room, Sal returns a little while later, reporting that a party of two Germans has arrived and reserved one table, 16 chairs and four sunbeds, for what turns out to be a party of ten. Is nowhere in the world safe?

On Saturday, my first peep through the window reveals the Germans' coach leaving bright and early, so I don't feel the need to run to the breakfast room and throw a towel on one of the tables.

The drive to Oakland is a mere 160 miles, a drop in the ocean compared to the previous two days. The scenery is very green, but quite dull, until we turn west and head for the coast. The green becomes golden brown, the flat becomes very hilly, and the tops of the hills are covered by wind farms—literally hundreds of the things. Rather than spoiling the landscape, I feel they make it more dramatic, giving the appearance of an invasion from another world.

After finding a hotel and resting up, we set out in search of fun and food. I try to find a famous baseball bar, but with no luck, so we drive around Lake Merritt, and eventually end up in Old Oakland. Sal has spotted a place that looks as if it might offer a good drink, so we walk towards it, and discover it is a fairly up-market restaurant called B. By up-market, I mean that the prices are about the same as a reasonable restaurant at home.

We are greeted by a wonderfully camp waiter, with the figure of a liquorice stick, who enquires if he will have the pleasure of our company for dinner. He will indeed, and we select our table. Sal has asparagus, which is served on a bed of something with a French name which escapes me. Sal enquires what this is, and receives such a wonderful explanation from our waiter that to have something else would be plain rude — it is basically egg, lemon and herbs.

I eat chicken wings and ribs, both of which sound bog standard dishes, but are elevated to the ranks of haute cuisine by the sauces and the sourcing — you can actually taste the chicken. The menu also offers five draft beers, all from small West coast breweries. The two I choose are excellent, particularly the Deschutes porter, which is served in a large wine glass so that you can actually savour the taste and smell.

I politely enquire if there is dessert, as the menu did not show any. The waiter is grossly offended, produces a separate dessert menu, and whispers, "I will say just two words— French toast," before swanning away. The dessert to which he refers turns out to be covered with berries and Grand Marnier, and I'm not a berries man, so on the waiter's return the following conversation occurs.

ME: *I'm sorry to disappoint you, but I'm going to have the chocolate and walnut bread and butter pudding.*
WAITER: *Your loss ... and Madame?*
SAL: *I can't actually manage a dessert, but I'd like you to know that if I could, I would choose the French toast.*
WAITER: *You're just saying that to appease me!*

I awake on Sunday feeling my redemption is complete, as I am to attend my first baseball game since May 27. In the meantime, we have a guest, my friend Susie, whom I have known since college days of the early seventies. She is visiting Los Angeles to attend her niece's graduation ceremony, and has flown up to join us for the day. A ridiculously early start has meant that she is with us for breakfast.

The morning is spent catching up, sorting out and napping, before we leave for the game, which has a lunchtime start. The Oakland Coliseum (or the McAfee Coliseum, to give it its corporate name) is visible from the hotel.

Walking to it, as opposed to driving, is another matter, and we eventually have to walk to the railway station before finding a pedestrian walkway into the ground.

I'm sorry to report that this probably wins the award for the ugliest stadium I have yet to visit, at least from the outside. It is one of a generation of stadia built in the sixties, which were all practically identical. They are often referred to as cookie cutters, because that's what they look like from the air.

Inside is slightly more pleasant, and has the full range of concessions. This is Sue's first ballgame, and only Sal's second, so I have my fair share of explaining to do. The concession stalls are impressive, with a good range of local beers, and hot dogs to match. A chicken parmesan hot dog proves more than an adequate lunch.

Susan, being a baseball virgin, asks many incisive questions, and at one point is able to make a comparison which might help some of my English readers to better understand the game. After St. Louis scores the first run, the Oakland inning reaches a point where they have runners on base, but have not yet scored. "It would appear," says Susan, "that Oakland is doing better at this stage."

"Yes," I reply, "but they need to get the runners home, otherwise none of them will count."

"A bit like Ludo, then," she concludes.

The game is played at a fair pace, and after the St. Louis Cardinals open the scoring, the Oakland Athletics reply by batting around in the first, and opening up a 5–1 lead. The Cardinals hang in there, gradually work their way back into the game, and six runs in the final two innings give them a 10–6 victory, much to the chagrin of the home supporters. The game is very well attended, possibly because it is Fathers' Day, and a trip to the ballgame is very much the thing to do.

Alaska

Monday June 18–Friday June 22

Monday is a day of decision-making for Sal. She has booked to return home from Seattle on Sunday, but is considering bringing this forward a few days, to coincide with my departure for Alaska. The conditions attached to the ticket she has booked, however, prove so inflexible that the Sunday departure appears set in stone. So we bid farewell to Susan, who is to return to Los Angeles, and head north, for probably the most contrasting and spectacular day's driving yet.

Oakland, to put it politely, is dull urban sprawl although, as we leave the metropolis, we are afforded some decent views of the bay. The city soon disappears, and we are once more travelling through verdant fruit-growing areas. About 60 miles along the road, a small white triangle becomes visible ahead of us. This gradually becomes larger and unmistakeably a snow-capped mountain.

We take a break in Harrison, California. While I am filling the car, my daughter Anya phones from home. When I return from paying, Sal informs me that she will call back in five minutes, as she wants us to be together for this piece of news. The news, when it comes, is what I am expecting, but wonderful nonetheless. Anya and her husband have been trying to adopt a child for several months, and the call is to tell us that we are to be grandparents to a baby girl named Joanna, date of arrival to be announced. I grin so much that there is a danger of my head splitting in half, and Sal sobs! Harrison, California, will stay forever in our memory.

Continuing north on I-5, we approach the area around Lake Shasta, and the scenery becomes the most stunning I have yet to see on this trip. It could be Scandinavian, Finnish more than anything. The colours are incredible; the deep green of the fir trees, the iridescent blue of the lake, terra cotta rocks and a bright blue sky. Looming above it all is the aforementioned mountain, Mount Shasta as it turns out, which is completely white and grey. It is so out of place compared with the bright colours of the rest of the landscape, that it looks as if someone has done a very bad cut and paste, and inserted a monochrome mountain into a coloured picture.

As evening approaches so does our 400-mile target for the day, and we find a hotel in Grants Pass, Oregon, a small town completely surrounded by hills and pine forests. It is at this point that I discover that I will remember Harrison, California, for yet another reason — it was the last time I saw my debit card.

So, after a good meal at a local diner (Sal still has two-thirds of her salad in the fridge, and she ate well), we settle down to administrative stuff. It takes ages to find a number to register the loss of my card, but we eventually manage, although the cell phone cuts me off before I have finished. It also proves impossible for Sal to find a cheap flight to join me in Alaska so, unless something miraculously appears this evening, she will take the rental car and do her own thing while I sample the midnight sun.

On Tuesday we leave Grants Pass with another 400 miles ahead of us, and me driving. I manage more than half of the journey, my longest stint since the operation. The journey is fairly devoid of incident, the one exception being when we stop for gas and food in Cottage Grove, Oregon. As I climb out of the driver's seat to fill up the car, I am suddenly aware of a figure close beside me. Now he turns out to be a very pleasant young man, but at first glance could have been mistaken for a bit part player from *Deliverance*.

He asks what I want, and I tell him I am intending to fill up with regular. "Are you going to do that for me?" I enquire.

"Have you filled up in the state of Oregon before?" he replies. I have to think.

"No, I don't believe I have," I surmise.

"In Oregon," he informs me, "it is a requirement of state law that the pumping mechanism is only operated by an attendant." He proceeds to fill the tank and clean the windscreen with a smile and a happy word or two.

After passing Portland, we enter the state of Washington, and soon enter the urban sprawl of Tacoma and Seattle, making our way to the motel I have booked, originally just for myself. We check in, and I am delighted to find there is a lake within walking distance, and a bus stop to the city centre directly opposite. We have failed in our last-ditch attempt to get Sal on the flight to Alaska, so I must abandon her for a couple of days—hence the environs of the motel are more important to me than usual.

For those who regard this trip as inspirational, this part is the most inspired. For those who think it's total madness, this is where the mania reaches its height. My taxi collects me at 5:45 A.M., for Sea-Tac airport. The check-in and security procedures are relatively brief, so I have time for a quick Starbucks before boarding my plane for the 1,444-mile, three-hour trip to Anchorage. Leaving Seattle is wonderful—there is no cloud cover for the first half-hour, and the landscape is a lattice of coast, lakes, bridges, greenery and the odd mountain. We lose visibility then, and I pass a couple of hours writing and dozing before the plane begins its descent. The scenery this end even puts Seattle in the shade, and is like nothing I have ever seen. The whole vista is full of snow-capped mountains, sometimes with the snow appearing to come all the way down to the sea, and there are vast glaciers clearly visible. Awesome is an overused word these days, particularly on this continent, but I think on this occasion it is appropriate.

Alaska, it appears, is bigger than Texas! I wonder if, when Alaska was admitted to the United States in 1959, Texas voted against, or at least sulked a little.

Anchorage Airport is small and friendly, and I have time for a quick snack before completing my journey with a 260-mile hop to Fairbanks. Inland Alaska is fairly dull compared with the coastal views I experienced, but I must try not to get too blasé. The short trip seems like a climb followed immediately by a descent, and I am in Fairbanks before I know it. At the airport I find an advert telling me that my hotel offers a shuttle service, so I ring the number and am soon collected by a kind gentleman who quizzes me about my stay and seems impressed with my answers.

My only knowledge of things Alaskan comes from watching the TV programme "Northern Exposure," which I have since learned was filmed elsewhere. So, after a couple of hours relaxing in my room, I go exploring. I have travelled light, so that I don't have to check any luggage. I soon find out I have made two errors. I have not brought the accessories to my camera, which now runs out of charge and, as I am approaching the Arctic Circle, I have brought slightly warmer clothes. I smile ironically to myself as the digital thermometer on the bank shows 101 degrees.

The town is not much different from other American towns, but certain aspects seem about 50 years in the past. But the heat defeats me, so I retire to the hotel, hoping that Midsummer Day proves cooler. The hotel is one of the more pleasant of my trip, and features its own bar, restaurant and ice-cream parlour. So a night in isn't exactly a hardship, as I'm planning a very late night tomorrow!

The reason I am in Fairbanks at this particular time is for the Midnight Sun Game, a local tradition that can be traced back to a bar bet in 1906. After passing through the hands of various institutions, it has become the responsibility of a local club, the Alaska Goldpanners, reputedly the northernmost baseball club on earth.

The game starts at 10:30 P.M., just as the sun is setting — in the north! It usually finishes between 1:00 and 2:00 A.M., by which time the sun is beginning to rise again, also in the north! To date, artificial light has never been necessary for the completion of the game.

So I plan my day with some care, to take into account the heat, my tendency still to fatigue and the fact that I am not a late night person. I decide to explore the town again, and then take a rest before leaving for the game around 8:00.

The temperature is still a mystery, and not just to me. As I wander around town, I find that two banks are displaying the temperature. One says 76 degrees, the other 91. Perhaps one is buying and one selling. Try as I may, I can't make it last for much more than a couple of hours. So, after finding a coffee shop with a balcony and writing a few cards, I return to my hotel and grab a couple of hours' sleep.

I have booked a cab for 8:00, although first pitch is not until 10:30. I spend a little while just walking about the perimeter of the park, and have a good conversation with one of the locals, who informs me that this is something special. "They won't turn the lights on," he assures me. "Whatever happens, they won't turn the lights on!" He then proceeds to recount the time in 1996 when the Chinese national team provided the opposition, as part of their Olympic preparation. Apparently, after six innings, the Chinese coach forfeited the game, as it was so dark that he feared his players receiving injuries. But they still didn't turn the lights on.

This really is a low-tech affair. Speeches and entertainment can hardly be heard, volunteers staff the concessions, manning large dustbins filled with ice and beer cans. The stands are pure aluminium, with no reserved seats so, by the time the sun disappears behind me shortly after 9:00, space is at a premium.

At 9:25, the home team, to roars of approval, begins to warm up, which includes watering the field.

Around 10:00, things begin in earnest. The teams are introduced, just like in the World Series. The commanding officer of the local Air Force base throws out the first pitch, the National Anthem is sung, and four jet planes rather impressively fly past.

The home team begins poorly. They can't pitch straight, and they continually strand runners. So by the middle of the third, although both teams have the same number of hits, the visiting Oceanside Waves, from San Diego, lead 5–0. At this point, volunteers throw whistling candy to the spectators, and the ground becomes full of demented skylarks. In the middle of the fourth, at the stroke of midnight, the game is halted. The guest singer again takes the field, this time to sing the Alaskan Flag Song. Another ceremonial first pitch is thrown, this one by Shaun Timmins. Mr. Timmins thus becomes the only person to throw out the actual first pitch, the ceremonial first pitch at the start of the game, and the ceremonial first pitch after midnight. He has been the winning pitcher in the Midnight Sun Game three times, more than anyone else, and the shirt he wore in the 100th Midnight Sun Game is now enshrined in the Baseball Hall of Fame in Cooperstown. So there!

The new day has an immediate effect on the home team, which scores a run. The game again takes its own path in the middle of the seventh. Instead of the ever popular "Take Me Out to the Ballgame," we are treated to something I have never before experienced. A song is played which involves the crowd shouting, at various key moments, "Happy Boy! Happy Boy! Hubba, hubba, hubba, hubba, hubba!" Perhaps it's something to do with the long winters.

Egged on by an increasingly enthusiastic, yet numerically dwindling crowd, the home team huffs and puffs, but the one remaining run is scored by the visitors, who end up 6–1 winners. The light between 12:30 and 1:30 is poor, but by no means unplayable.

The absence of taxis at the end of the game causes me to walk back to my hotel, which takes about 40 minutes. Everywhere is still open, there are lots of people about and, although I can't actually claim to see the sun rise, it is light as I arrive at 2:00 A.M. I manage to sleep until almost 8:00, and laze around until check-out at 11:00. The shuttle bus is far too prompt for my liking, so I find myself at the airport with three hours to spare. Security is again painless, although they do confiscate my toothpaste which, although almost empty, is too large. Two days ago it was the same size, and even fuller, when I apparently smuggled it in!

The rest of the day is really quite uneventful. The only unfortunate part of the journey occurs back in Sea-Tac, when the taxi driver insists on proving that there are two Motel 6s locally, by taking me to the wrong one first, and then I am reunited, however briefly, with Sal. It has been a week for strange reunions—first meeting a friend from back home in a motel in Oakland, and then meeting my wife in Seattle after being apart for a couple of days. There's something not quite right about it.

Washington
Saturday June 23–Sunday June 24

On Saturday, we pack the room into the car and, before 9:00, set off on the 20-mile drive to the northern side of Seattle, where we are to be provided with hospitality at the home of Rick Robertson. Neither Sally nor I have met Rick, who is an old school friend of our neighbour and friend Greg. Greg has very kindly arranged accommodation for me at various points on the journey, and this is the first occasion on which I have taken advantage of such.

We are not the only visitors this weekend, as quite a crowd has gathered, seemingly in my honour. Awaiting us at the house, besides Rick, are Greg's sister Susie, and her offspring Emily and David, aged 21 and 19 respectively. These three people we have met before, so they are familiar faces. We are also introduced to Rick's six-year-old son Will, and the Irish Water Spaniel, Cutter.

As there are other friends in town who are to be involved in the weekend's activities, plans must be made. So after much negotiation, Sally and I head off, with Susie, David and Will, to the centre of Seattle, where we are met by Rick's wife, Johanna. The first activity involves the Experience Music Project, a fairly new exhibit in the Seattle Centre. This started life as a tribute to Jimi Hendrix, himself a son of Seattle, but has blossomed into something altogether more expansive.

We cannot dally, as we have a 3:00 appointment elsewhere. We are being taken around an organic chocolate factory, which has set up shop in the former premises of the Red Hook Brewery. The whole affair is splendid, but the chocolate is truly remarkable, not just for its quality, but for the innovation of some of its flavours. My favourite has to be coconut curry, although the mint confection tastes as if it has an actual leaf of mint in the middle, and the thyme with sea salt is an interesting variation.

At the factory we meet two more of Greg's former classmates, Miles and Ludlow, and their respective partners, Alexandra and Nani, and we are told that we are to dine with these people that evening. So, after a rest and a change, we head to Ponti's, a local seafood restaurant. There we are joined by another former classmate, Todd, and his wife Donna. The meal is nothing short of splendid, and I happily suggest a toast to my friend Greg, who is the common factor amongst the people around the table, and has been instrumental in setting up this occasion, but sadly is at home in England while we drink his health. Here's to you, pal, and the generosity and hospitality of your lovely friends!

Sunday's first job is not a pleasant one; I have to drive Sal to the airport for her flight home. She has been with me for just over three weeks, and I can honestly say that this trip would have derailed completely without her mercy mission. The airport is still full of roadworks and suchlike so, despite it being a Sunday morning, there is a fair amount of chaos, which makes lengthy farewells impossible. But a few tears are shed, and I drive back in sadness, marvelling at the hand that fate has dealt me, and how I come to be married to the most selfless woman in the world. Most people wouldn't fly that far to fulfil their own dreams, let alone to support someone else in fulfilling theirs.

The major activity of the day, for which most of last night's guests reassemble, is a visit to Safeco Park, home of the Seattle Mariners, for the final game of a three-game series with the Cincinnati Reds. The series is notable for the return to Seattle of Ken Griffey, Jr., one of the foremost hitters and outfielders in the game. Although it is now several years since Griffey left Seattle, it is his first time back. This is because Seattle and Cincinnati are in different leagues, and interleague play constitutes such a small part of the season that this is the first time the computer has scheduled a homecoming for Griffey.

Returning heroes in baseball, as in other sports, can receive a variety of welcomes from the fans they left behind, anything from polite applause to vicious abuse. In Friday night's series opener, Griffey received a standing ovation, even though the Reds condemned the Mariners to their worst-ever defeat, 16–1. The Mariners won the second game, and Griffey got another ovation, so the stage is set.

We reach our seats just as the game is about to start. Griffey is the third batter to appear, receives his by now customary standing ovation, and plants the third pitch he receives into the centre field stand for a home run; 1–0 Cincinnati. In the next inning, Seattle appears to have got a hit to right field, but a late sprint and dive from Griffey turns it into an excellent catch. Someone, it appears, is writing this guy's script. On his next at bat, he hits a single, but his teammates fail to get him home. Then in the fifth inning, he again places the ball in the centre field crowd, only 15 rows further back this time; 2–0 Cincinnati.

Seattle's present-day hero is the Japanese import, Ichiro Suzuki. Whereas Griffey is a slugger, Ichiro nurdles, nudges, bunts and places the ball to such effect that, combined with his great speed, he gets hits where other batters are run out. Inspired by their wily teammate, Seattle gets back into the game, 2–2.

At this point, three noteworthy things happen in fairly rapid succession. First, it starts to rain, and we are treated to the impressive sight of the roof closing. It appears to be supported by a series of girders which run along train tracks on the top of the perimeter wall. I'm sure an engineer could describe that more accurately, but it all happens very impressively and quite quickly.

Next, at the bottom of the sixth, my attention is diverted to the huge scoreboard, on which people can arrange to have written birthday messages, marriage proposals and the like. At this juncture, the scoreboard reads, "Welcome to Safeco Field, Peter Taylor from Birmingham, England." It's too quick for me to get my camera working, so you'll just have to take my word for it.

Finally, in the bottom of the seventh, we are treated to one of the most exciting sights in baseball, the suicide squeeze. This is not a common sight, as it has a high risk factor, but if it works, it's both spectacular and effective. There has to be a runner on third base. The runner and the hitter are both given a prearranged signal by one of the coaches and, as the pitcher releases the ball, the runner heads for home. The hitter's job is just to put the ball fair. If he succeeds, the runner gets home; if he fails, the runner is dead. This one succeeds, 3–2 Seattle, and that's how it ends, with Griffey graciously doffing his cap as he leaves the field.

Montana
Monday June 25 – Wednesday June 26

Although Monday is day 86, in some ways it's a second day 1. Sal has arrived safely back in Byfield, my hosts in Seattle leave for work and school, and the lonesome traveller is back on the road. Saying I'm pleased to be on my own again would be both ungrateful and untrue but, as I leave Seattle, I can't help but feel that I have overcome my setbacks and am really back on course.

Seattle is definitely one of those cities to which I would return — I feel I have hardly scratched the surface of what appears a fascinating place. It seems totally inappropriate that such a lovely city should be blighted with such an excess of traffic. Just getting out of the place takes forever. Patience is rewarded, however, and the scenery for the first hour of the I-90 is absolutely stunning. The automatic gears in the car earn their corn as we take on and conquer Snoqualmie, one of the many mountains surrounding the interstate. The weather is not perfect, but this only serves to add to the impressiveness of the surroundings. The snow-flecked tips are surrounded by wispy clouds, and sharp showers fight with bright sunshine for air time. Just when you think you might be getting used to it, someone arranges to have a lake placed casually at the side of the road, which just adds to the drama of the whole thing.

Eventually the landscape starts to level out, turning more into farming country. But the lakes remain. I stop at one rest area, and on top of a cliff is a sculpture. I had spotted this on a postcard earlier and it's called, from memory, "The Old Man Releases the Horses." It's supposed to symbolise the moment

God placed creatures on the earth, and certainly looks very impressive in its chosen location.

I drive on, and eventually stop for the night in Spokane, where I try to catch up on all the organisational stuff that this journey demands—three days without internet certainly stacks up the jobs. I make sure there are complementary tickets waiting for me in Boise, Idaho, change the venue of my Oregon game from Salem to Portland to fit in with my host's plans, arrange a rendezvous with my daughter in San Francisco, and get back into the old routine of calling home. Sometimes old routines are just comfortable.

On Tuesday I soon leave Washington, and cross the border into Idaho. This part of the journey is very impressive. There are so many fir trees in this part of Idaho that it could be Christmas every day for ten years and you wouldn't even see a scratch. Once again the interstate decides to take on the mountains rather than go around them. At one point I realise I have been going uphill without a break for what seems like miles, and then notice that the altitude marker is 1,800 feet higher than the previous one.

At some point in the journey Idaho becomes Montana. I decide to stop and stretch my legs at a rest area which looks as if it might have a decent view, and find myself looking down into a river valley. The information boards at this particular place are all about the bald eagle, which is still a protected species in Montana. As I am reading all about them one of these magnificent birds soars overhead. I run back to my car for binoculars by which time, of course, it has disappeared. I continue to read the notice, and am informed that one of the trees on the opposite bank is a regular nesting place, and that the pole next to the board has a hole drilled through which is lined up with the nest. Using this as a guide I train my binoculars on the appropriate tree, and am rewarded with a view of the nest, with a bald eagle sitting guarding it.

Going from Idaho to Montana also means a return to Mountain Time from Pacific Time. It doesn't make much difference really. But when you don't realise until mid-afternoon, it means arriving at your hotel later than you have planned. But arrive at my hotel in Helena I eventually do, and confirm that we have internet before checking in. That, of course, is the kiss of death, and I fail to get a connection. Phoning the support line, I am informed that they are working on my hotel at that very moment. Good time for dinner is my conclusion.

Reading brochures over Wednesday's breakfast, it seems there is more to Helena than would appear at first sight, so I decide on a bit of tourism. But first, there is laundry and e-mails to be dealt with. My cousin needs to know where to send my All-Star Game tickets, my website buddy needs stats and photos, my hosts in Cincinnati want to confirm dates, and so on.

Once you leave behind the industrial, commercial fringe that seems to exist in every town, Helena is a quaint, leafy, almost Edwardian place. It caters for the tourist, but in the same subtle way of, say, Hay-on-Wye — gift shops, book shops, the odd bistro. The town centre boasts an elegant twin-spired cathedral, and a main street of handsome stone buildings, with a late-nineteenth-century feel to them. There are also interesting statues commemorating the mining history of the city. The street, incidentally, retains the name of Last Chance Gulch!

I spend an enjoyable couple of hours just mooching around the place then, after a break, I set out for the game at the local Kindrick Stadium, which is fairly tawdry, but has a homely feel about it. Only two sides have seats, so the outfield boasts a fine Montana skyline. The car park is a gravelled affair, with no white lines to inform the drivers.

Once inside, I find a stall belonging to the Montana Historical Society, which is sponsoring tonight's hot dogs, $1 each. The concessions also boast the products of the Lewis and Clark Brewery, which graced yesterday's brewhouse dinner. There is a board paying tribute to former Helena Brewers, the most famous of which are probably Gary Sheffield and Ryne Sandberg.

We have the obligatory national anthem, but with a difference. A pony-tailed, Stetson-wearing gentleman, of indeterminate age, plays the anthem on an electric guitar, in a style redolent of Hendrix at Woodstock; it makes a wonderful change from the endless procession of children's choirs.

The home team has a third baseman, named Wheeler, who wears the number 13 and boasts the given name of Zealous. I wonder if his parents read the Bible, or Colin Dexter! The first six innings see the pitching dominate, with only one run to each side. But in the seventh the visiting Missoula Ospreys put some hits together and take a 4–1 lead. This proves to be enough, despite a desperate last-inning rally from the Brewers which brings in one run and leaves the bases loaded.

Baseball is primarily a non-contact sport, but when contact occurs it can be quite violent. At one point we are treated to the sight of a runner being tagged out at home. When this happens, the catcher gloves the ball and covers the plate, i.e., positions himself between the plate and the onrushing runner. The runner is entitled to run through, over, or around the catcher to reach the plate—on this occasion he chooses a combination of the first two—and the rule is that if the catcher is still holding the ball when he gets up, or regains consciousness, the runner is out. Catchers often have fairly short careers, but this one keeps hold and gets the out.

Wyoming

Thursday June 28–Friday June 29

As I leave Helena, I realise more than ever that my knowledge of American geography is not what it could be. I am surprised, therefore, that the river I cross early on today's journey is the Missouri. I'm in the northwest of this huge country, and I have always associated the Missouri with southerly parts. I guess it must be a long river. I check a map to reassure myself and find, to my further confusion, that where I cross it, it's flowing north! How does that work?

I stop for lunch in Big Timber, Montana, and eat in a restaurant with more than a hint of what is supposed to represent the Old West. I decide that I need to do around 100 miles more to complete my quota for the day. This takes me through Billings, the last big town for a while, and I realise that I am coming close to the Little Bighorn, where Custer met his fate. In fact, as I sit in a hotel in Hardin, I am less than 15 miles from the spot. I can practically sense the ghost of Errol Flynn looking over my shoulder.

I spend the evening reviewing the remainder of the trip. I conclude that Colorado will have to be consigned to next year, along with Arizona and Southern California. I had thought I might fit it in after Las Vegas, but the driving distances are, I think, prohibitive.

There is also the great unknown of October to contend with, assuming I hear from the immigration people about my extension. I already have Hawaii, Nashville and Cooperstown that I would like to fit in somewhere. Hmmm! I always did enjoy jigsaws!

High temperatures are threatened again on Friday, and it's already mid-80s when I leave the hotel. As I said yesterday, the site of the Battle of the Little Bighorn is just a few miles away, and I feel I can't go so close without taking a quick look.

It's actually quite a tasteful place, not commercialised at all. They leave that to the gift shops on the other side of the highway. The site itself is just a commemoration of the event, and a wider memorial to the losses both sides suffered in the Indian Wars. It came about as a result of a meeting between survivors of the wars on the 50th anniversary of the Last Stand. A hatchet was symbolically buried, and it was agreed that the site would be developed as a joint memorial.

Travelling on, the landscape remains the same — rolling plains extending into shallow hillsides; and space, so much space. Arriving in Casper, I find my hotel is decorated like a riverboat, which makes a change. Although, from the front, it appears like any other edge of the interstate location, enquiries reveal that it borders a river. Not only that, but the ballpark is a ten-minute walk along the river bank. So, with the late afternoon temperature in the high 90s, I set off.

The park is fairly mundane, but its surroundings make it a pleasant place to spend a summer evening. The outfield backs on to the trees of the river bank, above which can be seen the Wyoming hills. Combine this with local brews and a mean barbecue stall, and it gets better. Minor league baseball is full of novelties, to try and attract the fans. Tonight, it turns out, is Bass Ackward night (it's an American Spoonerism), so everything happens the wrong way round. The groundsmen wear their shirts back to front, the players have their numbers back to front, and we start with the ninth inning. This means that the seventh inning stretch, together with its customary singing, comes in the third!

There is also a designated beer batter. One of the opposition is given this designation, and if he strikes out, there is cheap beer for ten minutes. The home crowd, naturally, encourages him to do so. The game is fairly even until the home pitching goes into meltdown, and the visitors score nine runs through a mixture of walks and errors. It ends Ogden Raptors 9, Casper Rockies 3.

At the end of the game we have the national anthem, and then the teams are introduced to the crowd. But I'm on my way out by then — you can take a joke too far!

Utah

Saturday June 30 – Sunday July 1

I have a decision to make on Saturday: a drive of 400 miles, followed by two nights in the same hotel, or a drive of 200 miles, followed by the same again tomorrow. I opt for the former, so am on my way well before 9:00. My journey is long, but enjoyable. The scenery again consists of rolling prairies and distant hills and mountains, much the same as the last couple of days. I must be starting to sound blasé. I hope not, because it really is very impressive — but I've already told you that and I'm beginning to run out of adjectives.

I stop for lunch at a buffet, which is extremely busy. I find a seat, and the waitress brings me a glass of water. A minute later, an elderly chap arrives carrying his food, and tells me that this is his place, and his water. I apologise, and explain that the waitress actually gave me the water, without saying the seat was taken. I move to another seat, and as I am about to fetch some food, the old chap approaches again, apologises for having been short, and explains that he complained to the waitress, who insisted that she had given the water to him. So he told her, "The man you actually gave the water to was taller, younger, had a beard, and was wearing a white shirt..."

"And was not nearly as good-looking!" I venture.

He slaps me on the back, with a grin, and we part as friends.

Utah turns out to be full of mountains, and ski resorts. I don't know why, but I had not expected that. Ogden is right in the middle of them, and is surrounded by stunning scenery. I arrive at a hotel which I have selected from a discount book, and find myself waiting at the desk behind twelve members of a motorcycle club from Las Vegas—not Hell's Angels but something broadly similar. They are very amusing, but slightly less so when they take all the available rooms. So I select another hotel from my book, which is a little more expensive, but has a pool, a garden, a restaurant, and splendid surroundings.

Sunday is the start of month four, and it certainly seems a long time since the day I left home. My plan for today is to catch up with paperwork this morning, and leave around 1:30 to have a look at the town centre, before getting to the ballpark around 3:00, first pitch being 4:00. It's a good plan, in theory. The first part goes swimmingly—a good breakfast in the restaurant next to the hotel, which appears to be very popular, and I'm ready for my chores. I'm trying to plan four weeks ahead, but it doesn't always work that way. So today I'm contacted by my host in Portland, to confirm that she is in receipt of my tickets for San Francisco, I hear from Las Vegas to confirm hotel and tickets, and similarly for Omaha.

The second half doesn't fall into line quite so easily. The brochures tell me that historic 25th Street is full of interesting shops and cafes—it doesn't tell me that they all but one are closed on Sunday. So that takes all of 20 minutes. After doing all I can to kill time, I still arrive at the ballpark 20 minutes earlier than planned. Strolling towards the ticket office, the only other fan in sight tells me that the start time has been put back to 7:00. Fortunately the ground is only a few minutes drive from the hotel, so I return to seek refuge from the heat.

So, for the second time today, I set off for the game. Lindquist Park is a comfortable little stadium in the town centre, and has recently been voted as having the best view in the whole of professional baseball. I find it impossible to argue, although I'm looking forward to San Francisco, where the park stands on the bay. Here, the mountains loom over the outfield, and on this sunny evening the aspect is absolutely magnificent. Rooster local brews, and a splendid Philly Cheesesteak, set me up for the action, and we're off.

The most notable piece of action in the game, sadly, is an injury. In the second inning, with the home team fielding, the second baseman runs to field a simple groundball as a runner tries to get to second base. They clash, and the home player stays down an awfully long time before being removed strapped to a stretcher.

The other notable feature comes when the ground crew sweeps the infield in drag, to the tune of "Do You Think I'm Sexy?" I think it's a rhetorical question. The match is fairly even, but the visiting Idaho Falls Chukars make better use of the chances that come their way, and win 4–2.

The sunset, regrettably, is over the stand rather than over the mountains, but the consolation of this is the wonderful colours and shadows that reflect from the rocks as the sun sinks. The mountains start the evening a sandy brown colour but, as the game progresses and the sun gradually sets, they turn gold,

Ogden, Utah — voted the best view in professional baseball. As the sun sets the mountains change from brown to gold to pink.

which then takes on a reddish pink tinge. San Francisco will have to go some to beat that.

Idaho

Monday July 2–Tuesday July 3

A relatively early start sees me heading northwest. We slowly lose the mountains, and by the time Utah becomes Idaho the landscape is as flat as a pancake. Traffic signs tell me that, in the event of a dust storm, I should not stop on the highway. Personally, I would prefer a traffic sign to tell me what I should do, rather than what I should not, never having experienced a dust storm.

The remoteness of the landscape around here really makes it difficult to plan a journey. Having 300 miles to travel, I have determined to put 100 miles behind me before stopping for breakfast. That quickly becomes 140 in the absence of any services. I have chosen to give a first outing to the Janis Joplin T-shirt I bought back in Port Arthur, Texas. The back bears a quote from the lady herself; "It's hard to be free, but when it works, it sure is worth it." As I await the arrival of my breakfast, a voice suddenly proclaims, "What a great quote!" The gentleman concerned insists on acquiring a pen from the waitress, and copying the phrase on to a napkin. He then treats me to a couple of lines from one of Ms. Joplin's songs, "Me and Bobby McGee," which contains a similar line, or, at least, a line containing the word "freedom."

The drive is so straightforward that I am in Boise by 2:30, and find the hotel has a swimming pool. After relaxing for a while, I take a cab into the town centre, which turns out to be both attractive and interesting, and I make a note to spend a couple of hours here tomorrow.

Having thus decided, I retire to a brewhouse for dinner. Now I know I might give the impression of being an obsessive in these matters, but these establishments, as well as their obvious eponymous charms, also frequently provide good food. This particular one, besides the usual pub fare, offers many fish dishes with international variations. I won't go into detail, but let's just say I was comfortable — a dish of paella, with chicken, chorizo, prawns and scallops, a home brewed barley wine, weighing in at 10.3 percent, and the Cubs on TV, winning 7–1 in Washington.

The first thing on Tuesday's agenda is 7:35 P.M. At least I can allow myself to wake up naturally instead of forcing the issue. As I said yesterday, my intention is to have a better look at the centre of Boise, which looks quite promising. But before I can do that, my diary reminds me that there are jobs to be done. It's almost like a day at work.

First, I have to call the car rental people. I've put 12,000 miles on the car already, and it hasn't been checked or serviced. I arrange with the company in Virginia Beach that I will sort it out with their San Francisco branch next week. They still can't seem to understand what it is that I'm doing, and make helpful suggestions like, "Bring it back to us and we'll change it."

"But I'm in Idaho."

"Well, bring it in when you get back to Virginia Beach."

"At the end of October?"

I remember the car park in front of last night's restaurant, and that seems a reasonable base from which to explore. I start my day with an iced coffee at a sidewalk table, and, as it is beginning to get warm, continue at a leisurely pace. Boise is as enjoyable as it promised to be, and contradicts most of the generalisations I have made about American towns. It has a compact centre, with shops, restaurants, an old town district, where buildings have been restored rather than replaced, and a plaza with a fountain, which youngsters are making use of due to the heat.

It even boasts a record exchange, and a second-hand book shop, in both of which I lose myself for a while. I treat myself to a collection of quotes, "The Wit and Wisdom of Baseball." But when even the locals are fighting you for the shade, you know it's too hot. It's so hot that, when I stop for lunch at yet another brewpub, I drink iced tea! So eventually I retire to the hotel for another solitary swim, and a little break before tonight's game.

The ballpark is nothing out of the ordinary, but America is in a festive mood, as tomorrow is a national holiday. It has been decided that tonight is Mardi Gras, and we are all given decorative beads as we go in. The Boise Hawks are one of the teams that responded to my request for a free ticket, and I am delighted to find myself directly behind home plate, 12 rows back in a sharply sloping stand. It's probably the best view I've had yet.

Apart from nuts and popcorn, most ballpark snacks consist of meat in bread; the secret lies in trying to find local variations on the theme. Tonight the local grill offers kielbasa, which turned out to be the thickest sausage I have yet sampled, a Polish variety with subtle spicing and a delicious flavour.

The game turns out to be a walkover; the visitors take an early lead, but can then do nothing right. The home team hits well, and takes advantage of the away team's mistakes, to end up winning 11–1. The home team is called the Boise Hawks, so when the little boy next to me says that he can see a hawk, he is largely ignored. But sure enough, a hawk has landed on top of one of the floodlight supports, and closer inspection shows that there is a nest up there. We see the occasional flutter of wings as it settles down for the evening, and then someone finds it necessary to have a test run for the evening's fireworks.

The hawk disgustedly leaves the building, with something small, headless, and apparently very tasty dangling from its talons. But I find myself wondering if this is the start of a trend — will we get a beaver at tomorrow's game in Portland? And should I reconsider my planned visit to the Detroit Tigers?

Oregon

Wednesday July 4–Thursday July 5

Independence Day is not a bad day for driving 400 odd miles, as very few people have any intention of doing anything similar. I'm on my way to Portland to visit Susie Stragnell — if you don't know who Susie is you haven't been paying attention. I know it gets confusing, because most of my female friends are called Susie, but you'll just have to concentrate.

There has been a slight change of plan. I was due to go to Salem, Oregon, tomorrow, to see a game there, but Susie has pointed out that there is a game in Portland, which would save us an 80-mile round trip. So she has got us some tickets, and Salem is cancelled. The only big difference is that the game is tonight, so I need to make a relatively early start. My early start becomes even earlier when I cross into Oregon, and my watch goes back an hour again. I am further reminded that I am back in Oregon when I stop for gas and breakfast, and there's that man again, reminding me that I should not attempt to break the law and fill up my own car.

The waitress has a brief moan about having to work on the holiday, but as I leave I am wished Happy Independence Day. I consider briefly explaining that we don't celebrate the robbery of one of our colonies by a bunch of guerrillas who refused to fight properly and would not wear bright colours, but decide that, at best, this will delay me for a while and, at worst, I could end up on top of a bonfire!

So I continue on my way, and make pretty good time to Portland. I find Susie's house fairly quickly, and relax for a couple of hours before setting off for the game. We take the bus, and Portland appears to be a lovely, casual city. The ballpark is in the centre, very well appointed, and almost to a major league standard. It even has some greenery on the outfield wall, à la Wrigley. Susie has got us some good seats, and we are meeting several of her friends. But we hide amongst the concessions until the sun has set far enough for our seats to be in the shade.

Susie's friends are good company, and all very knowledgeable about baseball. One of them tells a very repeatable story. One of the common collectables in baseball is the bobblehead, a small doll, the head of which bobs around. It is considered a minor honour for a player to have his own bobblehead. Apparently the Seattle Mariners are having a bobblehead evening for one of their players at an upcoming game and, to add to the novelty, have searched the telephone directory to see if it contained any guys named Head, with the first name Robert and the middle initial L. They have found two, and so the game is due to have two guests of honour, each going by the name of Bob L. Head!!

Tonight's game is very watchable — both teams score in the first, and that's how it stays until the bottom of the ninth. With one out, and extra innings looming, the home team hits into a double play. But the second baseman drops the ball, and a runner comes in to score — Tacoma Rainiers 1, Portland Beavers 2.

We are then treated to a splendid Fourth of July firework display, and wend our way to the bus stop, where a ponytailed guitarist offers a rendition of Del Shannon classics which is not exactly word perfect. Portland by night looks good fun!

All-Star Week

Thursday July 5–Tuesday July 10

My small basement bed is surprisingly comfortable, and I awake feeling very refreshed. In those early waking moments, I start to contemplate the next couple of days, and realise that, if I stay in Portland tonight, I will have 640 miles to drive by 12:00 on Saturday. So, after discussing it with Susie, I decide to make a move after lunch, and do the first few hours today.

First, I phone the San Francisco branch of my car rental firm, and, to my surprise, speak to someone with a brain. She tells me that she has made a note on my file, and if I drive to San Francisco Airport sometime next week, they will exchange my car for one that doesn't need servicing. I'll believe it when it happens!

Next, Susie insists on taking me out for breakfast to the local coffee shop. It's a charming place, with good coffee and home made cakes and pastries. The cakes are made with whole grain and fruit, so that you can eat chocolate and convince yourself it's a healthy breakfast. We sit outside, as it's a warm morning, say hallo to passing acquaintances of Susie, and put the world to rights.

Back at the house, we finish drying my laundry, and I set off. The journey is the opposite of the one I made with Sal when we drove from Oakland to Seattle, so I know it's going to be fairly spectacular. I am not disappointed, and by 5:00 I have put 180 miles behind me, and find myself in Roseburg.

Not a lot else happens on Friday, except that I move 340 miles south. I return through all the beautiful scenery around Lake Shasta, but I've already waxed lyrical about that. The major difference in the return journey is that it is ridiculously hot — 107 degrees when I stop at one particular rest area. It is still in the hundreds quite late into the evening, when I stop at Williams, California.

Tomorrow I move into San Francisco, where I will remain for a week. On Monday evening I will be joined by my younger daughter Nina, who will be travelling with me for a couple of weeks. In many respects it's the halfway stage of the journey. It's certainly the halfway stage of the baseball season. As I have explained before, baseball is an everyday game; teams play 162 games in six months, and never have more than one day off at a time. The exception to this is the All-Star Game break, during which matches are suspended for three days. The reason is that the best players in the major leagues take part in the All-Star Game, which this year is to take place in San Francisco. There are also lots of other festivities organised around this game, and I have managed to get tickets for all of them. I'll explain each of them as we go along next week.

Being the halfway stage of the season, it is usually considered a time for review, when teams decide whether they still have a chance, or whether to cut their losses and start planning for next year. The going has been fairly static so far. If the season ended today, the Boston Red Sox, Cleveland Indians, Anaheim Angels and Detroit Tigers would represent the American League in the playoffs. I think that's the same four teams that I mentioned last time I did this exercise, which was probably a couple of months ago. The New York Yankees are still way back, something like 12 games behind the Red Sox.

In the National League it's the New York Mets, Milwaukee Brewers, San Diego Padres and Los Angeles Dodgers. Again, I think three out of the four are the same as before. The big movers recently have been my Chicago Cubs, who have the best record in baseball over the past month. They are, as it is dubbed in baseball, "making a move," so maybe I won't have to rewrite the last chapter of the book after all.

No internet connection at this hotel, so this morning I switch on my phone to text home and let them know what's happening. Within seconds, it is making all sorts of noises, telling me that there are texts and voicemails awaiting me. Alarm bells start to ring but, as it turns out, it's a good panic.

There is urgent news. On Wednesday night, it seems, Jonny and Josh, the two pundits from Channel 5's baseball show, read out a letter from my neighbour Greg informing them of my trip. After dozens of e-mails and phone calls I gave up hope, but here it is at last. Their stated intention is to contact me and interview me in San Francisco when they come over for the All-Star Game. I shall do all I can to facilitate their endeavours.

Boosted by this news, I hit the road for San Francisco. The first stage of the All-Star festivities is the Fan Fest. As demand is so great, the tickets have entry times on them, and mine is for 12:00. The journey is just over 100 miles, and I have allowed myself plenty of time, so I believe. The journey is fairly straightforward although, after the wide open spaces of the northwest, five-lane highways and one-way systems take some getting used to again.

Having reached San Francisco and parked, I head out into a surprisingly cool city — that's cool as in temperature, not as in fashion — and walk the two blocks to the Moscone Centre, arriving at precisely 11:59. See, I told you I had allowed plenty of time.

The Fan Fest is an amazing medley of baseball-related activities, some of them with queues which put Alton Towers to shame. There is everything from the historical, displays on loan from the Hall of Fame and the Negro Leagues Museum, to the hysterical. You can stand behind a cardboard, decapitated figure of Barry Bonds, placing your head where his should be, and be photographed hitting your record breaking home run; or stand in a gap in the team lineup, and be photographed as a member of the San Francisco Giants; or stick your head on top of an outfielder leaping high to rob some poor hitter of a home run. It's a bit like the fat lady and scrawny man figures at Blackpool, except that people take this a little more seriously, and form some fairly long queues.

There are hitting cages, fielding practices, and chances for you to race against your dad while you both try to steal home. Then there are the collectables, which are a huge business in baseball — figurines, bobble head dolls, signed balls and baseball cards. One stall, which has something like a 90-minute queue, features a couple of retired players of renown, signing whatever people put in front of them. The thing I am most pleased to see is an acknowledgement of the women's league which appeared during World War II, and on the second occasion I pass this stall, there are a number of veterans from this league signing baseballs for yet another significant queue.

Eventually sated of this paraphernalia, I retrieve my car, and find my hotel. I am hardly enamoured of my return to city life but, by the time I have sorted the car, found a nearby Starbucks, and got my internet working, I feel ready to face the week ahead. My e-mails include one from my aforementioned neighbour, who has loaded the extract from the Channel 5 show onto the net for the world, and me in particular, to see. I am, it appears, on the verge of becoming an international superstar.

Feeling suitably famous, I set out in search of dinner. San Francisco does not, it appears, receive Channel 5, so I am not mobbed. The place I am seeking is just a few minutes' walk — Lefty O'Doul's, "the best deal on the square," Union Square, that is. This is a dark, wooden place, named after a local character with baseball connections. The walls are covered with local memorabilia, and the TVs are showing current games. The bar is lined with a vast selection of draught beers, but on the other side of the room is what can only be described as a cafeteria. You pick up your tray, choose from a fairly limited menu, one meat, two sides, one salad, bread, find a seat and off you go. The meat is carved from vast joints, and can in no way be described as rare. I opt for beef, with mash and gravy; it's comfort food, pure and simple — just the stuff for a poor lad experiencing a 40-degree drop in temperature over the last 24hours.

On Sunday morning there are important discussions to be had with those at home, before they leave for Manchester Airport. My daughter Nina is due in San Francisco tomorrow evening, so the last-minute instructions have to be given and received. The ethermail also brings lots of excitement from the mother country concerning my upcoming television interview.

All-Star Week Fan Fest, San Francisco — these women are veterans of the wartime women's league, inspiration for the movie "A League of Their Own."

Then it's on to the game, and the first chore is to collect the tickets. You may remember that Nina was successful in the All-Star Game ticket ballot, and she has arranged for the tickets to be collected by my good self. This is duly effected, but at this point I wish to have a serious moan. I managed to secure a ticket for the Fan Fest six months ago, when they first came on the market. Then came the tickets for the Futures Game, one of which I also acquired. I found a Home Run Derby ticket online, through an agency. But then, when Nina was successful in the ballot, the only way we could get the All-Star Game ticket was by buying a package which also contained the other three events. So after collecting the tickets this morning, I am left with several duplicates. I manage to sell the Home Run Derby ticket, at a loss, but the other two remain unused. This ridiculous system may explain why there are so many empty seats in the stadium. Even the touts are complaining that there are too many tickets about!

The only slight advantage of this surfeit of riches is, when I sit in what I think is the better of my two seats, the view is quite restricted. So I move to my other seat which, although a little further back, has a better view, both of the field and the surroundings.

AT&T Park is built on the edge of San Francisco Bay. Although I enjoyed looking at the mountains from my seat in Ogden, Utah, I'm afraid my vote for the best view in professional baseball would go to this park. All that stands between it and the water is a slim promenade, and a small fleet of kayaks paddles around what has been dubbed McCovey Cove, to catch any home run balls hit in that direction. The views across the bay and ahead to the bridge are magnificent — it's just a lovely place to be even if you don't like baseball.

Today's event is the Futures Game, which is a contest between the best young players in the minor leagues. The teams are divided as to the players' origins — USA vs. the World! (Funny, but when similar contests occur in our country, we always say Great Britain v the Rest of the World, so I'm not sure what the Americans are trying to claim here). The game is played quite seriously, and the teams are managed by two legends of the game, Dave Winfield and Juan Marichal. It is very watchable, with four home runs, and ends up 7–2 to the World team.

The second event is a softball game featuring legends of the game and celebrities. It may say more about me than the people concerned, but I recognise all of the baseball legends, but only one of the celebrities, and he, Jerry Rice, was an American football player. The crowd seems happy enough with the selection of celebrities, however, one of whom is Miss World, another of whom is the mayor of San Francisco, and lots of whooping and hollering takes place.

While all this is happening, however, the temperature starts to drop noticeably. I have managed to wear long trousers instead of shorts, but a jacket would be very welcome. I had planned to take a gentle stroll back to the hotel, perhaps stopping for dinner on the way. This plan changes to a brisk walk to the hotel to pick up a jacket, and a short step to last night's venue, Lefty O'Doul's, for a glass of Black Butte porter and more comfort food. If the weather stays like this, I may end up here every night.

Monday is day 100 — I mentally raise my bat to the crowd. Some days it feels like 500. The day starts with texts from home announcing that Nina is on her way, so I know the journey will be uppermost in my mind for the rest of the day. I know she's 27, but you never stop being a parent.

After breakfast and an hour's administration — change the appointment at the optician, fax forms to the insurance company — I set out for the ballpark again. Today is the third part of the All-Star festivities, the Home Run Derby. I get there as soon as the gates open, and spend the first hour wandering around trying to work out a way of contacting the Channel 5 people. My efforts come to naught, and even though my seat overlooks the auxiliary press box, and I spend odd moments of the afternoon checking the faces, it seems stardom will have to wait.

I wrote previously about how close the ballpark is to the bay. Since the Barry Bonds hysteria began, the stretch of water just beyond right field, McCovey Cove, has been the habitat of small boats, each occupied by a would-be ball catcher, hoping to net a valuable souvenir. Yesterday, for the Futures Game, there were one or two kayaks sculling about. Today, for the Home Run Derby, there are so many boats that, should a ball be hit out of the park, there would be little chance of it actually hitting water.

The afternoon's entertainment begins with tomorrow's teams taking batting practice. This is a bit more entertaining than it might sound, and involves lots of introductions to the crowd. Baseball fans love nothing more than to catch a ball hit into the crowd, and today will provide myriad opportunities. Many of the players are obviously caught up in the occasion. It's quite easy to spot those who are at their first All-Star Game, as they are walking around the field with camcorders. Several players have brought their kids with them, and the kids are suited up and joining in the fielding.

After lengthy practices for both sides, we are treated to an appearance from Counting Crows. From the bit of the stadium where I am sitting, appearance is the appropriate term, as it seems that certain bits of the band's equipment have not been hooked up to the P.A. I get the drummer and the keyboard player, but not much else.

The Home Run Derby is really just a bit of crowd-pleasing nonsense. Eight players, renowned for their ability to hit a ball a long way, are invited to take part. They bring their own pitchers with them, so that the ball is thrown exactly how they like it, and they see how many home runs they can hit. At each stage, the less successful contenders are eliminated, until we are left with a head-to-head for the trophy. The trophy is won by Vladimir Guerrero, of the Anaheim Angels. As well as hitting the most homers, he also wins the award for the longest hit of the night, which clears the stadium and is measured at 503 feet!

I receive a text to tell me that Nina's flight is delayed an hour, so I stop for a bite to eat. I check my messages to find that she has arrived and is on the shuttle bus. I phone her, and she is in her hotel room already! I have just ordered a meal, so I give her directions to the restaurant, and cross my fingers. A few moments later, there she is, large as life and twice as lovely. The meal gets longer as Nina is ordering as I am finishing, and then we share a dessert. Returning to the hotel we both realise we are exhausted so, with promises of a diner breakfast tomorrow, off she goes to her room.

On Tuesday, we have our promised breakfast at the local diner, and then set out to walk to the ballpark. She has no ticket for the game, but there are things happening outside the park that she is interested in seeing.

Noon is the time of the Chevrolet Red Carpet, when the players are due to arrive at the park in open-top Chevrolets. I am expecting stretch limos, but, true to the American love affair with such, they arrive in Silverado pickup trucks. The man of the hour is Barry Bonds who, despite all the controversy surrounding him, is a hometown hero. The fans chant his name as he approaches and make it clear exactly where they stand in the "Bonds—hero or villain?" debate. The villains, as far as they are concerned, are the Los Angeles Dodgers players who, although they are on the same team as Bonds, are still roundly booed for belonging to the local rivals. There is a seemingly infinite number of these arrivals, and the American League players have not even started yet, so we decide we have had enough of standing and retire to Borders for a drink.

Nina goes off to shop San Francisco dry, while I head for the game, to try to find the Channel 5 crew. My ticket is standing room, which is both bad and good. The bad is, obviously, that my feet and back will be hurting by the end of the game. The good is that it gets me into ground level, so I can walk through the posh seats behind home plate and try to find these elusive people. All my searching comes to naught, so I work my way around to right field, where I have a good overall view, and train my binoculars on the press pack. I pick out Peter Gammons and Chris Berman, two respected U.S. commentators, and David Lengel, who sometimes works for Channel 5, and is probably doing a link for them as I watch. I head in his direction but he quickly disappears from my view. At this point I realise that, if I'm not careful, I could waste this golden opportunity looking for a face in a crowd, so I text home as to where I'm standing, and settle down to enjoy the spectacle.

In case you haven't worked it out, the All-Star Game is the best players in the American League against the best in the National League. The starting player in each position is chosen by fan ballot, and the others by player ballot. The manager for each side comes from last year's World Series teams, and they select extra pitchers, and control the sides on the night. There are quite a few substitutions, and the occasion sometimes is more of a spectacle than a competitive game. In an effort to make it more competitive, they changed the rules a couple of seasons ago, and the winning league now gives home advantage to its entrant in the World Series. The National League has not won since 1996, and we are in a National League stadium, so hopes are high.

The NL takes an early lead, but the fifth inning sees something quite special. Ichiro Suzuki, the Japanese player from the Seattle Mariners, hits a ball deep to right field, and starts to run. He's one of the fastest runners in the game.

The ball takes a nasty bounce off the wall, and Ichiro keeps going, scoring the first ever "inside-the-park" home run in All Star history, putting the AL ahead, 2–1. Both sides score again in the seventh, but in the eighth the AL opens up a 5–2 lead, and the score stays like that until the middle of the ninth. With the crowd leaving in droves, a hitter gets on base, and then Alfonso Soriano (from those Cubbies of mine) homers, bringing the score to 5–4. Suddenly the crowd stops leaving.

A pitching meltdown occurs and, with two men out, the next three batters all walk, so the bases are loaded. The final batter makes good contact, but the ball falls a couple of feet short of the fence, and is caught for the final out. Victory yet again to the American League; game 7 of the World Series, should it occur, will therefore be in an American League park. The final chapter of my book will have to be rewritten!

California (Part Two)
Wednesday July 11–Friday July 13

We are out of the hotel before 9:00, and stumble around trying to work out the buses before grabbing a taxi to take us to the eye specialist. We arrive on time, only to be told that my appointment is for next Wednesday. I patiently explain their error, and am told that there is no problem because the doctor is free anyway.

After drops, tests, and unbearably bright lights, I am told that my eye is fine. The doctor is from Seattle, and we talk baseball before Nina gives him one of my cards and explains my quest. He goes to fetch his senior colleague, and for a few moments I assume this is just to talk more baseball, as the guy becomes even more enthusiastic about my journey. Eventually he gets around to my eye, and gives high praise to my Albuquerque surgeon. I always thought he was brilliant, and to have this confirmed by a fellow professional is comforting. He says my sight will gradually improve, but that I will probably not be able to pick the seams on a slider (a type of pitch). I reply that if I could do that, I would be playing the game instead of watching it, and he chuckles, more at his own remark than my retort, I feel.

Suitably heartened, we retire for breakfast, and to plan the rest of our day. We take a couple of hours' break, and I take the chance to check my e-mails. There is a growing disappointment amongst my readership, many of whom have watched or recorded the All-Star Game, expecting to see me interviewed. I fear Channel 5 may not have heard the last of this.

On Thursday I spend a couple of hours eating a leisurely breakfast and buying cards. I want to write a note to my eye surgeon in Albuquerque with yesterday's news. That done, we set off for the airport, as I need to exchange my rental car, which is overdue a service. The young woman who attends to us is unique — a Dollar employee who understands exactly what I am doing with my summer, and effects all the changes necessary without so much as a troubled look. The choice of car is interesting — I am first offered what they call a minivan. I would call it a people carrier, far too large for my needs unless I intend to pick up a hitch-hiking baseball team. So I end up with a Chrysler PT Cruiser. I am not sure what PT stands for, unless they were expecting me, but the style is what I believe is known as "retro." It is a stand-up design, that would not look out of place in a 50s cop show, and all the handles, instruments and the like are round and chunky. But it's good to drive, and should suit me.

On Friday we see some of the sights of this lovely city, then set off for Nina's first, and my last visit to the ballpark. The San Francisco Giants are playing the hated Los Angeles Dodgers, and the game is a sell-out. Baseball clubs are franchises, and, if they are not proving economically viable, it is fairly commonplace for owners to sell or move. Thus the Atlanta Braves were once the Milwaukee Braves; only last season the Montreal Expos became the Washington Nationals. But the most famous, or notorious, of these moves came in the mid–1950s, when major league baseball could not be found any further west than St. Louis.

New York at the time boasted three major league clubs, the Yankees, the Giants and the Brooklyn Dodgers, who had all graced the city for decades. So it was a highly controversial decision that took the Giants to San Francisco and the Dodgers to Los Angeles. The one thing that remains is a bitter rivalry that predates their arrival on the West Coast by decades. We arrive early enough to enjoy the sights, and walk around this beautiful stadium to catch everything it has to offer. There is much to see, but one of my favourite sights is a board devoted to the sayings of Yogi Berra, a famous Yankees catcher, who is remembered for his ability to not quite make sense.

> *"The place gets so crowded that nobody goes there anymore."*
> *"When you come to a fork in the road, take it."*
> *"It's déjà vu all over again."*

We settle down for the game, at which point Nina turns into an eating machine, seeing off a hot dog, popcorn and ice cream.

The notorious Mr. Bonds is in attendance, but for him and his team it is a real Friday the 13th. In his first at-bat he hits into a double play, and then the Dodgers, while walking him twice, build up a 3–0 lead. In the bottom of the eighth he manages to drive in a run, but only at the cost of another double play. The Dodgers score six in the ninth, and it ends 9–1, with Bonds still needing four homers to tie Aaron's record.

The San Francisco Bay, by which, incidentally, earlier this evening, I was walking with my baby, treats us to a fabulous rolling mist, and the crowd disappears into the night, still hurling abuse at the now somewhat smug Dodgers fans.

Nevada

Saturday July 14–Sunday July 15

Off we set for Las Vegas, in the Chrysler, which appears to be doing the job very nicely. The plan is to get about 100 miles from Las Vegas, and then find a motel close enough to complete the journey tomorrow in time for a 12:05 first pitch. This is a good plan in theory, but in reality the last 100 miles before Las Vegas consist of nothing but desert. So we decide to keep going, in the hope that the hotel we have booked for tomorrow can fit us in tonight. They can, and here we are.

This really is a strange place! I must be honest and admit that Las Vegas held no attraction for me prior to arriving, and so far I have seen nothing to change my mind. As I said, there is nothing but desert for 100 miles or more, and then suddenly there is city, no suburbs, no outskirts; desert, then skyscrapers, many of which look like fairy castles.

As for the temperature, we left a misty San Francisco in the low 70s this morning. A few miles before Las Vegas we were up to 112 degrees. Even after dark it is 105 degrees. The hotel, however, is good, and boasts an excellent restaurant, where this evening I have the pleasure of watching my daughter eat a fine steak. For a devoted carnivore, watching a lapsed vegetarian eat steak is as good as it gets.

Sunday morning, shortly after 11:00, we are ready to leave for the ballpark which, fortunately, is only a ten-minute walk. The temperature is again stupidly high, and humid with it, so even a ten-minute stroll is exhausting. The stadium is very modern, part of a complex that includes a theatre and a conference centre, but we are horrified to find that our seats are not in the shade. So we ignore the numbers and sit in the shade, unchallenged by authority. The crowd is quite sparse, so we are not doing anyone out of a place.

The roof above the seats has fans and cold air blowers, which give the impression of dry ice in these temperatures. So we equip ourselves with cold drinks, and settle down to enjoy the game. A little way in, I am curious as to what the temperature might be. Looking around, I eventually locate the thermometer, which reads 104. A few minutes later it has risen to 109, and then to 114. At this point I realise I am looking at the clock. It's a good job I realise my mistake before the end of the game, by which time the temperature would have been 236!!

The shade, the fans and the blowers combine to make conditions bearable. We pass a pleasant couple of hours, and the presence of some salespeople distributing free samples of Starbuck's something or other with raspberry in it enhances the experience. The game finishes Salt Lake Bees 5, Las Vegas 51s 6 — the players have their own strategy for dealing with the heat. It's called the home run. There are six of them, which account for ten of the 11 runs scored. It stops you having to sprint to first, and means you can just saunter around the bases.

We decide on a lazy evening, mainly due to the fact that the temperature is still 113 degrees at 7:30 in the evening. But we realise that no trip to this city would be complete without a look at the Strip; so we wait until it drops dark, and drive from our hotel to the Strip, along the Strip and back again; 14 miles in two hours! In some ways it's what I expected, but the thing that surprises me is how narrow the road is. In the movies it always seems so full of space; in real life everything is on top of everything else. I see names that have made history; Harrah's, Caesars Palace, etc., etc.

I am pleased to have made the drive, although I still fail to understand why the place was ever built. It is an amazing sight. I try hard to think of positive things to say about this supposedly magical city, but the best I can come up with is— Blackpool on steroids!

North Dakota
Monday July 16–Friday July 20

The demands of the calendar regarding Alaska and San Francisco were always going to make this part of the journey long and illogical. My next destination is Fargo, North Dakota, which is some 1,700 miles away; the good news is that we have four days in which to get there. There will be some revisiting of previous routes, but also a lot that has yet to be seen.

As we move north, across a corner of Arizona and into Utah, the landscape improves markedly. First the dramatic red sandstone, with its angular crags, then the more mellow colours of Utah, with the mountains falling into deep blue lakes. The temperature drops from the Las Vegas high to the mid–70s during an afternoon storm, and is now a pleasant 83 degrees where we are, just across the border into Wyoming.

This particular corner of Wyoming provides us with a good and cheap motel, but deprives us of an hour, as we move back to Mountain Time. After a meal in Evanston, I catch up on some sport. I see that the Cubs have swept the Houston Astros, and send off a puerile e-mail to Karen in Houston in celebration. I recall my visit to the Astros stadium with Karen's daughter Lindsay, and remember her taking quite a fancy to Houston's young rookie outfielder, a certain Hunter Pence. This must be young Hunter's first visit to Wrigley Field, because there is a wonderful clip of a ball being driven over his head into the outfield ivy. He turns and waits for it to emerge. It doesn't!

Tuesday is all about Wyoming — starting bottom left and ending top right. It's a big place — we cover 521 miles and we don't leave it. It's also full of space; most of the time we are surrounded by vast open prairies. We eventually arrive in Gillette, where we have planned to stay the night. Half an hour cruising, and two motels later, we decide to move north, and end up in Sundance, home of the Kid, although he is no longer in residence.

The campaign to stir Channel 5 into action appears to be warming up. A whole host of friends and family has written in support of my cause, and today I receive a copy of the latest — an e-mail from cousin Jeff which has actually received a reply from Erik Janssen, the producer of the show, saying simply, "Have him e-mail me direct." So I do!

The baseball season is now back in swing following the All-Star Game break. The eight teams which would reach the playoffs, if the season finished today, are the same as reported earlier. The interest lies in those teams who are threatening to make a move; the Atlanta Braves, Chicago Cubs, Arizona Diamondbacks and Seattle Mariners are all looking threatening. The New York Yankees, ten games adrift at the break, have been written off. No one comes back from a ten-game deficit. One week on, they are eight games adrift, but it just can't happen, can it?

On the sports scene, today's two lead stories are very different. Michael Vick, an American football player from Atlanta, has been indicted on charges of implication in a dog fighting ring. I think there is concern in the game that, if he goes down, he could take others with him. The other story is, of course, much more serious. This coming weekend, Beckham arrives!

On Wednesday morning I am offered Marilyn Monroe for breakfast. But wait, I'm getting ahead of myself. Whilst eating dinner last night we realised that Sundance is not far from Mount Rushmore. I know it's got little or nothing to do with music or baseball, but we may never pass this way again, so off we set.

We pass through Deadwood and, looking for somewhere to eat, we come across the Boondocks Rock 'n' Roll Diner. Now this little treasure may be targeted at the tourist, but is nevertheless the genuine article. A tin can of a diner, seating about ten at the counter, with the cook at his griddle behind. No air conditioning, just a big fan; a genuine 50s table top juke box; and a chipping machine, because the French fries are made from real potatoes. The decoration includes pictures of Elvis, "I Love Lucy," and many more.

The menu contains many allusions to 50s characters. Hence the chicken sandwich is the Marilyn Monroe — plump breasts, tasty buns, loads of cheese!

Nina, meanwhile, deals with a foot-long Frankie. Now this is my younger daughter we're talking about, so you'll have to do your own jokes.

From there we proceed to Mount Rushmore. As with many such places, it's not quite what I imagined. Don't get me wrong, it's a spectacular piece of work, which took 14 years to complete. But I always thought it covered a whole cliff face, whereas it actually covers the top quarter. The circle is squared, however, as in the café there are pictures of the company baseball team from the 30s!

It's all about the journey, not the destination. That is never more true than Thursday. Our destination is Lake Norden, which houses the South Dakota Amateur Baseball Hall of Fame. I am not sure what to expect from the destination, but the journey soon proves exceedingly worthwhile. After 50 miles of interstate we head north on smaller roads, and are soon witnessing South Dakota's wildfowl protection scheme.

More delightful scenery leads us to Lake Norden, a tiny town whose centre consists of maybe six shops, and the South Dakota Amateur Baseball Hall of Fame, housed in a two-room building donated by a local dignitary. The word to bear in mind here is "amateur" as this institution has very little to do with the major leagues. It is a celebration of the amateur game in South Dakota, and is obviously a work of love and devotion. The exhibits are what you would expect, but a couple of the stories bear repeating. In July 1948, the longest game ever in this state took place, finishing Bonesteel 4, Platte 3, after 28 innings. The winning pitcher, Robert "Spud" Grosshuesch, pitched all 28 innings, and struck out 62 batters!

In 1964, when the local high school was appointing a new principal, the school board insisted that the person selected should be a catcher!

Ever onward, and our journey brings us to North Dakota, and the town of Fargo. In the last four days we have driven just over 1,700 miles, and the prospect of two nights in the same motel is very attractive. So after a couple of hours' relaxation, we head out to dine at a Greek restaurant next door to the motel.

The nation is stunned by the news that Beckham's swollen ankle may prevent his debut, but the Barry Bonds saga is reaching a climax. Over the last few weeks he has been rubbish, having one of the worst averages in the major leagues. On Sunday he told reporters that he was "f****** embarrassed to wear his f****** uniform. Now f*** off out of here!" This week his Giants have played four games against my Cubbies. He was rested for most of the first three games, but played yesterday, and hit two home runs, his first for weeks. (Don't worry, the Cubs won, 9–8). This gives him 753, two short of Aaron's record.

Today the Giants start a three-game series against Milwaukee. July 20 is the anniversary of the day Aaron hit his 755th home run! In Milwaukee! The right fielder that day was Bobby Bonds, Barry's dad! As I wrote a while back, baseball commissioner Bud Selig, because of the steroids issue, has yet to make a statement as to whether or not he will be in attendance when Bonds breaks the record; Aaron was his childhood idol, so he must feel a bit conflicted. Selig is a Milwaukee fan, lives and works in the city, and has a suite in the stadium. You couldn't make this stuff up, could you?

Inevitably, we make a gentle start to Friday. Nina sleeps in while I catch up with e-mails and such. We have a game tonight, but I want to see the Roger Maris Museum, and Nina has some shopping to do. Conveniently, the museum is located in a shopping centre ten minutes walk from our hotel, so two birds are killed with one stone. The museum consists of three shop windows, and a small room displaying a video on Maris' life. So who was Roger Maris, I hear you ask.

Back in the twenties, Babe Ruth hit 60 home runs in one season, and it was thought the record would stand forever. In 1961, two members of the same team, the New York Yankees, started to threaten the record. They were Mickey Mantle and Roger Maris. Mantle was a blond-haired, blue-eyed all–American boy, at the peak of his career. Maris was a quiet family man from Fargo, North Dakota, in his third season with New York.

As the season panned out, America became worried about its great hero, the Babe, being deprived of one of his records. It was pointed out to the Com-

The Roger Maris Museum, Fargo; a small display in a North Dakota shopping mall pays tribute to the man who, in 1961, broke Babe Ruth's near-sacred home run record.

missioner, Ford Frick, that Ruth set his record in a 154-game season, while in 1961 the season had been extended to 162 games. Maris broke the record in the last game of the season, and for many years two records were entered in the game's statistics until in 1991, by which time Maris had suffered an early death from cancer, a committee decided that the record should be given solely to Maris. The video shows the effect of the mammoth season on Maris and his family, and how he saw out the rest of his career. It also shows in what high esteem he was held by his teammates, and how they were affected by his early death.

This evening's game sees the Fargo-Moorhead Redhawks entertain the Winnipeg Goldeyes. The first thing I notice after arriving at the pleasant but functional stadium is the number 8, Maris' number, on the far wall. This indicates that the club has retired his shirt number, which is the way a player is honoured by his club. There is a homely atmosphere. The game is sponsored by the Northern Plains Potato Growers Association, which means that some poor unfortunate is walking around wearing a giant potato suit.

Two obviously devoted fans just behind us have devised a little rhyming chant for each batter, which they shout out as he takes his place: "Hit it far, Salazar!; Knock it to Boston, Austin!" (in North Dakota those final two words rhyme). They have obviously given it a lot of thought, but by the time each batter has been up for the fourth time, it loses a little of its charm.

The local brew is called Lenny's, which is short for a long German word ending in ... hausen. I partake of a creamy dark, not dissimilar to a dark mild, and a berry Weiss, which is a more than passable imitation of a Belgian fruit beer.

The game starts like a house on fire, with the home team scoring seven in the first, and forcing Winnipeg's starting pitcher out of the game. After that the game is more or less decided, and finishes 10–1 to the Redhawks.

Minnesota

Saturday July 21

Four miles out of Fargo, we are in Minnesota, the state of 10,000 lakes. We don't see all of them from the I-94, but there are a few nice ones. We continue into Minneapolis, check into a very pleasant hotel, and relax for an hour before setting off for tonight's game, an American League encounter between the Minnesota Twins and the Los Angeles Angels. The Twins play in the Metrodome which, as the name suggests, is a dome. Just to get this clear, this is not a modern stadium with a retractable roof, with the game played indoors on artificial turf. It is like a 60s concrete stadium, such as Oakland, but with a huge translucent tent for a roof. A unique and somewhat comforting notice welcomes us as we enter the stadium: "the Minnesota Twins Baseball Club bans guns in these premises"!

We sit next to two Angels fans, surrounded by Twins fans, and the game turns out to be one of the best of the trip so far. It starts off looking like a pitching duel, with defences on top. The Twins pitcher glories under the name of Boof Bonzer, and the fans show their appreciation of his efforts by shouting his first name, which sounds, of course, as if they are booing him. In the bottom of the sixth, the tie is broken with a solo home run from the Twins, and another in the seventh appears to have cemented the win. But in the eighth, the Angels manufacture two runs to bring it level.

At this point, Nina returns from a little wander with one of the best ballpark snacks to date, strawberries and bananas covered with chocolate sauce.

In the bottom of the eighth, the Twins fan behind me begins to rubbish the first batter, Nick Punto, who is having a poor year. Punto responds by hitting a double. I look at the fan and laugh, and he promises to lay off Punto until noon tomorrow! The next batter walks, putting the Twins in a good situation but, when the following batter comes up, Punto succeeds in getting picked off at second base. "The noon tomorrow deal is off!" yells the fan behind.

The next batter again walks, bringing the Twins catcher, Joe Mauer, to the plate. He lashes a pitch into the outfield, where the centre fielder gets a hand to it, preventing it from leaving the field. He injures himself in the process, and Mauer keeps going like a startled hare, achieving that rarity, an inside-the-park home run. Twins win, 5–2. We bid farewell to all our new friends, and stroll home through a warm Minnesota night, thinking what a friendly and amenable city this is.

Nebraska

Sunday July 22nd–Monday July 23rd

Faced with another 370 miles today, we make a reasonably early exit from Minneapolis, heading south along I-35. It's not too long before we are in Iowa ... or is it heaven? On this occasion we are just passing through en route to Nebraska, and are scheduled to return on Thursday for the real Iowa chapter of this voyage. But ironically, when we become ready for a late breakfast, the first available place to stop is Clear Lake, which is our scheduled stop for Thursday.

Funnily enough, after being accused of being Dutch, German, New Zealander and various other nationalities during this trip, the three people who speak to us today spot us as English straight away. The attendant in the gas station, having ascertained our nationality, then asks a strange question. "What does my accent sound like to you?" How are you supposed to answer a question like that? American? Just plain wrong?

We find our hotel in Omaha and, after a couple of hours, decide to eat. We end up in the Village Inn, one of the franchises not yet tried, and meet our waitress, A.J. Arianna Joan, we later discover it stands for, although her first name is Bernadette. She is entranced by our Englishness, and immediately tells us all the places we should go in Omaha, despite being informed we are leaving lunchtime tomorrow. She recommends the Old Spaghetti Factory, a restaurant which serves "the best spaghetti in the world." She then announces that she wants to visit Europe, particularly England and Italy. I suggest that, when she gets to Italy, she doesn't tell them that Omaha has the best spaghetti in the world!

I eat my first pot roast of the tour, which turns out to be an excellent beef stew, and we decline dessert, despite A.J. threatening to hold us hostage until we sample "the best pies in the world!" We arrange to meet her at the game tomorrow, and escape into the night.

Monday has a backwards feeling to it, as we are going to a ball game, and then travelling. I have checked the net several times, to make sure that the game really is starting at 12:05, and it seems to be true. So just after 11:00 we set off for Rosenblatt Stadium, to see the Omaha Royals entertain the Memphis Redbirds. Before leaving, I check my e-mails, and find one from someone I have never heard of, congratulating me on my trip, and saying how he had heard it mentioned last night on Channel 5. I am curious.

The weather is odd too. The sun is hidden behind a thin, hazy cloud, and it is humid, so that it feels hotter than the 83 degrees indicated by the thermometer. Arriving at the ground, I remember that Nina received a message on my phone, so I switch it on and pass it to her, while I go to collect the tickets. Suddenly she appears to be in a state of high excitement, and it appears that the message is from Jonny Gould, the presenter of the Channel 5 baseball programme. He is very apologetic about missing me in San Francisco, and was trying to contact me to be interviewed on the programme. We then start to receive texts and messages from home. It seems I did indeed get a mention, as did several of my supporters, including my sister (???) Nina, who is travelling with me on my quest to visit "every single ballpark in the States!!????!!" Never let the truth spoil a good story!

We find our seats, and cover ourselves with sun cream, as we can feel ourselves burning despite the fact that there is no sun. I must, at this point, say a word in support of Omaha Beef. The word is "tasty," and today is half-price steak burger day, certainly a cut above the usual ballpark burger. The stadium is sparsely populated at the front, with people who have nothing else to do on a Monday afternoon, and crowded at the back, with seemingly every school in Omaha providing a group, and a noisy group at that.

The game starts at a fair lick. Memphis hits a single, a double and a home run in the first, to lead 3–0. Omaha pulls a run back in the second, and we look forward to a high-scoring game. But, despite Omaha pushing hard, even loading the bases at one stage, there are no more runs. We sit and melt gently as the game progresses, and can't believe the temperature is still only in the 80s.

We have decided to do a couple of hours' driving after the game, to make tomorrow more bearable. We pass through a quite spectacular storm, which is preceded by the most bizarre sky. Arriving at the motel, I return Mr. Gould's call. He is extremely apologetic for San Francisco, and for upsetting my entire family. He advises me to contact his producer, and it appears I am pencilled in for Wednesday or Sunday.

South Dakota

Tuesday July 24 – Wednesday July 25

We are headed for St. Paul, a small town which houses the Nebraska Baseball Hall of Fame. It is a little larger than its South Dakotan equivalent, but still very homely. We park up, Nina notices an elderly lady running a stall about recycling, and they are soon deep in conversation. It appears that Marion (for that is her name) knows the whole town, and we are told who runs the museum, and, as we head in that direction, she is on the phone to the woman who runs the local newspaper.

The museum is a two-roomed building, with one room dedicated to the people of Nebraska who have played major league baseball, and the other devoted to the six players from the state who have been inducted into the National Baseball Hall of Fame. Pride of place is given to Grover Cleveland Alexander, possibly one of the best pitchers to ever play the game, and a native of St. Paul. The curator is extremely knowledgeable, and reels off information about her six precious charges without pausing for breath.

The best, and probably the worst, thing about small town America is that everyone knows everyone else. So the curator tells us to lunch in the Sweet Shoppe, which has "the best pies in the world." Obviously the title has changed hands since Sunday night — perhaps there was a bake-off yesterday.

We set off for Sioux Falls — the motel is easily found, and we settle in, then go looking for dinner. Nina fancies pasta, and the place at the top of the road is called "Old Chicago" — pizza and pasta. Easy! Good menu, excellent beer list — I begin with a pint of Moose Drool! Our waitress, Alison, is also fascinated by our journey, and when our bill arrives it has a lovely message and a baseball drawn on the back. Yes, she gets a good tip!

Back to the hotel to check e-mails before bed; one from my neighbour attaching a video clip from Channel 5's Sunday show, where I am mentioned and am to be interviewed; one from a friend offering to write to his senator in Washington to speed up my visa extension; one from my elder daughter telling me that she and her husband have just crossed one more major administrative barrier on the way to adoptive parenthood, and the arrival of a small bundle is imminent. TV star, cause celebre, and grandparent — how many more new roles will this extraordinary summer bring?

Iowa

Wednesday July 25–Sunday July 29

Wednesday starts on a very positive note. Last evening I e-mailed Erik, the producer of Channel 5 Baseball, and this morning he calls me in my hotel room. He says that they want to feature me in the show for the rest of the season, and that the first spot will be on Sunday evening. He also offers me some support for the rest of the trip, so I'm feeling very positive about the whole thing.

Today our game is the Sioux Falls Canaries playing host to the Shreveport Sports. Again it's a noon start on a weekday, but I'm beginning to understand why. The other day I referred to groups of school kids. The schools are, of course, on vacation, and I realise now that the groups in attendance come from summer play schemes and the like. The clubs can boast a 3,000 crowd, and the groups have something to do. The park, known as the Birdcage, is nice enough but there is no shade at all. Bearing in mind this is a noon start, and the temperature is in the 90s, this is a potential problem. But with hats, sun block and cold drinks galore, we brave it.

The game is dominated by pitchers. The Canaries' pitchers throw 14 strikeouts, but errors and walks cost them dearly. The Sports' pitchers only allow five runners throughout the whole game, and none of them manages to score — Sports win, 5–0.

There is also some sort of educational programme going on with all the kids' groups present, as the Canaries' mascot, Cagey, is expected to chase off someone dressed up as a cigarette end, known as Ciggy Butt, while the kids all boo. It's more like a pantomime than a sports event.

After the game, we drive the 220 miles from South Dakota, through Minnesota, to Iowa. Because of the vagaries of the schedules, it feels like we have been to each of this group of states at least twice. Tonight's motel is literally yards from where we had lunch on Sunday. The morning sun is beginning to take effect as we consider the possibilities for the evening, so we opt to stroll over to the aforementioned restaurant, grab some carry out, and fall over in our rooms. The TV is showing my Cubbies making mincemeat of their arch rival Cardinals, 7–1. They are now one game off a playoff spot. I go to bed and dream of a World Series!

No baseball on Thursday, so we devote the day to Clear Lake's most memorable event, the 1959 plane crash which took the lives of Buddy Holly and two other musicians. Firstly we drive to the north of the town, along a dirt road, until we find a sign indicating the path to the crash site. A ten-minute walk along the side of a field of corn brings us to the site, where a small memorial has been placed. The memorial appears hand-made, from sheet metal, and depicts a guitar topped by three discs, each inscribed with the name of one of the artistes and the name of his greatest hit.

The second part of the pilgrimage takes us back into Clear Lake, a pretty little town on the bank of a huge lake. The Surf Ballroom is where the three performed on the evening before the crash. The Surf is still a functioning venue, and is largely unchanged since the 50s. The foyer, corridors and lounge are covered with photographs and mementoes. The foyer has a display about the crash, and one wall of the lounge has a display of photographs for each of the three men.

Friday's first destination is Dyersville, a small Iowa town whose life changed in 1989 when the Lansing Farm, just outside the town, was chosen as the location for the film *Field of Dreams*. In case there is anyone out there who has never seen the movie, it tells the tale of an Iowa farmer who hears voices telling him to build a baseball field on his farm, and the field then attracts the ghosts of several former players, the most notable being Joe Jackson. The film is based on the book *Shoeless Joe*, by W.P. Kinsella.

The location of the film has been preserved, and is now a popular tourist sight. The rest of the farm is still in working order, and visitors are only able to visit the field. So you hang around, read about the film, run the bases, play catch, sit in the bleachers and just enjoy this unique site.

Two things make the visit a little odd. Firstly, we happen to be in Dyersville on the one day in the year when some strange cycling event is also happening. So we have to share the town with 4,000 cyclists. The event also includes the Field of Dreams on its itinerary, so a few of the cyclists are sharing the field with us when we arrive. The second odd thing concerns the ownership of the farm. Part of the left and centre outfield never belonged to the Lansing Farm, but to a neighbour. When the movie was completed, Lansing decided to leave the field as it stood, to be seen by friends and family. The neighbour differed, and ploughed up his bit and replanted it with corn. A few years later, he sold that piece of land to an out-of-state commercial company, who agreed to recreate the field in its original form. Each side has its own agenda, and when you arrive you find two entrances, and two gift shops. Unfortunately, driving from Dyersville, the first one we reach is the commercial one. Ironically, we decide to leave our shopping until the end of our visit, so once we find out the facts, we are able to shop in the Lansing store.

The field is a delight. Apart from the shops and notice boards, it is exactly as it appears in the film. As with the Buddy Holly crash site yesterday, it is a good feeling just to experience something that has meant so much to you. We do all the tourist stuff, and read all about the making of the film, which probably doesn't sound very exciting, but it certainly is one of the highlights of the trip. They built it, and we came!

Our trip to Cedar Rapids is only around 60 miles, which is a welcome change from some of the marathons we have done lately. We have taken to picking up free magazines with hotel discounts in them, and so we are heading for the Quality Inn, for no other reason than that — they have a discount voucher. The baseball game we are here to see is not until Sunday afternoon, so we are going to spend three nights in the same place.

We arrive and check in, and it appears a very nice hotel. The broadband works, and the first message I pick up is from Erik, at Channel 5, arranging the niceties of my first interview on Sunday. I am to be phoned between 6:00 and 6:30.

Saturday is a very welcome day, with no alarms or wake up calls; we just do our own thing until we are good and ready. My own thing includes, as always, planning the next phase of the trip. So this morning I am busy confirming complementary tickets for Cincinnati and Florence, and continuing to sort out tickets and accommodation for my brother-in-law when he meets up with me in New York.

Nina leaves for home in four days, so there is an obvious need for shopping. Fortunately our hotel is a few hundred metres from a large shopping centre, so we have a leisurely lunch and spend the rest of the afternoon viewing the delights of the mall.

Field of Dreams, Dyersville, Iowa — They built it, so we came. The part of Shoeless Joe Jackson is played here by my daughter Nina.

Returning to the hotel after a good dinner, I watch with delight the last couple of innings of the Cubs' 8–1 victory over the Reds. Life gets even better when news comes in that the Brewers, whom the Cubs are chasing in their division, have lost both games of a doubleheader. This leaves the Cubs just one and a half games back.

Changing channels, I watch Barry Bonds playing for the Giants against the Marlins. Last night, Bonds hit another home run. This brings his career total to 754, just one short of Aaron's record. Commissioner Selig, after his prevarication, has announced his intention to be present when Bonds breaks the record, if possible. But there are big celebrations in Cooperstown this weekend, so he has an excuse to be absent. In the ninth inning the Giants, who are losing, mount a comeback. With the scores level and two men on base, Ray Durham comes to the plate. The next batter is Bonds. Durham knocks a double, the Giants win the game, and the Bonds roadshow has to continue tomorrow.

Sunday also starts gently. Our game does not start until 2:00, so the morning is taken up with sleep, showers, laundry, and all those things that a couple of spare hours permit. Once ready, we head off for the stadium, arriving about 45 minutes before the first pitch. It's surprising, therefore, as we approach the park, to hear the announcer getting very excited and loud about something. It transpires that a local company is staging a home run derby, and several guys are stood somewhere around second base, doing a reasonable job of hitting the ball into the bleachers. All for charity, mate!

The game, between the Cedar Rapids Kernels and the West Michigan Whitecaps, is somewhat of an anticlimax. The home team commits four errors, plus some wild pitching, and even a balk to second base, which ultimately comes back to haunt them. The away team plays steadily, and cruises to a 6–1 victory.

I return to the hotel with 45 minutes to prepare for my TV interview — massage, voice coach, meditation. Erik phones as agreed, explains what's going to happen, and arranges to phone back in ten minutes. When this happens, I am put through to the studio, where Jonny and Josh explain what they will ask me, and then proceed to do so. It's all over very quickly, two minutes and 15 seconds apparently. It's all fairly straightforward, where I've been so far, favourite parks, where did I get the time and money from. Oh yes, and why I'm doing it! Had to think a bit about that one! The nice thing is that I am going to become a regular spot, so my fans will have to get used to sitting up late on Sundays, or preset their videos. We pop next door to the Granite City Brewery for another delightful dinner, and return to a message from home that the interview was shown between the third and fourth innings.

I will leave you with an unusual story. Baseball, because of its open-ended structure, has a greater propensity than most sports for unusual scores. But check this out! San Diego Padres vs. Houston Astros; score after one inning

Padres 11, Astros 0; score at the end, Padres 18, Astros 11. A fun one for the fans.

Wisconsin
Monday July 30–Tuesday July 31

Monday starts very busily, with lots of positive response from back home to my TV interview. My technology support team has been very prompt, and the interview is now there on the website for all to see. I am also receiving e-mails from complete strangers, who have heard the show and looked up the website.

After dealing with all the correspondence, we set off east on the 151, and cross the border into Wisconsin at Dubuque. Our first destination today is Madison, which also turns out to be larger than I expected, and stands on two beautiful lakes. On December 10, 1967, the smaller of these, Lake Monona, was the scene of a plane crash in which Otis Redding and four members of his backing group lost their lives. He was just 26 years old.

On the bank of this lake stands Monona Terrace, a convention centre, which contains a memorial to the singer. After parking the car, we set off in search of the spot, but find no signposts. I see a catering worker taking a break, so ask for directions. He points us towards the location.

We find the roof garden, which is beautifully designed and tended, and has an amazing view over the lake. The memorial is a plaque set into the terrace. It's a simple memorial, put there by his appreciation society, and we spend a couple of minutes sitting admiring it and remembering the man's music. In terms of location, this place certainly has the edge over an Iowa cornfield, no disrespect intended. The view of the lake is stunning, and restful, and appropriate.

We move on to Milwaukee and check into the hotel. It seems that, after three weeks, I have succeeded in exhausting my daughter, so we settle for a quiet evening in. While Nina rests, I set off in search of food, and conclude that the hotel is not in a very salubrious neighbourhood. There are no decent take-aways in sight, so I return to the hotel and phone some in. ESPN is showing the Cubs, so I don't need much persuasion to stay in. Sadly, they lose, missing the chance to go to the top of their division. One game at a time!

Tuesday in Milwaukee concentrates on two things: getting Nina ready to go home, and a ball game. As reported yesterday, the pace (and this humidity!) is beginning to take its toll with Nina, so it's noon before we get moving. Knowing we may not get a proper meal later, we have a good lunch in a Greek restaurant, and then buy an extra suitcase, to carry all the extra stuff Nina has acquired on her trip.

Tonight's game is the Milwaukee Brewers against the New York Mets. They both lead their respective divisions, so it threatens to be good. Usually neutral, tonight I'm rooting for the Mets, as the Brewers are the team the Cubs are trying to catch in the National League Central.

Watching the TV before leaving, the pundits are pointing out that this could be one of baseball's biggest nights for years. Bonds needs one home run to equal Aaron's record, Alex Rodriguez of the Yankees needs one home run to reach 500 for his career, and Tom Glavine needs one win to reach 300 for his career. It could all happen tonight and, as Glavine is the starting pitcher for the Mets, we could be there to witness a little piece of sporting history.

The front desk of the hotel has little maps with walking directions to the ground and, for once, pedestrians are catered for. Crossing the car park of the hospital opposite, a footpath through a small park takes us to Miller Park, home of the Milwaukee Brewers—one of the more obvious sponsorship opportunities. It's a nice modern ground, but the evening is very humid, so the park is sweltering, especially as it contains a sellout crowd of 41,790.

Milwaukee is known for two things, beer and sausage, so we sample both in the name of research, and I have to say they are not the best of either — quite palatable, but not enough to justify their reputation.

The game is a good one, and the atmosphere is improved by a very vocal Mets fan just behind us, who provokes reaction from the home fans. The Brewers take a one-run lead in the fourth, and the Mets come back with two in the sixth. At this point we get the highlight of the evening, the famous Milwaukee sausage race. Five guys in sausage costumes race against each other while the crowd bets on the result. Bratwurst wins.

Glavine leaves the game in the seventh, to a standing ovation from both sets of fans, and so is on course for his 300th win. For a pitcher to be credited with a win, his team has to have taken the lead while he is pitching, still be ahead when he leaves the game, and not lose that lead for the rest of the game. Sadly the Brewers tie the game in the eighth, so our chance of witnessing a special moment disappears into the Milwaukee night.

The game is still tied after nine, so we go to extra innings. We know by now that the Cubs have won, so defeat for the Brewers would take the Cubs to the top of the division. Both sides come close to breaking the deadlock, but not close enough. At the end of the 12th things are so tense that we get a bonus sausage race. Hot dog wins this one.

By the time the game reaches the 13th inning, we just want someone to win, so that we can go to bed. Geoff Jenkins, a pinch-hitter for the Brewers, obliges with a two-run homer, and Milwaukee wins, 4–2. It is now 11:30, a four-hour, 25-minute game.

Collapsing on my bed, I flick on the TV to see how the other two potential history makers have fared. Bonds has again failed, which leaves Alex Rodriguez as the story of the night. The Yankees have beaten the Chicago White Sox 16–3, scoring a team record eight home runs, shared amongst seven players. Rodriguez has contributed precisely nothing! History will have to wait.

Indiana

Wednesday August 1–Thursday August 2

I suppose if you're reading the story of someone who is fulfilling a long held ambition, and has been allowed seven months off work, it might grate a bit if they start whining. But Wednesday's a bitch! While I am waiting for Nina to get ready to leave, I receive a phone call from my car rental people in Virginia Beach. They are trying to fax me my third voucher, but, since I was a day late reminding them, their computer can't cope. They want me to phone the company in England which issued the contract, because England won't talk to them. So I phone Manchester — on a pay as you go cell phone — and they tell me Virginia Beach is talking rubbish. It's like being a teacher again. When you saw two kids separately and got two different versions of the same incident, each blaming the other. So I give each the other's phone number — they can sort it out.

We leave Milwaukee and set off for Chicago's O'Hare Airport. The plan is to stop somewhere for something to eat, as we have plenty of time. But we see nowhere, except for one place when I miss the slip road. We decide to head to the airport, where we miss the turn for the car park, and have to go round again. Eventually we park and head for the terminal, where the check-in is mercifully quick. Turning the corner and expecting to see some restaurants, all there is is the queue for security. So it's straight into the tearful farewell — and she's nearly as bad! What is supposed to be a gentle goodbye over a nice meal is over in seconds and she is gone.

Onwards into Indiana, and to Fort Wayne. It's getting into the evening as I find 1401 Washington, and am puzzled to find it's not a hotel. So I phone my hotel and find that there are two Washingtons in Fort Wayne, and I need the other one. Eventually I arrive, check in, find that my key won't open my room, sort that out, and decide to treat myself to a nice meal. Driving around Fort Wayne, I fail dismally to find a decent restaurant, and end up in a fast food Italian (which is actually quite palatable).

Back in my room, the day ends on a comparative high. The Brewers are being shown live (in case you're wondering, the chorizo won tonight), and they are beaten by the Mets. The Cubs win a close one, and move to the top of their division.

What a difference a day makes! Before I have got round to showering on Thursday, I have learnt that Nina has landed safely at Manchester Airport, I have sorted out the problem with the car rental company, and...

At this point, I must refer you back to when I was travelling through California with Sal, and we heard we were to become adoptive grandparents in about four weeks. We were asked to keep it a secret until everything was official, as things can always go wrong. Well, it's taken 45 days, a bit longer than four weeks.

But today they have gone right, and I am very happy and very proud to welcome to our family Miss Joanna Gulliver, aged around 14 weeks. Mother and baby are fine; father required seven stitches to his wallet.

Immediately I discover a strange thing about travelling alone. You can cope with the bad times. You just sit in your room, eat crap food, blow your nose a lot and go to sleep. But when you get good news, you have no one to share it with. So I jump up and down a bit, and tell the woman at the car rental company, who is very pleased for me!

I follow this with a nice breakfast, and proceed to the park for today's game, Fort Wayne Wizards vs. Beloit Snappers. The stadium is fairly nondescript, but is set in a park which has a camping area, a welcome green spot in the middle of an urban sprawl. The day is hot, in the 90s, but is also humid, so within minutes of finding my seat I am wringing wet. Still bursting with the news, I decide to phone cousin Pam in Virginia Beach, because I know she will be happy and make all the right noises. She is, and she does! That's what family's for!

The game is entertaining, and is the story of missed opportunity, a common story in sport. The visitors put 17 men on base, but manage only one run, while the home team has ten runners, but brings two of them home to win, 2–1.

Today's drive to Indianapolis is only 137 miles, two hours down the interstate. But a traffic accident and roadworks conspire to turn it into three. I find the hotel easily, and am delighted to see a Red Lobster almost opposite — a good place to celebrate. A quick check of e-mails finds my first photographs of Joanna — a cute little thing with a round face and big blue eyes — so my joy is reinforced as I leave for dinner.

I feel ridiculously smug entering the restaurant, but my waitress refuses to engage me in conversation, so I celebrate quietly with some good seafood and a bottle of wine. As I near the end of my wine, I have a crazy desire to leap to my feet and announce my happiness to everyone in the restaurant. But my English reserve gets the better of me, and I just smile to myself.

Kentucky

Friday August 3–Monday August 6

Friday morning sees me off to a comparatively early start, for the short trip to Jasper, Indiana. For a nice change, my computer tells me to ignore interstates and take to the little roads, which actually go through places.

The problem with this sort of journey is that you don't pass the same range of amenities, so I get to Jasper in need of a late breakfast/early lunch. Jasper boasts one of the better welcome signs, which reads, "Jasper — if you lived here you'd be home now!" You can't fault the logic. I also have a couple of bits of shopping to do; I need a new scorebook for the games, and I have to post a greeting to my new granddaughter. I flagrantly use this as an excuse to tell the post office clerk my news.

Jasper obviously has strong German roots. Many of the businesses have Germanic names, and there are more German flags in the town than American ones. I make a mental note to strike football and military history from my list of potential conversation topics. The restaurant I select for my repast is called Schnitzelbank, and features German specialities.

After a fine lunch, I move on to my excuse for coming to Jasper, the Indiana Baseball Hall of Fame. This turns out to be on a college campus, and occupies a small corner of an education building. As usual, it covers college baseball as well as the professional game. It is no different to the ones I have seen before, but each one has unique stories of individuals who have dedicated their lives to the sport.

I drive on to Louisville, where I have decided to spend the night. This turns out to be a unique place — the only American city that does not have dozens of cheap motels visible from the interstate. As I have no booking, and no magazine coupon, I drive around for ages, and eventually end up somewhere above my usual budget, but which serves the purpose nevertheless.

The daily e-mail check brings mainly notes of congratulation on my newly acquired grandparental status. But one is very different. A couple of baseball fans from Ullapool in Scotland write. They have heard of my exploits on Channel 5, have checked my schedule on the website, and are planning to be at the same game as me in Washington in September. Could we meet up? That sounds like a distinct possibility.

A short drive into the city takes me to Saturday's first destination, the Louisville Slugger Museum. For those not acquainted with the name, the Louisville Slugger is not a nickname for a pre-war boxer, it is a bat, the world's most famous baseball bat, the one favoured by the majority of major league players. The museum is located in downtown Louisville, and you can't really miss it. Standing outside the entrance is the world's biggest baseball bat, taller than the building itself.

The visit begins with a video showing various notable players hitting, and talking about hitting. This features one of the most remarkable slow motion shots I've seen, with a close-up of a runner straining every sinew to reach base, and the ball slowly coming into the picture behind his shoulder, and overtaking him frame by frame.

We are then given a tour of the manufacturing process, which is fascinating. The computerised lathe which shapes a bat from a piece of wood in under a minute is particularly impressive. The museum is well constructed and informative, but my favourite part has to be the special exhibition. This features a display of Charlie Brown cartoons. If you are a fan you will know that baseball is one of Charles Schulz's most recurring themes, and the display bridges a seemingly unbridgeable gap between these cartoon kids and professional baseball.

Back on the interstate, I only have to contend with a short hop to Cincinnati, the domain of the Scheurer family. Steve Scheurer and I have been good friends since meeting in 1968, and I have known his wife Liz almost as long. I did once, in 1972, meet the rest of his family here in Cincinnati, but that encounter is clouded by time, so most of these people are new to me. Steve and Liz now live in Pittsburgh, although they are in attendance this weekend, so I'm staying with sister Judy and her husband Bruce.

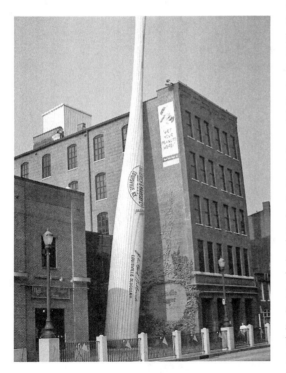

Louisville Slugger Museum, Kentucky—a fascinating tribute to the most famous of baseball bats. I wouldn't want to meet the guy who could swing this one.

I arrive at the house to a warm welcome, pink balloons, and pictures of my new granddaughter pasted all over the house. I mean *all* over the house; on the fridge, on the head of my bed, on the toilet! Her picture even adorns the wine bottles on the dinner table! It seems her arrival has created as much joy here as it has at home. I have been warned over the last 30 years of the madness of this family, and now I am experiencing it at first hand. I can attest that it is a joy to behold.

I can't tell you what a refreshing change this is to motels and restaurants. Fairly predictably, while I have better things to do than watch TV, Alex Rodriguez hits his 500th home run, and Barry Bonds his 755th, thus tying Aaron's record. The commissioner is in attendance, and issues a fairly brief congratulatory statement. Now we just have to wait for number 756.

On Sunday I awaken to the gentle sound of raindrops on my bedroom skylight, politely listening for my hosts to be up and around. Hearing no sound, I lie in bed writing, until nature eventually insists that I get up. At this point, I smell coffee, and go downstairs to say good morning before showering. I find Judy sitting on the porch. The rain has not been enough to relieve the intense humidity, but I decide to join her for a cup of coffee before showering. We start to chat, and one cup turns to two or more before Steve arrives for breakfast.

At this point I decide I should shower and dress but, finding the shower occupied, return downstairs for more coffee, realising in the dim depths of my mind that this, a lazy Sunday morning, is exactly what I need. At this point, I am introduced to the appallingly attractive family tradition of Bailey's in Sunday morning coffee. By the time I shower and we eat breakfast it's technically early afternoon.

Around three Judy drives me into the city to see her workplace, the WCPO Channel 9 TV studio. I am given a tour by Judy's boss, Bob, whom I met last night. I see all the exciting computerised gizmos, and am introduced to the head of sport, who intends to interview me at the Reds game on Tuesday. We agree that I should contact Channel 5 and let them know this is happening, in case they want to pick it up.

There are time constraints, however, as I have to be back at base by 7:00 for my second interview with Channel 5. I locate myself in a wonderfully cool lounge, and the whole process goes very smoothly. The first thing they ask me is about young Joanna, so she gets her first mention on TV. Then there are some fairly straightforward questions about the difference between minor league and major league games, and we chat about fatigue, and the oppressive weather. First reports from home are that it has gone OK.

Monday morning again begins gently. I pack my bags, do a few jobs on e-mail, and eventually phone Steve's other sister, Gail, to say that I am heading in her direction. The drive to Gail and Tim's takes only ten minutes. I am exchanging a beautiful, rambling old house on the edge of town for a luxury condominium on a hillside overlooking the river, the ballpark and downtown. I think this is what's called a no-lose situation.

After settling in, Gail and I go visiting the household of the youngest Scheurer brother, Andy. Gail's nephew, James, is a baseball fanatic, and is impressed by stories of my trip. He shares his card collection with me. His knowledge is impressive in one so young. He has a duplicate of Kerry Wood, the Cubs pitcher, which he allows me to keep. I am honoured!

Back at the condo, the afternoon drifts away with cold drinks and nibbles, until it is time for the evening's festivities to begin. I have tickets for a minor league game in Florence, Kentucky, which is really a suburb of Cincinnati.

Because of our destination, my hosts have selected a restaurant in Newport, Kentucky, for an early dinner. Newport was, apparently, a major location for the mob before it relocated to Las Vegas, and Walt's Rib House was one of their favourite haunts. As we are early, the place is almost empty, but the walls are lined with portraits of gentlemen whose hair is much younger than the rest of them, and matriarchs in evening dress. The ribs are excellent, as is the rest of the meal. But even if it hadn't been, I don't think I would have complained!

It is a short drive from there to the ballpark, where Liz joins us for the evening's main event, Florence Freedom vs. Chillicothe Paints. These teams belong to the independent Frontier League, which means they are not affiliated to any major league team.

The humidity is oppressive, with hot dogs giving way to ice cream. Predictably, the game turns into a long one, even including a floodlight failure. There are runs galore, what the sporting press might dub a slugfest, and after six innings the Paints lead 7–6. At this point the visitors put the game to bed, with a seven-run seventh. The game eventually finishes 15–6, and we retire to the air conditioning of the car and the condo.

Ohio

Tuesday August 7–Friday August 10

On Tuesday morning Gail arrives back from a couple of hours of work with nephew James in tow. The Reds have given me a free pass for their Hall of Fame, so we're going to do that around noon instead of before the game.

The Hall of Fame is at present enhanced by a Pete Rose exhibit. As I have mentioned before, Rose was a Reds player between the 60s and 80s, and broke Ty Cobb's all-time hits record. Although he has pride of place in the Reds' Hall of Fame, he is barred from what would have been automatic entry to the National Baseball Hall of Fame by his involvement with gambling towards the end of his career, which earned him a lifetime ban from the game.

While we are meandering around the exhibits, Gail receives a call from John Popovich, whom I met on Sunday, and who is the Head of Sport at WCPO. He would like to bring forward my interview from this evening to now! So, as we leave the museum, John arrives with a cameraman in tow, and we do the interview in a small open area in front of the stadium. They then take some shots of me looking intently at exhibits I have already seen an hour ago, and it's in the can, as I believe these people say.

And so to the game; the Reds, with a little encouragement from Judy, have laid on a complete package for me. We have the WCPO seats, and are met there by Bob, who showed me around on Sunday. My package includes a parking pass, and we progress from the underground car park through what appears to be an exclusive entrance. As we emerge into daylight, we find that the seats are just behind home plate. I'm used to this at minor league games, but at major league games I have never been anywhere near this close. As we are marvelling at the padded seats, we are approached by Bernie, our waiter ... yes, that's waiter ... who says we can order stuff all through the game and it will be delivered to our seats!

Laurie, from the Community Relations Department, comes to make sure I'm OK, and at that point the scoreboard displays a message welcoming me to the game. I am also promised a visit from Mr. Red, the mascot. This occurs in the sixth, and I wave merrily to him before he produces a spray gun and drenches me — which is actually a blessed relief!

Oh yes, and there was a game! The Reds, who are not good this year, score three in the first and add a homer in the third. The Reds pitcher, long blond-haired, guitar-playing local boy Bronson Arroyo, throws a blinder, and the Reds win, 4–0. The scoreboard informs us that the temperature of 97 degrees is a record for game time at this stadium.

Gail has taped the six o'clock news, and we are treated to a clip of what will hopefully be a longer story on Friday — me expounding on the difference between fan behaviour at baseball games and cricket games. That wasn't exactly my best bit but, hey, there's no such thing as bad publicity.

On Wednesday I awake to the news that I should, perhaps, have stayed up a little longer last night. Barry Bonds, at long last, struck his 756th home run to take sole possession of the career record. The spectator who caught the ball is reported as suffering several grazes, as he disappeared under a pile of 30 bodies, but managed to hold on to a piece of baseball memorabilia estimated to be worth between a quarter and a half a million dollars.

After fond farewells, I head north on I-71 towards Cleveland, and then take a detour east on I-76, to the town of Kent, Ohio, the home of Kent State University. Readers of my age may not require an explanation, but for the rest of you there is a story to be told. In 1970, with the Vietnam war dragging on, President Nixon ordered the invasion of Cambodia. This sparked protest up and down the land, one of the most notable being on this campus. Student protesters burnt down a building used for military training, and the state governor ordered the mobilisation of the National Guard. This produced one of the most memorable images of the era, with the newspapers full of pictures of students walking up to guardsmen, and placing flowers in the barrels of their guns.

The following day, the students again protested in front of the guardsmen. The guardsmen drove them back and, in the face of student taunts, opened fire.

Four students were killed — Allison Krause, Jeffrey Miller, Sandra Scheuer and William Schroeder — and nine were wounded.

Signposts on the campus direct me to a small memorial, and a marker describing the events of the day. There are four spaces in the car park which are fenced off. These are the spots where the four students fell, each with a small triangular plaque in the corner. The Report of the President's Commission on Campus Unrest stated that the shootings were "unnecessary, unwarranted and inexcusable."

On to Cleveland, and three nights in the same hotel; after settling in, I walk down to the ballpark, in search of a bar named Cooperstown, which is owned by Alice Cooper. For those of you ignorant of the lore of baseball, the name not only acknowledges the owner's name, it pays homage to one of the most sacred sites in baseball. Cooperstown is the home of the Baseball Hall of Fame, so when a player is said to be "headed for Cooperstown," it means he will join the ranks of the game's immortals.

It takes a little longer to find than I had hoped, because it has changed its name to Local Heroes. Whether that means it has changed ownership I cannot say, but it still provides good beer and food regardless.

For many years, Cleveland was largely associated with Municipal Stadium, known as "the mistake by the lake." A little harsh, perhaps, but they have started to do something about it. This reputation is one of the two reasons that are cited as the reason why the Rock 'n' Roll Hall of Fame was located here, the other being that this is where disc jockey Alan Freed was working when he first used the phrase "rock 'n' roll."

Either way, this is my destination for Thursday. I came to the Hall of Fame three years ago with Sally and Nina but, due to us not realising that there is an hour's time difference between Chicago and Cleveland, we left ourselves a little short of time. But this time I have allowed a whole day.

I arrive at the Hall around 11. It is a beautiful glass pyramid, fronted by several larger than life guitars designed by a variety of artists. From the lobby, you descend into the main exhibition hall. This is obviously the largest part (it's a pyramid, remember?). There is no obvious route through this hall, and you can pass several hours meandering amongst its exhibits.

By 4:00, my feet are hurting and my brain is full. Fortunately the hotel has an in house Chinese restaurant, so I'm not going far tonight.

While walking home, I noticed a baseball museum mentioned somewhere, so, as I have some free time on Friday, I go off in search of it in Cleveland city centre. It's quite easy to find, and is obviously a work in progress. There are extensive plans inside, but at present it's just a shop in an arcade. The exhibits look at the history of the game in Cleveland, with particular emphasis on black and Hispanic players. It's interesting, but fairly minimal.

I spend the next couple of hours buying and writing cards, and having lunch, before going back to the hotel and getting ready for tonight's game.

Jacobs Field was one of the first of the new wave of ballparks, and has a good reputation. It certainly proves to be very attractive, with wide corridors and lots of spaces for people to meet and talk. I particularly enjoy Heritage Park, a display of plaques honouring the club's all-time great players.

I wrote earlier in my trip of Jackie Robinson, the first black man to play in the major leagues. He played for the Brooklyn Dodgers, a National League club. The first American League club to sign a black man was the Cleveland Indians, in 1947, and that man was Larry Doby. Tonight's game is honouring Doby, and every Cleveland player wears number 14, Doby's number. I hope the umpires aren't too confused. Three of his children are there to throw out the first pitch, and the ceremony is treated with great respect by both sets of fans.

Tonight's visitors are the New York Yankees, whom I am looking forward to seeing. So are a lot of other people, if the attendance of 41,765 is anything to go by. There is a culture in baseball that if you're not a Yankees fan, you hate them, a bit like Manchester United in football. I don't subscribe to either and, although I'm a Cubs fan, the Yankees have my favourite player in Derek Jeter. The Yankees are not having a good season, and are five games behind Boston in their division. They are, however, only a half-game back in the wild card race. Cleveland leads the Central Division, so a good game is promised.

I wrote a few days back of Alex Rodriguez hitting his 500th home run. Tonight he hits his 501st, swatting the second pitch he receives to deep centre with a swing so effortless you have to check to make sure he isn't just taking a practice swing. Jeter has three hits, and plays faultless shortstop with seemingly all the effort of a Sunday stroll. The Yankees take a 6–0 lead and, although the Indians pull one back, the Yankees introduce Mariano Rivera, their famous closer, in the ninth. Rivera is nicknamed "the Sandman" because he's brought in to put the game to sleep! Sure enough, two groundouts and a fly ball and it's all over.

Michigan

Saturday August 11–Sunday August 12

My first destination on Saturday is a building in a residential area of Detroit which was bought by Berry Gordy in 1959, with a loan of $800 from his family, to start a record business. A couple of decades later he sold the business for several million dollars, and it now bears the legend, "Hitsville U.S.A." In between he produced a string of hits by artistes who quickly became household names, and are now enshrined in pop history: the Supremes, the Four Tops, the Temptations, Smokey Robinson and the Miracles, the Jackson Five and more.

Compared to similar venues I have visited on this trip, this one is quite homely, or amateurish, depending on where you're coming from. They are a staff member short, so there is quite a wait; the guide for the first part of the tour is a Diana Ross impersonator, who insists on joining in with all the songs in the video; one of the others is on his first day, and hasn't learnt his script. But the history of the place is still impressive, especially the business-like attitude; the company provided music teachers, choreographers, and even instructors to ensure that the artistes knew how to behave in public, so that they always reflected positively on the organisation.

Arriving at my hotel, I find that the room is not yet ready, so I take a walk around the surrounding area, a strange mix of elegance and deprivation. The stadium, Comerica Park, is extremely impressive, and I am looking forward to tomorrow's visit. The Detroit team is known as the Tigers; anyone not knowing that would only have to take a glance at the décor and engravings on the outside of the stadium to remove any doubt.

Eventually I can get into my room. The hotel is in the heart of the city, and so is a tall and thin building. My room is on the top floor, and from my little window I can see over the roofs to the ballpark and, in the other direction, a bar which advertises home-brewed beer. When the sun starts to drop a little I investigate. Previous experience might lead you to expect me to write about decent beer and reasonably priced, wholesome food. Well, you'd be right!

Sunday's game does not start until 1:05. The ballpark is a beautiful stadium, built in an area that also includes the football stadium and the opera house. The stadium is much more open than the previous two I have visited, which provides a very attractive vista. The tiger motif which I mentioned yesterday is even more visible inside the park — there are tigers everywhere, statues, pictures, probably more than in India.

The Cincinnati connection has been at work again, and provided me with an excellent seat just behind first base. Although the temperature peaks at 86 degrees, the early afternoon sun makes it feel hotter, and people take regular breaks to go and stand by the concessions in the shade. The stadium is so well designed that there is even a good view from there. The visitors are the Oakland Athletics, and their third baseman, Marco Scutaro, opens the scoring with a two-run homer in the second. This just serves to wake the sleeping Tigers, and their right fielder Magglio Ordonez opens the bottom of the second with a solo home run. This is the prologue to a remarkable sequence of events, and a series of walks and singles puts the Tigers 5–2 ahead. This brings Ordonez to the plate again, with two on and two outs. He homers again, a three-run shot this time, to put the home team 8–2 ahead, and become only the second man in team history, and the first for 40 years, to hit two home runs in the same inning.

This basically decides the game, although both sides chip away and the final score is 11–5. At the end of the game it is announced that the Tigers shortstop, Placido Polanco, has just played his 143rd consecutive game of error-free baseball, tying a major league record.

The early finish to the game gives me the opportunity to see a little of Detroit, so I head off to the waterfront. It's a very pleasant area, with an impressive monument marking the "underground" which helped slaves escape from the U.S. into Canada. There is also a Caribbean festival, with people milling around enjoying the heat of the evening and the reggae band.

But there are no restaurants open (it's Sunday again!), so, after a lengthy walk, I end up back at the brewhouse opposite the hotel. I'm not really complaining.

Canada

Monday August 13 – Tuesday August 14

Before the complaints start pouring in, I know Canada is not one of the 50 states — but it does have one surviving major league baseball club, so it has to be done.

So I'm leaving the country for a couple of days. My destination is not too far over the border, and the drive is easy. Before too long I am at the border, and the guard gives me a gentle cross examination before sending me on my way with a smile. I wonder if it will be so easy going back to the U.S. in a couple of days' time.

My first port of call is the small town of St. Mary's, which houses the Canadian Baseball Hall of Fame. It takes me a while to find the correct exit from the main road, but after that, it's relatively straightforward. St. Mary's turns out to be a holiday resort, with swimming and walking areas. I see a sign to the Hall, and end up driving around the woods for 15 minutes, seeing my destination in the distance but not being able to get the car round to it. I eventually go back to the road and return to my original instructions, thus finding it easily. It certainly wins the prettiest location award among all the museums I have visited, being set on the edge of the forest, next to a couple of well-kept baseball diamonds used, presumably, by local teams.

I have to ring for entry, and am met by the curator, whose knowledge of the game is obviously deep, and who delights in sharing such with you as you process through the four rooms of memorabilia.

After a brief look around the town centre, which includes lunch, I head towards Toronto, phoning my hosts to say I am en route. Another explanation is perhaps due as to how I know these people. Back in the 70s, when my wife Sally was newly qualified as a nursery nurse, she came to Toronto to work as nanny to the Kennedy family, looking after their two small girls, Liane and Jalyn. The latter, now Mrs. Anderson, is my host for this visit.

Eventually I find the tall, slim townhouse in the heart of the city, and am warmly greeted. Sally has never lost touch, and I have known Jalyn since she was a teenager. On my last visit I met her husband, Bill, and on this occasion I am introduced to their son Jack, now 18 months old, and eager to demonstrate his ball skills; fortunately I picked up a foam baseball at the Hall of Fame, and he knows what to do with it; a pitcher in the making, I'm sure.

Here are some interesting facts about Toronto! Toronto has yellow parking tickets! Toronto has door locks where you can put the key in, but not get it out again! Guess how I spent Tuesday morning!

Having been left home alone by my hosts, I check my car, to find it has a parking ticket, despite the fact that I have been told to leave it there. Returning to the house, I open the door, but then cannot extract the key from the lock. So my plans to spend a couple of hours wandering around the city are somewhat compromised. Jalyn arrives home at one, hits the door such that the key immediately comes out, and tells me to leave the parking ticket for them to sort. She says I will get another one tomorrow, but it's cheaper and easier for them to pay the ticket than find me a legitimate space!

We set off for lunch on the rooftop terrace of a lovely Mediterranean restaurant, and spend the rest of the afternoon around Toronto, visiting, shopping, drinking coffee. Then we have to co-ordinate operations as regards getting tickets for the game, getting Jack from day care, getting a ticket to Bill and getting me to the stadium. Jalyn drops me at the ground and I call her to let her know that I have my ticket, and I have left one under Bill's name at the ticket office.

The tickets, which have been laid on by the club in response to my request, are superb. The seats are level with third base, about 30 rows back. The Rogers Centre, formerly known as the SkyDome, is an interesting building. Although now a little dated, it is very spacious and comfortable. It is a beautiful evening, and the roof is open, giving a perfect view of the huge needle-like tower which looms over the park.

Tonight's game is the Toronto Blue Jays against the Los Angeles Angels, and both teams have star pitchers on the mound. So it is a little surprising when the Angels score in the first, and the Blue Jays immediately reply with four runs. That turns out to be the end of the scoring. Both pitchers perform well, but Roy Halladay, the Blue Jays' pitcher, goes all nine innings, a complete game, and receives a rapturous ovation from the crowd.

Meanwhile the seat next to me is still empty; Bill never made it, the demands of a new job being so great. I grab a taxi, and find Jack is still awake, so Jalyn and I enjoy an hour of his company before he eventually passes out. We share a bottle of "Chateau Joanna," courtesy of the Cincinnati connection, and I make my farewells, knowing that my hosts will have left the house before

I rise tomorrow. One of the joys of this trip is looking up old friends, one of the great sorrows is always leaving again so quickly.

New York
Wednesday August 15–Tuesday August 21

Before saying our farewells last night, Jalyn asked if I wanted food for today's journey. I said that would not be necessary, and so came down this morning to find a bag containing muffins with cheese, coffee cake, fresh fruit, soft drinks and several cans of beer. If I had answered in the affirmative I would have needed a trailer for the car. So I pluck the latest parking ticket from my car, leave it for the locals to sort, and set off for the United States.

After wrestling with the morning traffic, I make good progress to the border. Here my love affair with the U.S. Immigration Department continues. The man in the booth says I need a travel document, gives me a ticket, pulls me over and sends me into an office. After a short wait my name is called, and the conversation goes something like this.

"Why are you in the United States?"

"I'm touring the country watching baseball games, and writing about them."

"How long were you in Canada?"

"Two nights."

"Why were you in Canada?"

"To see a baseball game."

"Who did you see play?"

"The Blue Jays."

"Where are you staying tonight?"

"With friends in Lake George."

"What's the address?"

"I don't know. I have directions but not an address."

"I must have an address."

"I don't have it. I have the address where I'm staying after that, in New York."

"OK, give me that address."

"It's in my address book, which is in my car."

He then gives me permission to leave the building and return to my car, phoning ahead to the guards in the car park, presumably so that I'm not gunned down while attempting escape. Deciding on a belt and braces approach, I grab my address book, my directions to Lake George, and a photocopy of my visa application extension. He writes down an address, and asks why I don't have a white card which was issued on my arrival. I explain that I had to send in the card with my application for a visa extension. He looks at the photocopy.

"Why do you need this?"

"Because I want to stay to the end of October, until after the World Series."

"But you've just left the country."

"What do you mean?"

"You've arrived back in the U.S. today, so your visa is valid for six months from today. You don't need this."

"But I was told I had to apply, even though I was going to Canada."

Shrug!

"But they charged me $200."

Bigger shrug! "$6 please! Have a nice day!"

I continue with my journey, not knowing whether to be pleased that I have my visa extension, or annoyed that I'm down $200.

I eventually reach my destination on the banks of Lake George, the holiday home of my neighbours Greg and Penny, of whom I have written previously. This is an annual ritual, the coming together of the Stragnell clan, and various parents, siblings and offspring are in attendance. One of the brothers, Sandy, lives here permanently with his wife Pam, and I am billeted in their house. My room has a stunning view of the lake, and humming birds feeding outside the window.

The rest of Wednesday and the whole of Thursday have nothing to do with my project. This is a remote place with no broadband and no cell phone reception. So out of touch with the real world that I have to resort to such things as walking in the forest, taking boat rides, and swimming in the lake. Having well and truly recharged my batteries, my mission will continue on Friday.

From one extreme to the other! I have arranged to give Greg and Penny a lift to the city, so on Friday we all bid fond farewells to the Stragnell clan, fit ourselves miraculously into the PT cruiser, and head southeast. The journey is a comfortable one, and we don't hit debilitating traffic until we reach the city itself. It comes upon us very rapidly; I know there are suburbs, but they are certainly not visible from the interstate, which provides verdant surroundings almost until the city is upon us.

Then there it is—the familiar skyline, even though I have not been there for 35 years. We drive past the famous Yankee Stadium, which will provide tomorrow's entertainment, and soon find Park Avenue, which is my passengers' destination. Despite their claims as to the opulence of their accommodation, the first 20 blocks or so take us through East Harlem, hardly synonymous with opulence.

Eventually the train line bisecting the thoroughfare disappears underground, and the avenue opens out into its true glory. We throw a U-turn and there, waiting as arranged, is Marcus. Anally retentive superfans will remember

Marcus; for the benefit of the others, he is my cousin's son, last encountered on vacation in Florida, but normally resident in the city.

We deposit Greg and Pen, and head off towards Brooklyn. We pass the 59th Street Bridge and, just for the record, it doesn't make me feel groovy. Reaching the apartment, we play the parking game, which involves driving around the neighbourhood until you see someone threatening to leave, and then waiting in the middle of the road until they actually go.

After settling in, we head off to eat. One of my inspirations, the late Pete McCarthy, wrote in "McCarthy's Bar" that one of his rules for travelling was never to walk past a bar with his name on it. So I am delighted to dine in Pete's Ale House, and raise a glass of locally brewed stout in Mr. McCarthy's memory.

On to the subway, and we travel to Coney Island, where we plan to see the Brooklyn Cyclones play. Coney Island has all the appearance of a miniature seaside resort, and between the station and the ballpark there is a funfair and several fast food stands of a seaside nature. As we leave the station it starts to rain heavily, so we hurry to the ground, find some shelter, and await Marcus's friends, who arrive in various bedraggled states. We enter the ground, get refreshments, and stand around a trash can (it provides somewhere to put the drinks) awaiting developments. When the rain stops, the ground crew removes the tarpaulin. Seconds later, the rain starts again, and the tarpaulin is replaced.

The Cyclones staff tries desperately to entertain us, with dances, men in snorkels and wacky mascots. Eventually the rain stops, the tarpaulin is lifted, white lines are painted, and players begin to show an interest. Then it pours down again! This time the tarpaulin is not replaced, so the writing is on the wall. The game is officially postponed, at which point the rain stops for the rest of the evening.

We return to Brooklyn, and Montero's, Marcus's favourite local watering hole. There we are eventually joined by Marcus's wife, Jenny, and my brother-in-law Alan, who is joining me for this leg of the journey. He has just flown in from visiting his son in Banff, grabbed a cab to Marcus and Jenny's flat, and been led down here. Once again I suffer the disorientation of encountering someone from home in a strange setting — I don't think I'll ever get used to it!

New York claims to be the city that never sleeps, where you can get anything at any time. Brooklyn, where I am temporarily based, would seem to be the residential epicentre. Living space is at a premium, which leads to some oddities in daily practice. On Saturday, I get up and start to write. I am soon joined by Marcus, who offers me a coffee. When I accept, he gets dressed, goes out and buys me one, explaining that counter space is at a premium in the flat — sorry, apartment — and they can't justify the space a coffee maker would occupy.

After a lazy morning, we take the subway to somewhere near Union Square, and meet a couple of friends for an excellent pizza lunch, during which

I book accommodation for the Philadelphia leg of the trip. Marcus has an extensive network of friends, but insists Pete should be auditioned before I agree to let him host me. Pete has been renamed Football Pete, not because he has any great love of football, but because I am Baseball Pete! Anyway, he passes the audition with flying colours, and I am told I know his wife Alice from Marcus and Jenny's wedding.

We then stroll to the square where we meet up with the rest of our party, 16 in all, and head for Yankee Stadium. There is a palpable buzz as for many of us this is the first visit to the most famous stadium in baseball. Within the next year or so it will be replaced, and we can see the skeleton of the new stadium as we arrive. But for the time being it is still there, the "House that Ruth Built," the Bronx Zoo. All the greats in the game have played here — Babe Ruth, Joe DiMaggio, Mickey Mantle.

Marcus has achieved the notable feat of arranging tickets for 16 people in close proximity to each other, but there is an uncomfortable hiatus while the ticket office tries to convince him that his order was for two days ago. Eventually he returns victorious, to be almost blown away by 15 people simultaneously exhaling in relief.

Old Yankee Stadium — Cousin Marcus displays the 16 tickets for our party. The manic grin disguises the fact that the ticket clerk tried to claim that he had actually booked tickets for the game two days earlier!

The seats are good, with a view down the first base foul line. I sit next to Alan, and attempt to ease him through his first game. Every now and then we are momentarily distracted by the hat game, in which one of our party has decided we must all participate. When the first batter comes up to the plate, the first person takes the hat and places a dollar therein. If the batter achieves a hit, the dollar is kept and the hat passes on; if the batter does not get a hit, the hat is passed on with the dollar. With 16 of us and two hats, it's quite an amusing pastime.

The Yankees are playing the Detroit Tigers, who are in contention in the American League Central. The Yankees still trail Boston in their division, but are only a half-game back in the wild card race. The Yankees' pitcher is Roger Clemens, "the Rocket," possibly the best in the game over the last 15 years, and who now keeps coming out of retirement for one last season. The Yankees score in the second, but a run in each of the fourth and fifth give Detroit the lead. In the sixth, the Yankees' bats come alive to the tune of four runs. Clemens pitches six strong innings, and Rivera, whom I have mentioned before, puts the game to bed in the ninth; Yankees win, 5–2.

There are two highlights to a Yankees home game, even if you know nothing about baseball. When the ground crew tidies up the infield, they have a synchronised routine in time to the music. Then, when the Yankees win, the announcer plays "New York, New York" by Frank Sinatra, and most of the crowd joins in while exiting the stadium.

Sunday's special treat is the Staten Island Yankees vs. Brooklyn Cyclones, the Triple A teams of the Yankees and Mets respectively. So, after another imported coffee, complete with breakfast this time, we set off for the Staten Island ferry. By the time the motley crew, a mixture of familiar and unfamiliar faces, has assembled, we are nine. We board the ferry, which is provided free of charge, and take the 25-minute trip. The boat provides a spectacular view of downtown Manhattan, the Statue of Liberty and Ellis Island, as well as having one of the cheapest bars in New York.

The ballpark is next to the ferry terminal, and is another small, homely minor league park. The unique thing here is the view beyond the outfield, a classic New York skyline above the water.

The game is a local derby, played out before a 7,000 crowd. The Yankees post two runs in the fourth and two more in the fifth. The rain threatens, and occasionally moves us from our seats, but the game is completed without interruption. The Cyclones rally briefly in the ninth, but it is too little too late and the Yankees take the game, 4–1. As Staten Island is the Yankees' affiliate, that can mean only one thing—cue Frank Sinatra—"Start spreading the news..."

Returning on the ferry, we bid farewell to most of our party, and four of us pause at Pete's Waterfront Alehouse for a pre-dinner beer. My cell phone rings, and Erik from Channel 5 asks if I can do an interview in an hour's time. I slow down my beer intake so as to be relatively sober, and the interview is conducted in a doorway in a rainy Brooklyn street. I am asked to elucidate on the differences between watching the New York Yankees and the Staten Island Yankees, which I do; then I am asked to choose between them, which I decline to do, as they have both been memorable parts of my journey.

We return to the apartment, where Jenny has prepared a lovely dinner for us. Coffee is suggested, which of course means going out again. We make our choices at the local Starbucks, and stroll along the boardwalk for one of the most memorable moments of the trip. We are facing the Manhattan skyline by night; you have seen the poster on a thousand lounge walls, and there it is for real, large as life and twice as beautiful. Although it is a very familiar image, the reality of it is something that will remain with me.

Monday is the only day in the city on which I do not have a baseball game scheduled, so we decide to take advantage of the lull to see some other bits of New York that fit into my general framework. We start off in the local deli, buying coffee and pastries for breakfast. This is an amazing place, with all sorts of coffee, milk, cakes, breakfast sandwiches, as well as a full range of other foods.

Heading into the city, we leave the subway in the Central Park area, and head for the Museum of Modern Art. Sotheby's, Marcus's employer, has a corporate membership which gets us in free of charge, and we roam for a while looking at the various exhibits.

Lunch beckons, and we move on to Mickey Mantle's, a restaurant on the edge of the park. I think I've mentioned Mantle before, but, just in case, he was a Yankees great from the 50s and 60s. It is a good place, full of both sporting and entertainment memorabilia — but the odd thing is that all the pieces are labelled and priced, there to be sold rather than looked at.

We return to the apartment for some respite, and then set out again for the evening's festivities. Alan and I have decided to repay our respective hosts in some small part by buying dinner. The train takes us to the East Village, and McSorley's, the oldest alehouse in New York. They have an extensive drinks list — light or dark. If you don't like beer you're in the wrong place. The beers come in half-pint jugs, a good half of which is foam; there is sawdust on the floor, and the walls are lined with ancient photographs.

We cut across the edge of Chinatown to Little Italy, where stands our chosen restaurant. In the mid-seventies Dylan recorded "Joey," a song about mobster Joey Gallo, which describes his death after being shot in a Little Italy clam bar. Well, this is the clam bar! Admittedly, the original was a few doors away, but a good story nonetheless. We dine handsomely on clams, pasta and Chianti and, following Joey's example, stagger out into the streets of Little Italy. During the time it has taken us to eat, it has become dark, and the area has come alive. Each restaurant has tables on the sidewalk, and a greeter trying to persuade you that this restaurant is the best in a row of maybe 30 Italian restaurants.

A smaller version of our party leaves the train a few stops early, to make the last part of our journey home on foot, across the Brooklyn Bridge. This is another marvellous night time sight, and rounds off the evening perfectly. We put Alan and his host Mike in a taxi and, as we turn for home, Marcus points out a plaque on the wall of a bank. This was the site of the offices of the Brooklyn Dodgers, and it was on this spot that Jackie Robinson signed his contract, thus becoming the first black man to play major league baseball.

Tuesday turns out to be one of the worst day's weather since I arrived in the States. It rains, almost non-stop. After a morning of writing and laundry, we decide we can't prevaricate any longer, and set off through the rain. There is an exhibit in New York at present which fits within the parameters of my trip, so we jump on a bus and head for the Museum of the City of New York. The exhibit is called "Glory Days: New York Baseball 1947–1957." During this decade, the game was being revitalised by the end of wartime and the integration process, led by Jackie Robinson. The city's three teams dominated the game in a way that has never happened before or since, and in only one season was the city not represented in the World Series.

In 1957, the owners of the Dodgers and the Giants, tempted by richer audiences, moved their clubs to Los Angeles and San Francisco respectively, and the city was left with just the Yankees for the next five years. The exhibit shows the involvement of the city in the game during that decade, and lovingly outlines key games, players, and incidents which led to the title of the Glory Days.

From there we move to Times Square, where we grab an early dinner at ESPN Zone. ESPN is the American equivalent of Sky Sports, so there is no doubting where the establishment's theming lies. But the food is fine and filling and, as we leave the restaurant to find our train, the rain is stopping and the sky is brightening; not by much, but enough, we hope, to allow for a game of baseball.

Tonight's venue is Shea Stadium, which older readers will remember for a rather remarkable concert in 1965 when the Beatles broke America. But its day job is the home of the New York Mets, who were formed in 1962 when the league was expanded, thus giving New York back a National League team. The Mets are doing well this year, leading their division. Tonight's visitors, the San Diego Padres, are leading the wild card race. Both teams are fielding strong pitchers, so a good game is promised. The weather is damp and cold, which perhaps explains why neither pitcher is at his best. The Mets score two in the first, with a Carlos Beltran home run. The Padres pull one back in the third, with a Mike Cameron homer, but the Mets, with Beltran again to the fore, immediately post two more.

In the sixth the Padres pull it back to 4–3, and next inning take the lead 5–4. The Mets equalise in the eighth. The Padres score what appears to be the winner in the top of the ninth, but in the bottom of the ninth the Mets, in front of a buoyant crowd, score two to steal the game, 7–6, probably the most exciting game I have seen on my trip.

West Virginia

Wednesday August 22–Thursday August 23

My car is legally parked until 8:00 Wednesday morning, so an early start is in order. For Marcus and Jenny this is just another working day, so Alan and

I bid our fond farewells and hit the road. New York is always going to be congested, but the bridges take us away from New York and into New Jersey. From there we enter the green, wooded countryside of Pennsylvania, on into Maryland, and finally West Virginia.

The weather is cool, not getting out of the 60s, and a low misty cloud makes the scenery almost British. As we crest the top of the final hill that brings us to West Virginia, the sun emerges and the temperature climbs rapidly. By the time we reach our hotel it is 84 degrees and humid.

We decide to explore the town centre, and discover that Morgantown is a university town, and already quite busy. Alan fancies a look at the river and a couple of decent beers, and a local points us to the West Virginia Brewing Company, which turns out to have a balcony with a river view. The food and beer go down well, and we return to the hotel more than satisfied.

At this point in the trip the baseball season is three-quarters of the way through, and the trip itself has a third to run. The run for the play-offs is starting to look interesting. Although many of the same teams that I mentioned earlier are still in pole position, no one as yet has a completely convincing lead. In the American League, Boston and Anaheim remain on top of the East and West respectively, while Cleveland is now edging Detroit in the Central. Seattle is going strong, and has pushed Detroit from the wild card spot.

The National League still has the Mets topping the East, but elsewhere there has been some change. The Cubs lead the Central, neck and neck with Milwaukee, and the Arizona Diamondbacks have gone to the top of the West, leaving San Diego in the wild card spot. But there are still 40 games left.

As far as the trip is concerned, I have five major league parks left, and 12 states. The questions to be considered are how do I fit in Hawaii, when do I go to Cooperstown, and what I'll be doing during the playoffs.

Thursday is our easy day, so we make a gentle start. But our destination is Charleston, in time for the main event, West Virginia Power vs. Lexington Legends. These are the Single A affiliates of Milwaukee and Houston respectively. We arrive to find an elegant, town centre ballpark which, like some of its major league counterparts, has the walls of original town buildings incorporated into its design.

We find our seats, in the front row of section 107. This is between home plate and third base, and there is one seat between us and the gangway. This seat is occupied by Rod, who is dressed in a bright shirt, and has several chains around his neck. He is somewhat surprised to see us, especially when he discovers we are from England. "They don't usually put visitors here," he says. "Did they tell you this was the Toast Section?"

"No," I reply.

"Do you know what the Toast Section is?" he asks.

Since Rod already has beers in my cup holder as well as his own, I assume this involves a fair amount of raising of glasses, and ask if this is the case.

"It might be!" he replies, still affecting suspicion. "How did you get these tickets?"

"On the internet."

"Did you make any special requests?"

"Yes!" I lie, "I specifically asked not to be put next to anyone loud with chains around his neck."

"Did you?" he asks incredulously.

"No!" I grin, and from that point on we are best friends. I suddenly observe the real reason for it being called the Toast Section.

Rod has in front of him a toaster, plugged in to a convenient power point, and is busy making small piles of toast. This, we discover, is for when an opposition batter strikes out, at which point Rod leads the crowd in pointing at the batter as he returns to the dugout, and chanting "You are toast, you are toast!" This is followed by the distribution of slices of toast to the crowd.

Rod is, by his own admission, obsessive compulsive, and keeps detailed statistics on the opposition players. This is so that he can, in a very loud voice, remind them of their failings in great detail at the appropriate juncture. So pitchers are mercilessly reminded of the number of runs conceded, fielders of their errors, and batters of their failures, which are all correlated on pieces of paper in front of him.

He has a great rapport with the people in this section, who are prepared to act as his stooges when required. So, as the opposition introduces a new pitcher, Rod shouts, "Hey, Mike!"

"What, Rod?" enquires a voice from several rows back, right on cue.

"We call this pitcher the Foreman."

"Why is that, Rod?"

"Because he gave up four runs in the first inning at Augusta, four in the fifth in Columbus, and four in the second at Greenville!" exclaims Rod triumphantly.

When he requires action from the crowd, he either holds up a placard, or shouts, "I say..." followed by his prompt, and "You say..." followed by the crowd's expected response. One of the Lexington players is Kobi Clemens, son of the famous Roger Clemens who we saw pitch in Yankee Stadium. He is given no mercy, and his father's reputation only provides more ammunition for Rod's barracking. He informs the crowd, "Ladies and gentlemen, may I introduce to you Kobi Clemens? Those of you who were here yesterday will know that young Kobi had a career night. He hit two home runs! But what young Kobi must realise is that last night is now history! I say 'Last night,' you say 'History.'" The chant of "Last night — history" resounds through the section. Kobi strikes out!

Rod also has placards prepared for each home team batter, and a host of other props. Thus, when one of the opposition pitchers starts to display his frustration, Rod produces a puppet of Darth Vader, and a sign which reads, "Give in to your anger!"

I get to know Rod and talk about my trip in between innings, and in between several rounds of beers. We are even introduced to the beer seller. I come to realise that, apart from its primary purpose, dry toast is also useful as a counterbalance to an excess of beer! Towards the end of the game, he announces to the crowd in our section the nature of my trip, eliciting several rounds of applause. When an opposition player who shares my surname comes to bat, Rod leads the crowd in a chant of "Pete Taylor is better than your Taylor!"

The heat in Charleston today has been up to 96 degrees and humid, so by the end of the game we are sweaty, tipsy and amazed at the evening of which we have been part. Oh yes, and there was a game — lots of impressive hitting by both sides and the Power wins, 12–5. The crowd, especially section 107, goes home happy, and small children appear from nowhere to beg pieces of toast. Surreal!

Vermont
Friday August 24–Saturday August 25

Friday is purely a driving day — we haven't had many of those lately. Our destination is Vermont, over 800 miles from Charleston, and we plan to break the back of it. The drive is the exact reverse of the one two days ago, so there is nothing much to report. When the journey clock tells us we have done over 500 miles, we look for a hotel, which is why we find ourselves in Parsippany. It's not a made-up name! After checking in, we decide to find the local township, and set off along the road on which the hotel stands. Suddenly it becomes an interstate, so we decide to do a U-turn. Our first effort takes us onto another highway. We manage to turn around on that, and get back on the interstate. Unfortunately we are still going in the same direction. Eventually we get off again, turn around and eat in a Chinese restaurant two blocks from the hotel. The longest U-turn in history, around 20 miles!

The first part of Saturday continues the theme of retracing footsteps. From New Jersey we pick up I-87, which goes through New York state, and is the reverse of the route I took last Friday down to the city. We even take the same exit that I took for Lake George, and repeat the next miles of my journey, until we head into Vermont. We grab some lunch in Fair Haven, and leave the main roads behind as we head for Burlington. This certainly is one lovely state, and the drive is very enjoyable. Burlington, Colchester and Winooski are all really parts of the same town, which makes it quite a big place. Being a holiday area, a lot of the motels are full, but we eventually find one with vacancies about a mile and a half from the ground.

We decide to walk to the ground, which is a little further than we thought, but it's a pleasant walk across a river bridge and past several converted mills. The ground is tucked away behind some houses and surrounded by trees, certainly one of the more picturesque backdrops for a game. As we enter along a dirt track, we pass the visiting team, leaving their bus already in uniform and walking into the stadium.

The club has provided us with complementary tickets for the game, Vermont Lake Monsters vs. Brooklyn Cyclones. Anyone paying attention will spot that the opposition is the same as for last Sunday's game on Staten Island, where the backdrop was Manhattan. The change in scenery does not appear to affect the Cyclones. In the second inning they score seven, and chase the starting pitcher. This heralds a rather abject performance by the home side; they fail to turn simple double plays, they are twice caught stealing at third, and the pitchers walk any number of hitters. They get through so many pitchers that the first baseman has to pitch the ninth—faultlessly, with two strikeouts! The Cyclones take full advantage and win, 14–3.

Maine

Sunday August 26–Monday August 27

A nice gentle start to the morning sees us leave Colchester around 11:00 and, largely ignoring interstates, head due east across Vermont, New Hampshire and Maine. The landscape is an upscale combination of Scotland and the Lake District, made even more dramatic by the light drizzle, which brings clouds to sit on top of the mountains.

Lunch is taken in the small town of St. Johnsbury, at the local diner. The diner seems to be an integral part of American culture, in much the same way as the local pub in England. On a Sunday lunchtime, the place is heaving, and I think we are the only non-locals in there. The journey continues with a succession of lakes, mountains and rustic towns, and a surprising amount of traffic; but then it is an August weekend in a popular holiday area.

Eventually we arrive in Portland and find our hotel. We have a few hours to kill before I receive my now customary phone call from the guys at Channel 5. This time the interview seems a little longer, and the questions a little more thought provoking. What's my best baseball experience so far? Is it better to watch a game with or without company? Is there a big difference between the different minor league levels? I think I give a decent account of myself, and prepare for dinner.

Monday is Alan's last full day of travelling with me, so I suggest that he should choose how we spend it. He chooses wisely. The decision is that we should get a boat and see some of the islands that stand off Portland, so Al does his research. We can either spend a lot of money on the cruise with full commentary and sit-down meal, or we can take the mail ferry for $13. This is the boat that takes the residents to four or five inhabited islands, as well as the mail and a car or two.

So by 10:00 we have driven into Portland, parked up, bought tickets, gone to the bakery for carry-out coffee, croissants and scones, and are waiting on the quay for the ferry. The trip is relaxing and interesting, affording some memorable views and a few bits of wildlife. At one island we have a 40-minute wait, so we are able to take a brief walk. The next island has a general store where we treat ourselves to an ice cream. It really is a delightful way to spend a morning.

Back to the hotel for a nap, and then out to tonight's game, Portland Sea Dogs vs. Trenton Thunder. These teams are the Double A affiliates of the Boston Red Sox and the New York Yankees, and I wonder if their extreme rivalry will extend to this level.

I always book in advance, even for minor league games, and so far it has proved an unnecessary safeguard. But tonight I am surprised to find the car park almost full, and the "sold out" notices outside the ground. Enquiring of a steward as to why, it seems that the Boston Red Sox have sent one of their starting pitchers, Jon Lester, down to pitch here. Lester broke into the major leagues last season, but then contracted lymphoma. He has made a strong recovery from the cancer, and the Red Sox are trying to get him ready for major league play, with a view to the playoffs. His promised appearance has certainly put a few thousand on the attendance.

The Sea Dogs start with two in the second, the Thunder pull one back but Portland adds two more in the third. Then the pitchers take charge. Lester pitches into the seventh. Both teams score again in the eighth, and it finishes 5–2. The Yankees rivalry is there to be seen, not just as the Sea Dogs win, but as news of a drubbing for the major league Yankees trickles through on the scoreboard.

Portland tops the table on two of the lists for minor league grounds—a 7,000 attendance, and a microbrew stall with eight different beers!

Rhode Island

Tuesday August 28–Wednesday August 29

The main task for today is to get Alan to Boston's Logan Airport by mid-afternoon. It's only 100 miles from Portland, so there is no time pressure on us. We steer clear of the interstate for a while, and head south on Highway 1.

We decide to breakfast at Wells Beach but, although it is a lovely spot, it doesn't run to a restaurant, so we return to the highway and soon find an appropriate eatery. The drive through this particular part of the country makes it easy to see why it's called New England. As well as Wells, we pass Portsmouth, Worcester, Coggeshall, and many others. Climbing on to the interstate for the final leg of the drive, we even pass an exit for Byfield, my home village. Eventually we reach the airport, bid each other farewell, and I am once again the lonesome traveller.

It's only 50 miles south to Pawtucket, where I am to see a game tomorrow. The hotels in the town are a bit pricy, so I have picked one out in Smithfield, a few miles away. From the map, it looks to be a typical arterial road location, so on arrival I am delighted to find it back from the road, surrounded by woodland.

After dinner I return to the hotel, and settle down to an evening of baseball. A couple of divisions are in a really interesting situation. In the American League East, Boston leads the Yankees by a seemingly insurmountable eight games. But the Yankees are still looking for the wild card spot, and the two teams are starting a three-game series tonight. In the National League Central the top two, the Cubs and Milwaukee, also start a three-game series tonight. The Cubs lead Milwaukee by a game and a half, but St. Louis is only two games back, and waiting for the top two to slip up.

The Yankees, win 5–3, to close the gap to seven games, and are only a game and a half out of the wild card. The Cubs beat the Brewers to go two and a half games ahead of them, but the Cardinals win to remain just two behind. It's going down to the wire.

Wednesday morning I don't even leave the hotel. Given a nice room, a pool, a great internet connection, and a long list of things to do, it's an opportunity not to be wasted. So, shortly after 2:00, I jump in the car and head for Pawtucket. I have a vision of Rhode Island as a rich person's playground, with lots of waterfront and yachts and stuff; so I am a little put out when Pawtucket turns out to be one of the most run-down areas I have yet come across. My plan is to find the ground, drive around and find something to eat, and sit in a coffee shop by the water writing postcards.

Eventually I locate the ground, which is in a fairly isolated spot. So I drive along a main road looking for somewhere to eat, but sadly most places have closed down. Eventually I drive past a park with a notice board advertising a seafood restaurant. Café more like, but at least they sell food, and the shrimp is fresh. So it's just postcards left, and I soon discover how run down Pawtucket really is—they don't want you to send pictures of it to people!

By now it's 5:30, so I head for the ground and people are already going in. As I enter the ground, I notice that most of the memorabilia on display refers to a certain night in 1981, when the Pawtucket Red Sox played host to the Rochester Red Wings, with first pitch at 8:00. Rochester scored in the seventh, and the Pawsox, as they are known locally, equalised in the ninth, taking the game into extra innings. In the 21st inning, Rochester scored a second run, but in the bottom of the 21st, the home team made it 2–2. After 32 innings, by which time it was 4:00 A.M., the umpires suspended the game after eight hours of play, declaring that the game should be finished when the schedule permitted. This was 65 days later, when the second part of the game lasted precisely 19 minutes, with the Pawsox winning, 3–2, in the bottom of the 33rd inning. This remains the longest game in the history of professional baseball.

Tonight's visitors are the Buffalo Bisons, and they make a good start, scoring once in the first and twice in the second. The Pawsox score in the fourth and fifth, but the visitors score three in the sixth. By the bottom of the ninth Rochester leads, 6–3, and most of the crowd has drifted away. The first two batters single, and then the third, Kottaras, hits the first pitch he gets over the

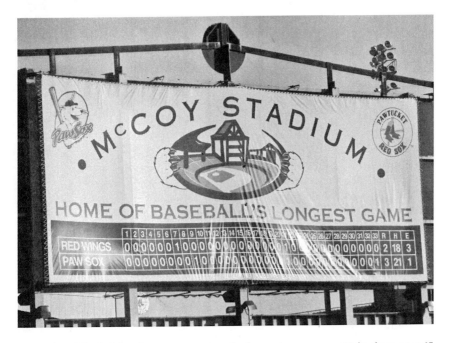

Pawtucket, Rhode Island — monument to the longest game ever, 33 innings over 65 days. Tonight we only got to 10.

right field wall, taking the game to extras. Visions of 33 innings and 4:00 A.M. flash through my head. But the Pawsox score again in the bottom of the tenth to send the remnants of the crowd home happy.

New Hampshire
Thursday August 30–Friday August 31

Compared to the rest of the country, some of these northeastern states are really small. I leave Rhode Island, drive through part of Massachusetts, and am now in New Hampshire; total distance, 92 miles. That really is Thursday's agenda; the rest of the time is spent relaxing, messing around in the hotel, and going to dinner. I return to keep an eye on what's happening in the baseball world. A couple of days ago I wrote that there are important series in a couple of the divisions; what I haven't realised is that, in five of the six divisions, the first-place team is playing the second-place team.

In the American League East, the Yankees sweep the Red Sox in three games, reducing the gap between them to five. It's still probably too big a gap to close. In the AL West the Angels sweep Seattle, to extend their lead to five and a half games, so they are looking a fair bet too. And the Yankees have overtaken Seattle in the wild card.

In the National League, the effect of these series is different. In the East, Philadelphia sweeps the Mets in four games, thus reducing the Mets' lead to two. The Central sees the Cubs beat Milwaukee 2–1, and increase their lead to two and a half; and in the West San Diego wins three straight against Arizona to draw level. In tonight's late game, Arizona gets one back over the Padres to go back to the top of the division. So, if the season ended today, the playoffs would feature Boston, Cleveland, the Angels, the Yankees, the Mets, the Cubs, Arizona and San Diego. But there's a month to go yet.

With two months of my trip remaining, things are drawing to a conclusion. I have just seen the dates for the postseason and, for the first time in years, the World Series is scheduled to run into November. My plane home is booked for October 31st, so something will have to be done. There's also Hawaii to squeeze in somehow.

The only scheduled event Friday is the evening's game, so I decide to find some postcards. There is a large mall less than half a mile away, and it's a while since I risked my life in the pedestrian cause, so I decide to walk. An eventful ten minutes of dodging traffic and scrambling down embankments and I'm there. The first shop I see sells postcards, so I buy half a dozen, get some coffee, and sit and write them.

And so to the game — New Hampshire Fisher Cats vs. Trenton Thunder; a short drive takes me into town, and a car park opposite the ground. Manchester has the distinction of having the most expensive parking lots in minor league baseball, at $10 more than twice as expensive as anywhere else. I am begrudging this charge as I enter the ground, when I see a sign proclaiming "Welcome to the Fisher Cats entertainment experience!" That's OK then — $10 may be steep for a minor league baseball game, but for an entertainment experience, very reasonable!

The food stalls are good — a clam roll (I have to wait while the clams are cooked), and a local beer called Smuttynose (I think it's a kind of seal). When the game begins, it does so explosively; in the bottom of the first the Cats' leadoff hitter puts the first pitch he receives out of the ground, the second hitter singles off his first pitch, and the third hitter is walked on four pitches. The pitcher then recovers and strikes out the side.

In the bottom of the second the Cats' first batter again homers off his first pitch, almost to the same spot as his colleague in the first, 2–0 to the Cats. In the top of the fourth Trenton's first batter homers, and then three more runs score; in the bottom of the fourth the Cats score two: 4–4. In the fifth another home run for Trenton is followed by a run for the Cats: 5–5.

At this point both teams change pitchers, and there is no more score; extra innings again, in successive games. In the tenth and 11th, Trenton get runners to third with no outs, but fail to bring either home. In the bottom of the 11th three singles win the game for the Cats, and we finish with a firework display!

Delaware

Saturday September 1–Sunday September 2

The demands of various league schedules mean that, once again, I am driving more miles than I would have done in a perfect world. Going from points north of New York City to points south thereof almost inevitably means using I-95 and the New Jersey Turnpike, a stretch of road always busy, often congested, and with no scenery worth mentioning. If you think of the stretch of the M1 between Luton and North London, multiply by 20, and add some toll booths, you're pretty close. But it's done, at least until Monday when I will do the journey in reverse, and I'm in Delaware, in a motel by the side of the interstate, ready for tomorrow's game.

I can now confirm plans for the rest of my trip. I have decided to go to Hawaii for four days at the end of September, to complete my set of the states.

I'm also receiving reassuring noises from Channel 5 regarding post-season tickets; the fly in the ointment is that late start for the World Series, and what to do about my return flight, currently booked for October 31st. Hmmmm!

Sunday's game has a lunchtime start, so after an easy morning I take the ten-minute drive to the park. The car park is free, so we are obviously over our entertainment experiences and back to good old minor league baseball. The stadium is next to Wilmington Riverfront, more of which later, but unfortunately, it faces the wrong way to take advantage of the fact. Instead, the view from the stands is of the beloved I-95. Not as bad as it might seem, but it does appear a little odd to watch cars zipping past above the level of the scoreboard!

The game is Wilmington Blue Rocks vs. Potomac Nationals, Single A affiliates of the Kansas City Royals and the Washington Nationals and, as the gentleman next to me remarks, "It's a beautiful day for a ballgame!" While I'm waiting for the game to start, I get a call from Erik at Channel 5, to arrange this evening's interview. It seems that this week I'm going to be accompanied by a graphic, so it's all very exciting.

The game is a tight one, and very entertaining. The Nationals score first, oddly enough from a strikeout. As the hitter strikes out, the man on first is attempting to steal a base. The throw to second catches him in a rundown between first and second. While the fielding side is thus distracted, the man on third heads for home, and the throw comes in too late to prevent him from scoring.

I have mentioned before that a good performer on the PA has pieces of music earmarked for various parts of the game. When an opposition pitcher is pulled, a favourite is "Should I Stay or Should I Go," but today this is outdone. The departure of the opposing pitcher is greeted by "Happy Trails to You" by Roy Rogers! In the fifth a couple of singles and a double put the home side ahead 2–1, and some excellent defence and pitching make sure it stays that way.

Wilmington Waterfront is a shopping complex and leisure area on the banks of the Christina River, so I pop down there for a little exploration. It turns out that it was once a thriving ship building area, responsible for many U.S. Navy ships. It has been renovated into this complex, but several of the cranes have been left there as a reminder of what it once was. Many of the shops are closed, but the ice cream parlour remains open so, in the interests of research...

I return to the hotel and, after awhile, Erik phones again. They are having technical problems, so we are going to have to "go live." So I go for an early dinner, and return to do my stuff.

The interview goes well. It's in two parts this week, and the graphics turn out to be my August and September schedules. I, unfortunately, am not aware of this at the time so, when they ask me for my August highlight, they have a list in front of them and I don't. But I clutch at a couple of straws, crack a couple of jokes, and move a couple of steps nearer to the inevitable BAFTA (British Academy of Film and Television Arts).

Connecticut

Monday September 3–Thursday September 6

Monday sees the start of a motel-free spell of ten days. But as part of life's quid pro quo there's I-95 to contend with again. All goes well until I reach New York City; one wrong turn is easily rectified, but then my instructions tell me to leave on exit 4, and the road has nothing between exits 3 and 5. So I keep going east, which feels sensible, until I notice an exit for one of the parkways further down my route. Following this, I soon come to the Merritt Parkway, which takes me deep into Connecticut.

This is a lovely, tree-lined highway which covers around 50 miles of my route. The drive takes me past some familiar names, such as Yale — I never knew where that was, now I do. I stop for lunch in Stamford, and continue to my destination, Glastonbury. No festival for me, instead the home of a very good friend. I have known Lee-Ann since 1974, and on my last visit here, six years ago, met husband Arthur, and offspring Christopher and Heather. In 2001, the kids were eight and 11 respectively, so you don't have to be a genius to realise what a change I find in them.

My accommodation is luxurious; lying on my bed I find an early birthday present from my daughter Anya, two T-shirts bearing the legend "Superstar Ultimate Road Trip King," with my name and web address on the back. They will be worn — maybe Sunday in Pittsburgh would be an appropriate place for their debut.

Today is Labor Day (no, that's not a spelling mistake!), so everyone is at home when I arrive. They have moved since my last visit, and the new house is a beautiful place, located in the middle of a heavily wooded area. So we sit with cold drinks, catching up on six years of news, photos and suchlike.

Tuesday starts quietly. The kids are off to school, Lee-Ann has to do a day's supply teaching, so Art and I hang around doing very little. We drive out for lunch at Doogie's Diner, purveyor of seafood, burgers and a 16-inch hot dog, and drive home again to recuperate, and prepare for what promises to be one of the big nights of the trip.

Many months ago, I wrote to all the clubs I was planning to visit asking for free tickets. I received a reply from Mary-Jane Foster, co-owner of tonight's hosts, the Bridgeport Bluefish, saying that a project such as mine should be "applauded and supported." Would I like to watch the game from the owners' seats and would I like to throw out the first pitch? Yes I would!

It appears that Anya has sent more than enough "ultimate road trip" T-shirts, so the kids are all kitted out as my travelling fan club. Lee-Ann has been detained at school, so Art, the kids and myself all pile into a car and off we go. We arrive at the club to be greeted by Mary-Jane, who shows me the offices and introduces me to the team manager, Tommy John. I recognise the name, one of the greatest left-handed pitchers of all time. He played for the Dodgers and the Yankees, but oddly is best remembered for the fact that, in 1974, he damaged his pitching arm. Surgeons replaced the ligament in his elbow with some taken from his other arm. The procedure is now relatively commonplace in the game, and is known as Tommy John surgery.

We are shown to our front row seats, and Art receives a phone call from Lee-Ann, who has arrived but is in the rest room feeling unwell. He disappears to sort this out, and they soon return, announcing that everything is well. Mary-Jane arrives to tell me that the time is nigh, and I am led out onto the field to meet the two mascots, BB Bluefish, a large blue fish, and Captain LI Sound, a gnarled old sea captain. I am introduced to the opposition manager, another former pitching great of Red Sox and Yankees fame, Sparky Lyle. I am led out onto the mound and deliver the first pitch. It's a bit low for a strike, but I manage to keep it out of the dirt.

At this point Capt. Sound approaches again, wanting a hug. I oblige, and can't understand why he won't let go. Just then a familiar voice, from deep within this huge costume, says, "It's me, Pete! I'm here!" My wife Sal, who had e-mailed me only this morning explaining why she could not travel again to the States, was in the costume. The crowd is treated to the shocking sight of me snogging an old sea captain.

We are then led inside, where we manage to rid Sal of the costume, and a newspaper reporter is waiting to interview us. This goes off well, and we eventually get back to our seat, where we are greeted with much hilarity. Next we are confronted by a TV reporter/cameraman, who asks more questions. I am questioned repeatedly by other fans, someone gives me a present, we drink some beer and ... oh yes, there's a baseball game on — Bluefish lose, 7–2.

I spend every spare moment questioning people about what has been happening, and it appears no one has spoken a word of truth to me for the last two days. Sal has been staying at Lee-Ann's since Saturday, and only moved into a hotel last night so that the surprise could be effected publicly. Lee-Ann has not been teaching, she has spent the day with Sal. The illness was feigned so that she could help Sal change. I may never believe a word anyone says to me ever again.

Wednesday passes quietly, with much catching up to do, and then I receive a phone call from Erik at Channel 5, reminding me that they want to do a

Wednesday interview this week, as well as my usual Sunday stint. They want to know all about the goings on of the previous evening, and it almost sounds weirder talking about it than watching it happen. Seasoned pro that I have become, I deal with the spontaneity with scarcely a falter; another one in the can, as they say.

The rest of the evening is spent watching my beloved Cubbies beat the Dodgers, 8–2. Whereas most of the playoff places seem to be sorting themselves out, the Cubs are still in a three-way race with Milwaukee and St. Louis. Milwaukee also won, to stay a half-game behind the Cubs, while St. Louis lost, to fall two games back. It's going down to the wire, I told you.

Thursday is my 57th birthday and starts, as all birthdays should, with cards in bed. My family, as usual, comes up with the goods, but pride of place must go to young Joanna, who evidently has made her first attempts at writing. I'm that proud!

I have been asked where I would like to go for my birthday lunch, and I have requested somewhere by the water. So at

Top and above: Before and after. My wife Sally prepares to surprise me in the costume of Capt. L.I. Sound. As far as I know I'm not related to the fish!

10:30 we leave for Old Saybrook, a lovely little town on the coast, where we have been booked into a seafood restaurant which overlooks the sea. The view is lovely, and the food is excellent, stuffed clams followed by crab cakes.

The afternoon passes in a gentle blur, we return home, spend more time on the porch, and are joined by the kids ready for the evening festivities. Once again we dine out, a steak and a pint of Octoberfest at Houlihan's. On my return, I am presented with gifts by my delightful hosts: a book of baseball short stories, and a beautiful picture frame bearing a picture of Nina and me on the boat in San Francisco Bay.

What a delightful day! Why some people choose not to celebrate birthdays I will never understand; I celebrate each one with increasing intensity and verve, and today has been made very special by the people around me. The only negative is that the Cubs throw away a lead to lose to the Dodgers. They are now in a tie in their division with Milwaukee, with St. Louis just one game behind. As Cubs fans well know — nobody said it would be easy!

Pennsylvania
Friday September 7–Thursday September 13

On Friday we commence stage two of the motel-free period, as we leave Lee-Ann and Arthur with sincere expressions of gratitude for the wondrous, and still unbelievable, events of the last few days. We manage to be on the road by 9:30, with 500 miles ahead of us. It turns out to be a beautiful drive, through Connecticut, New York and Pennsylvania.

Eventually we see the familiar skyline of Pittsburgh, familiar not just because of the skyscraper based on the Houses of Parliament, but because Sally and I have been here twice before. We try to come here each time we visit this country, as this is the home of our good friends Steve and Liz. If these names are not recognisable, you need to refer back to Cincinnati.

The focus of the visit is Sunday's game, where the local Pirates will face the Chicago Cubs. The three-game series starts tonight, and the top of the table Cubs are beaten 6–1 by the bottom of the table Pirates. This is a crazy division, as the second-place Brewers and third-place Cardinals are also beaten. So the situation in the division remains unaltered.

Saturday passes lazily, concluding with an excellent dinner, after which we return home to the last couple of innings of the Cubs' victory over Pittsburgh; frustratingly, Milwaukee wins also, so the two teams remain neck and neck on top of the National League Central.

Sunday is the day of the game — Pittsburgh Pirates vs. Chicago Cubs, first pitch 1:35. So, after an easy morning, the four of us set off, all clad in "superstar ultimate road trip king" T-shirts. It is another humid day, and the air hangs heavy over the city, with very little sunshine. PNC Park has recently been voted the best of the new ballparks in an American TV poll, and it is indeed beautiful, standing on the banks of the river with the Pittsburgh skyline in the background. Steve has managed to score some tickets from a previous employer, and they come complete with a parking pass, which enables us to park right in front of the stadium.

In the car park I buy chocolate from a little kid in aid of his school. Steve has six tickets, and there are only four of us, so he looks around for someone to give them to. Eventually an old black guy passes, and Steve asks if he wants some tickets. "I ain't got no money!" he replies. Steve shrugs expansively and hands over the tickets. The old guy beams, and runs off in search of his son.

We enter the stadium, and wander around, watching the warmups and catching some of the wonderful views. I have reached the stage of my journey where there is little new in ballparks. The local ales are different, but the food is largely the same. But Pittsburgh has pierogies, so I have to give them a go! These turn out to be large ravioli, made of some sort of dough, filled with a cheesy mixture, and served with sour cream; not exactly health food, but not unpleasant either.

The seats are excellent, just to the first base side of home plate, and not very far back, so we settle down to a good afternoon's baseball. But as the game starts, so does the drizzle. The neutrals tell me the game is a really good one — for a Cubs fan it's quite a frustrating afternoon. The Cubs start well, and take a two-run lead in the top of the second. The Cubs' starting pitcher is Steve Trachsel, recently acquired from Baltimore to add quality to the bottom of the rotation. It doesn't work! The Pirates score six in the bottom of the second, including a bases-clearing triple which would have been an inside-the-park home run if not for an excellent throw home which results in the hitter being out at the plate.

The Cubs struggle, but by the bottom of the seventh have pulled the score back to 7–5. But the comeback is crushed by three Pirates' runs in the bottom of the eighth. The out-of-town scoreboard is reporting news of a Milwaukee victory, so the Cubs slip off the top of their division by a game.

And it rains, and it rains, and it rains; sometimes it slows to a drizzle, but it never really stops. It's so wet that even the Pittsburgh Parrot, their mascot, dons a cape and sou'wester. I have to keep looking to my right to make sure that Sally is still in her seat, and not in the Parrot costume. The humidity at the start of the game is such that the rain is actually pleasant, but I have to acquire the new skill of scoring underneath a waterproof sheet.

We drive home, interrupted only by a phone call from Erik to arrange this evening's interview. We are all soaked through, so it takes some dry clothes, and a glass or two of honey porter and double chocolate stout, to restore us to something approaching normal. The interview goes well; I receive sympathy about the Cubbies' result, we talk about how lovely PNC Park is, and they ask about my plans for the rest of the trip. Then Jonny and Josh declare on air that Channel 5 is intending to do something with me in the post-season, which is really exciting news. After working to a schedule for six months, the prospect of a month not knowing where I'm going or when is exhilarating to say the least.

Monday is a day off—after a morning at the aviary, we move on to a late lunch at one of my favourite establishments, which I have visited on both of my previous visits to this city. The Church Brew Works is a deconsecrated church which has been converted to a brew pub. The brewing vats have been located where the altar once stood, and are still surrounded by stained glass windows. The restaurant area has seating made from the original church pews. For someone like me, who worships good food and beer, it is an ideal place.

There is a small but excellent list of beers, some of which are rotated or seasonal. The dark beer on offer is a hazelnut stout and, remarkably, it has a distinct taste of hazelnuts! This may sound bizarre to the average Guinness drinker but, believe me, it's worth the risk. The other beers are also excellent, as is the food, and I would recommend any visitor to this city to seek out this remarkable place.

We drive back along the Strip, which is the only part of the centre of the city which has not been redeveloped. It consists of a long row of original buildings, many of which are devoted to food supply. There is a fish market, a meat market, several Italian delicatessens and many other fine shops and restaurants. There is a wonderful fish and seafood lunch shop, called Bentkowich, which has no seats but where you can buy lunch and, allegedly, the best fried fish sandwich in Pittsburgh. I sampled this during my last visit, and would not dare to argue with the claim.

One of the things that were immediately confusing on my arrival in this strange land was the reversal of dates. Thus, when registering at a hotel, I had to remember that my birthday was 9/6, and not 6/9, as it has been for the past 50-odd years. The only reason I mention this now is that Tuesday is, therefore, 9/11, which is how most Americans refer to the attack on the twin towers which took place six years ago. So the TV and radio are full of commemoration, and people recounting where they were when. In our case, the answer would be halfway up a mountain in Scotland with, ironically, Steve and Liz, our present hosts. The fourth plane, you may remember, came down just outside Pittsburgh.

But it's our time to move on, so we say our goodbyes and hit the road. By this time it has started raining; and how it rains. Today is rainier than the rainiest day of the rainy season in the middle of the rain forest. We have been informed that the drive between these two cities takes us through some glorious countryside, and it probably does. But all we see is the spray from the trucks coming in the opposite direction. The best view of the day is a hot cup of coffee in Starbuck's.

At around 4:00 we reach the environs of Philadelphia, and easily locate the house of our latest hosts, Alice and Pete. Pete, the anal amongst you will recall, I met for lunch in New York; Alice we have both met, however briefly, at Marcus and Jenny's wedding three years ago. They live in a lovely old house, which they are renovating, in an area of the city called Manayunk. They have two rescued greyhounds, Roxie and Bebe, and we join them in walking the dogs around the area, which is oddly reminiscent of an English seaside town, but without the sea!

We walk to a Thai restaurant on Main Street and, en route, Pete explains that Manayunk is an old Indian word meaning "where we go to drink." I can't understand why most of the towns in the country don't have this name!

Wednesday is Sal's opportunity to buy gifts, baby clothes, and all the other things which are so much cheaper here, so the morning is spent wandering, in my case aimlessly, around Target and Walmart. We get back to Manayunk and have a delightful al fresco lunch before setting off for the game. We choose public transport, a suburban train into the city and a subway to the park. The change occurs in the centre of the city, so we at least get a small glimpse of this historic place.

Citizens' Bank Park is one of the new breed of ballparks, but is built outside of the centre in an open area near the old docks. It is beautifully built, with wide walkways which enable you to have a view of the game even whilst walking around the ground or queueing for beers.

Philadelphia is famous, some might say notorious, for the cheesesteak sandwich. I have sampled this at other parks—a sub roll, thinly sliced steak, melted cheese, onions and peppers—but have not yet had the definitive Philly version. I have missed the opportunity to compare and contrast the two rival city centre factions, and the queue for the ballpark version, which I am advised is inferior, is ridiculously long. So we opt for something which can only be found in this ballpark, the Schmitter. This is named (or might not be) after local baseball legend Mike Schmidt, and is the bastardised offspring of the Philly cheesesteak and the hoagie. It consists of the cheesesteak ingredients outlined above, plus grilled salami, fresh tomato and mayonnaise. The warm bun struggles to hold all these ingredients, and it looks one awful mess; but close your eyes and take a bite, and it's quite an experience. Just don't wear your best shirt!

We settle down for the game (not that we could go far after the "snack"), and it's really quite eventful. In the top of the first, Colorado puts the first two hitters on base. The third hitter, Matt Holliday, hits a very low line drive straight at the Philly third baseman, who takes the catch, thus dismissing the batter; the third baseman throws quickly to second, thus dismissing the runner who has left the base; the second baseman dashes at the runner from first, who I think is unaware that the catch has been taken cleanly, and tags him out; a triple play — it's only taken 57 games, but here it is, my first triple play!

In the bottom of the first Philly loads the bases, but strands all three. In the top of the second the Rockies' catcher, Torrealba, strikes out and evidently disagrees with the umpire's decision a little too vehemently. He is thrown out of the game and has to be removed physically by his own manager. It's happening everywhere except on the scoreboard!

In the top of the third the aforementioned Holliday decides to make amends for hitting into a triple play, by placing the ball over our heads deep into the crowd for a three-run homer. In the top of the fourth the first batter hits the ball hard, unfortunately straight at the knee of the pitcher, who has to withdraw from the game. The new pitcher fails to come to terms with his unexpected promotion, and puts eight batters on base, six of whom score; Phillies 0, Rockies 9!

In the meantime the Phillies, after the first, fail to put more than one runner on base for the remainder of the game. The Rockies add a solo homer in the sixth, and tack on runs in the eighth and ninth. The Phillies fans are not happy, and can only find solace in persuading each of the fans who catch the home run balls to throw them back; final result, 0–12!

At this point of the trip the emotions seem to be becoming more important than the hard facts. Thursday is Sal's last day with me, so whatever we decide to do I'm going to have to work hard not to be miserable. The first part of the day is spent repacking, and when we eventually decide to bid farewell to our hosts we head for Philadelphia Zoo. This is an excellent choice, as it's something we both enjoy and find distracting. To a large extent it works. The zoo is interesting and well stocked, and seems to care for its animals at least as much as the public.

Towards the end of the afternoon we head towards the airport. Sal's flight is not until 9:00, so I have decided to find an airport hotel. This will let me hang on at the airport if the flight is delayed, and not have to drive somewhere new in the dark. As it turns out, the hotel has a shuttle bus, so we are able to utilise that and leave the car parked up.

We get rid of Sal's luggage, which gives us 90 minutes to find somewhere to eat and relax for a while. We spend most of the time discussing what I have achieved so far, and what there is left to do. I have said from the start that I am not doing this trip alone, and the support, both practical and emotional, of my family has been immeasurable. I am really missing home now; so much has happened since I left. There are friends and neighbours I will never see again — one of the funerals is taking place as I write — and I have a grand-daughter I have yet to meet. As Sal disappears, I walk away feeling determined to see this thing through, knowing full well that everyone at home is behind me.

I return to my room, understandably a little low. But then the TV informs me that the Cubs have beaten Houston, and so returned to first place in their division. It doesn't make the parting any easier, but it makes the staying more bearable.

New Jersey
Friday September 14–Sunday September 16

I start Friday gently as usual, making sure my writing is up to date, and set out just after 10:00. The exits from Philadelphia are not very user friendly, but I manage to escape the city with only one U-turn.

My journey today is just over 70 miles, as I am visiting John and Dana, whom I have never met before. John is the son of a good friend, and I want to at least take the opportunity to stop off and say hello. The house is quiet when I arrive, and we are observed by a daft golden retriever and several cats. I am warned that we will shortly be invaded by female children. Have I stepped into a time warp? When the children arrive, they are accompanied by other children, and then by appropriate adults. I lose track of the number of children and adults to whom I am introduced during the course of the afternoon. Eventually those who remain are fed, and we depart for our big night out, at the Office Lounge.

This is a huge bar, full of TVs, on which various baseball games are showing. I am re-introduced to some of the people I met this afternoon, introduced to some new ones that I didn't meet this afternoon, bought drinks and generally shown a good time. John is also English, so we take the opportunity to exchange notes about the difference between these two countries. Things you hear in an American bar that you wouldn't hear in an English pub: "Whiskey, or Scotch?"

The main game being shown is the first of a three-game series between the Yankees and the Red Sox. The Red Sox open up a 7–2 lead. As the Yankees slowly come back into the game, it becomes apparent where the sympathies of the majority of the customers lie. When the Yankees take an 8–7 lead, there is applause and high-fives all round. The results show that the Cubs have won, and Milwaukee has lost, giving the Cubs a lead of a game and a half. Frankly, it's a good night all round.

On Saturday morning I leave my hosts and, as my route takes me near Belmar and Asbury, decide to check out some Springsteen trivia. Homage paid, I head north, deciding to use the coast road rather than the Turnpike. I see a sign for Mount Mitchill, and pull off to take a look. This turns out, at 266 feet, to be the highest part of the Atlantic seaboard between Maine and Mexico, and has a marvellous view over the Narrows to the New York skyline. Further investigation finds a touching memorial to the victims of 9/11, which states that many local citizens assembled here to watch the scenes across the water at first hand.

I continue to Somerset, find my hotel, and set off in good time for tonight's game, Somerset Patriots vs. Camden Riversharks. I arrive early, despite the threat of "pre-game Irish entertainment," an oxymoron if ever I saw one. This turns out to be Marty McLenan, a guitarist and vocalist, who seems oblivious to the historical roots of his music as he follows "The Minstrel Boy" with "McNamara's Band" without batting an eye. As he finishes, the PA system carries on the theme with some pipe band music, "Scotland the Brave" if I'm not mistaken!

The game is entertaining, finishing 7–4 to the visitors, and is interspersed with the usual gimmicks plus, on this occasion, a group of young girls performing Irish dances. We finish with fireworks, probably o'fireworks if I'd been paying attention, but not all of them are green.

My previous jaunts through New York and New Jersey have been subject to a strict schedule. On this occasion I don't have another game planned for a week, so I am taking the chance provided by this respite to see some of the things overlooked previously.

Lawrence Berra was a famous Yankees catcher from the end of the war until the early 60s. As a youngster, some of his friends thought he resembled a religious character in a film they had just seen, set in India. They nicknamed him Yogi, after this character; not only did the name stick, it even led to the naming of the famous cartoon character Yogi Bear, in the late 50s. Berra retired to Montclair, and the university there has a baseball field and museum in his honour. On Sunday morning I seek it out, and it's well worth the effort. The exhibits bear testament, not only to Berra's illustrious career as player, coach and manager, but also to the deep affection in which he is held by members of the baseball community.

Yogi is also responsible for some of the funny sayings that abound in baseball, which I wrote about in San Francisco. "It ain't over 'til it's over" originally came from him. You can buy books of the somewhat muddled pronouncements of the great man, and I'll leave you with one of my favourites. When asked by his wife whether she should cut his pizza into four slices or six, he replied "Just four, I'm not hungry enough to eat six!"

My next destination is just a short drive down the highway, but could be a million miles. Following the leafy avenues of the university, Paterson is one of the most run-down places I have yet visited, and yet there is a good reason for my being here. It is the birthplace of Lou Costello, half of the famous comedy duo, Abbott and Costello. Ironically, his partner, Bud Abbott, was born in Asbury, which I visited yesterday. I have directions to a small park which contains a statue of Costello, but when I come to the appropriate turn, it is blocked off, and there is traffic everywhere. The place is so busy that I drive around in circles and become completely lost, until I notice a small park to my right, containing a statue!

If you don't know what this man has got to do with baseball, get online and look up the "Who's on First?" sketch. The statue depicts Lou with a baseball bat on his shoulder, and bears the legend "Lou's on First!"

It takes ages to find my way out of the town; whichever way I go I keep returning to the centre. Eventually I find my way out of the mess and head west, until I find a motel for the night. If this country has any urban regeneration projects, I would like to nominate Paterson as the beneficiary of all of them!

Cooperstown

Monday September 17–Wednesday September 19

Whichever of the legends you believe about the birth of baseball, there is little doubt that the game has its roots in the northeast of this country. In fact, until the two New York teams upped and moved to the West Coast in the 50s, the first-class game went no further west than Chicago and St. Louis. The result of this is that there are a lot of sites in this area which are of interest to the baseball fan.

If you have only heard of one baseball player, it would probably be George Herman Ruth, known to all and sundry as Babe, and it is his grave in Hawthorne, New York, which is Monday's first port of call. After starting his career with a brief stint in Baltimore, Ruth was sold to the Boston Red Sox, with whom he won two World Series. But in 1919, the owner of the Red Sox sold his star to the rival New York Yankees — he needed the money to finance a Broadway musical — and the Babe began the most illustrious part of his career. Boston never recovered from the sale, and it was 86 years before they won another World Series; the 86-year drought was known to Boston fans as "the curse of the Bambino."

The Babe's career with the Yankees is well chronicled, but perhaps the highlight was in 1927 when he broke his own record and hit 60 home runs in a season — a figure which stood until 1961. Ruth died in 1948, and is buried in the Gates of Heaven cemetery in Hawthorne, with his second wife, who outlived him by almost 30 years. The grave is a fairly opulent affair, as are many in this cemetery; but this is the only one decorated with baseballs, cards, hats and other memorabilia left by the fans who still come to visit the great man.

Next I drive 100 miles north, to the town of Troy, a fairly insignificant place with a park in which stands a remarkable monument. The Troy baseball club joined the National League in 1879, but was required to stand down three years later to make room for teams from New York and Philadelphia, which had greater commercial potential. They were awarded honorary membership of the league, a status which they hold to this day. Most of the players joined the New York club, which was initially named the Gothams, but which later became the New York Giants, until it moved to San Francisco. So Troy, New York, actually gave birth to the San Francisco Giants!

One of the other boasts on this unique monument is that five of the Troy players went on to be elected to the Baseball Hall of Fame, a remarkable number by any standards. One of these five was a guy named Johnny Evers, who played for the Chicago Cubs when last they won a World Series in 1908. Together with two teammates, he formed one of the most notable infield combinations the game has ever seen, and the only one, to my knowledge, to become the subject of a poem!

Written by Franklin Pierce Adams from the point of view of a disgruntled Giants fan, it reads

> *These are the saddest of possible words:*
> *"Tinker to Evers to Chance."*
> *Trio of bear cubs, and fleeter than birds,*
> *Tinker and Evers and Chance.*
> *Ruthlessly pricking our gonfalon bubble,*
> *Making a Giant hit into a double—*
> *Words that are heavy with nothing but trouble:*
> *"Tinker to Evers to Chance."*

A gonfalon is a flag, and in this context refers to the National League pennant, or league title.

My final drive of the day brings me to Cooperstown, holiest of baseball holies. For once the computer takes me off the interstate and gives me a route through the forest which surrounds this town. Autumn is on its way, and the leaves are just starting to change; it's a beautiful place to be.

On the signs which welcome visitors, Cooperstown describes itself as a village; it certainly falls into that category somewhere between a large village and a small town, and it is in a beautiful spot. It sits on the southern shore of Lake Otsego, and is surrounded by thick forests. The Cooper after whom it is named was the father of James Fenimore Cooper, of "Last of the Mohicans" fame, and the writer was a long-term resident of the place. Many people choose this area as a holiday venue, and would have done so even if the baseball authorities had not chosen it as the location of the Baseball Hall of Fame.

But the building of the Hall of Fame has had a dramatic effect on the town, or village if you prefer. There are about 50 shops in Main Street, 40 of which are baseball themed. The restaurants have names like Home Run Café, and Extra Innings. If you choose this as a location for a holiday, and you don't like baseball, you may find it very uncomfortable; perhaps like walking through the average Cornish village if you don't like pasties or clotted cream.

But, at the risk of stating the obvious, it is to the Hall of Fame that I have come, and that is Tuesday's main event. It is a functional yet elegant building, which was instituted in 1936, and it serves two purposes. Firstly, there is an actual hall, which contains a plaque for each of the nearly 300 players and administrators elected to this honour. This is a sanctum, where people walk around with great respect, talking in hushed tones and quietly worshipping the heroes of the game. It is a beautiful room, with a canopy which, on a good day, projects a web of shadows and sunlight onto the gallery floor.

The rest of the building houses the official museum of Major League Baseball, which is a magnificent display. There are exhibits on the history of the game, the ballparks, artefacts from all the major league teams; there are sections on black baseball and women's baseball; there is a cinema showing trailers of the countless films featuring baseball; and, when you need some light relief, a video showing continuously the Abbott and Costello "Who's on First?" sketch.

As an institution it is very impressive. It makes no apology for being what it is, and there are few concessions to commercialism. There is no food or drink allowed in the building; your hand is stamped as you enter and you can come and go as you like — there are plenty of places to eat within 200 metres of the place. When I have had my fill of baseball information, I exit the building into a quiet garden, which contains several statues dedicated to various aspects of the game. I take some photographs and spend a few minutes relaxing and reflecting on the beauty of this place.

Suitably inspired, I pop into the Post Office, then walk down to the lake, planning the rest of my day, and of my week. I have decided to book an extra night at the hotel, so that I can spend the whole of tomorrow exploring the rest of Cooperstown.

With ten games left to the end of the regular season, things are hotting up; the Cubs lose tonight, while Milwaukee wins, so once again the two teams are level. In several other divisions, teams with seemingly unassailable leads are being pegged back. Philadelphia has pulled to within two games of the Mets, the Yankees to within two and a half games of Boston, and San Diego to within one of Arizona. The only teams who look certain division winners are Cleveland and Anaheim.

As I've noted before, holiday resorts in this country work to a pretty strict routine. Summer starts on Memorial Day, which is the last Monday in May, and ends on Labor Day, the first Monday in September. Some institutions take this literally, and open and close on these dates. In the case of somewhere like Cooperstown, a kind of schizophrenia kicks in. Some places, like the fast food joints between here and town, have all the furniture in a pile, presumably until next May. The Hall of Fame stays open all year, but its normal hours are extended during the summer season, so the other businesses in town get confused. The determined ones remain open, to eke each last drop of business out of the baseball faithful.

So on Wednesday I decide to explore these businesses; second-hand book shops, clothing stores, purveyors of memorabilia, all around the theme of base-ball. There are a lot of them, and there is a lot of rubbish. But every now and then a little gem surfaces, and I manage to do a little bit of buying among a lot of looking.

There is also a small baseball park, named Doubleday Field, after Abner Doubleday, who was claimed to have invented the game, with the first ever game supposedly having been played on the spot where the stadium now stands. That, at least, is the Cooperstown version of the legend. A more historically accurate version places the origins in Hoboken, New Jersey, though in truth the game's origins are more complicated, and is baseball the result of a gradual evolution. But this is where the Hall of Fame game is played every year, and it's a charming little stadium. So why let the truth spoil a good story?

The evening is spent watching baseball — happily for me the TV is broad-casting the Cubs against the Reds. The Cubs take an early lead, go behind 2–1, and come back to win, 3–2, in the bottom of the eighth. Meanwhile the scores from the Milwaukee game are flashed up regularly. They take an early lead, but are pegged back in the seventh. As the Cubs are taking the lead, Milwaukee goes behind 4–2 but, as the Cubs win in the ninth, Milwaukee ties their game in the top of the ninth, and it goes to extra innings. Houston scores in the bot-tom of the tenth to win, and once again the Cubs lead the division by a game.

As I wrote earlier, some of the races are getting very interesting, so watch-ing the scores come in is quite exciting. The story of the evening is that the Yankees win again, and Boston loses again. On May 29 Boston led the Yankees by 14½ games; the lead is now down to a game and a half. No team has ever lost a lead of more than 14 games in a divisional race!

D.C.

Thursday September 20 – Monday September 24

Leaving Cooperstown, I drive south, mostly away from interstates, and continue to be impressed by the beauty of this part of New York State; trees, rivers and lakes, and the sun continues to shine.

I head for Thursday's destination, Bethel Woods Centre for the Arts, a state of the art performing arts centre near the small town of Bethel. It is an elegant single-storey building, with enough parking for a very large-size crowd. But its main claim to fame is to be found on a small monument in the corner of one of the adjacent fields, which proclaims it as the site of the 1969 Woodstock Festival.

By the time I got to Woodstock we were half a dozen strong, and everywhere there was the sound of lawn mowers. The centre was closed for the winter, and the ground staff was busy keeping everywhere looking good. I spoke to one of them, who told me what was happening and directed me to the memorial.

It's a fairly simple affair, listing those who performed, and remembering the event which closed the New York State Thruway. In the middle of the field I could see a totem pole in the distance which, apparently, bears carvings of Jimi Hendrix and Janis Joplin, but I could not get close enough to see it properly. But the place certainly has an aura about it, and many artistes say it is a wonderful place to play.

I drive another 60 miles or so south, before finding a hotel. It makes tomorrow's journey a little bit shorter. I watch with pleasure the news of Milwaukee's defeat coming through. The Cubs have a night off, so their lead increases to a game and a half. The Mets lose again, Philadelphia wins again, reducing the lead to a game and a half; and San Diego wins its seventh in a row, reducing Arizona's lead to half a game. After leading clearly for the whole season, a couple of teams may just fall at the last.

On Friday I make a welcome return to a few of the great highways of North-Eastern America — I-95, I-295, the New Jersey Turnpike — crowded and monotonous every one. I appear to be making good time on my journey until the last 15 miles which, frustratingly, take forever due to a traffic accident, and 28 lanes trying to converge into three.

Eventually, I reach Bethesda, and the apartment of my good friend Phyllis. She and I worked together back in 1975 and, although we haven't seen that much of each other, have always kept in touch. Bethesda is ideally placed for both Washington and Baltimore, so I will stay here for five nights whilst seeing games in those two locations.

Then I do something which I have not done for a while — I iron a shirt, and make myself look as presentable as is possible after almost six months on the road, because I'm being taken out. Phyllis is Jewish, and this weekend is the biggest holiday in the Jewish calendar. It is also the Sabbath, so that makes tonight a double whammy. Those of you who know me will be aware that I am not an advocate of organised religion but, on this occasion, my rules of travelling kick in again. If I'm staying with someone and they invite me somewhere, I go!

The weekend also involves fasting (I have no intention of joining in that part), so the service is preceded by a gathering of about 20 friends for a final meal. We meet at an Indonesian restaurant and eat a buffet, which is excellent. I am introduced to everyone — no one thinks it odd that I'm joining in, and the conversation is more about baseball than religion. I should say at this point that this particular group is Reconstructionist. This is the less traditional end of the Jewish spectrum, and means that they do all sorts of things not found elsewhere, like allowing women to play an equal part, acknowledging gay and lesbian relationships, and welcoming other religions — and, I suppose, atheists like me!

We return home for some catching up, but Phyllis has a long day of celebration tomorrow, so it isn't too long before we call it a day. Friday, I think we call it.

On Saturday, Phyllis has left the apartment to do Jewish holiday things before I even wake. So I have the day and the apartment to myself. The morning is taken up with writing, downloading photographs and generally hanging about. I have the good intention of then exploring the neighbourhood, but I discover that Phyllis' cable TV has the channel that broadcasts Cubs games. So I make myself a sandwich and settle down to watch a very entertaining 9–5 victory. This puts the Cubs two games ahead in their division pending Milwaukee's game later in the day.

Towards the end of the afternoon I set out for today's game, the Washington Nationals against the Philadelphia Phillies. The Washington Metro proves relatively easy to master, not so the stadium, which has probably the most confusing numbering system I have yet to encounter. At this point, I have good news for Oakland fans; their stadium is no longer the worst I have visited. R.F. Kennedy Stadium is named in memory of the politician of that name, but its only other saving grace is that tonight is the last but one baseball game it will host.

Major league baseball returned to Washington at the beginning of last season, following a lengthy absence, when the Montreal Expos were closed down and the franchise moved here. Plans were made for the construction of a new stadium and, hopefully, it will be ready for the beginning of next season. But tonight, I wander around forever before finding my seat in something called the mezzanine. The view of the field is like watching the game from a post-box — you can't see balls hit to the fielder in front of you, and you can't see balls hit high. So I purchase a glass of locally brewed stout; tasty, but $6.50 for a small glass which is half foam, and settle down to enjoy what I can see of the game.

At this point I am joined by Murdo and Christine. These are two Scottish baseball fans who have heard of my journey on Channel 5, and, as they are in Washington, have offered to come and share a game with me. The company is more than welcome. The game still has relevance. Although Washington has long since been consigned to the list of also rans, Philadelphia is still in hot pursuit, both of the Mets in the Eastern division, and of San Diego in the wild card race. Philadelphia goes ahead in the first, and Washington levels in the sixth. This remains the score at the end of the ninth, which makes it sound like a pitching duel, but there were lots of hits, with each team stranding eight runners.

So it's extra innings, but not many. In the top of the tenth, the Phillies piece together three runs, which is enough to secure the win. News comes through that San Diego has lost, so Philadelphia only trails in the wild card race by half a game. The same scoreboard tells me that Milwaukee has been beaten, so the Cubs' lead is extended to two and a half.

Sunday morning I have chance to get on line. The Cubbies have announced that they are selling post-season tickets, both online and by phone. So I spend an hour or so staring at my computer screen, whilst at the same time phoning the ticket number and getting an engaged signal. It doesn't take too long until I get messages saying everything is sold out.

When Phyllis returns, we go out for a lovely pancake breakfast, see a bit more of Bethesda, and return in good time for Phyllis to prepare tomorrow's classes, and me to watch the Cubbies yet again. Wrigley Field looks a delightful place to spend a sunny Sunday afternoon, as the Cubbies wallop Pittsburgh, 8–0. The cheers greeting each Cubs run are nothing compared to those that greet each Atlanta run posted on the scoreboard, as they come from behind to beat Milwaukee, 7–4. The Chicago crowd even imitates the famous "tomahawk chop" gesture performed by the Atlanta crowd. The two results combined mean that the Cubs take a three and a half game lead into the final week.

One of Wrigley Field's great traditions is that, at each game, a celebrity will lead the crowd in the singing of "Take Me Out to the Ball Game" during the seventh-inning stretch. This is the last home game of the regular season, so the chosen celebrities are — the ground crew! A microphone is brought out onto the field and the guys in the blue shirts do a fine job!

Next on our busy schedule is an early dinner, at a local Pan Asian restaurant, which offers a fine menu combining Japanese, Thai and Indonesian food. We eat sushi, calamari and chicken satay — not a combination available on many menus. Returning to the apartment I do my now customary Sunday evening interview for Channel 5. I am quizzed as to my plans for the coming week, and preparations for the post-season. I am asked what I thought of RFK Stadium, and provide a more than forthright answer. Baltimore on Tuesday, I am promised, will be a great improvement.

It is a significant day in the baseball season, as the Cleveland Indians clinch the American League Central, and the Anaheim Angels the American League West. Boston is through, although it is not yet decided whether they will win the American League East or take the wild card. The other five playoff places are still up for grabs.

I spend Monday in Washington, and am compelled to visit the Vietnam Wall, the nation's memorial to the dead of that particular war. It is not as spectacular as I assumed and, because it is built into the contours of the area in which it stands, almost invisible from behind. It is constructed of black marble, and simply contains the names of the dead. The names, all 58,000 of them, are also contained in a book at the end of the wall. There are two and a half pages of Taylors.

I return to an empty apartment, as Phyllis is teaching tonight. The TV tells me that the Yankees have lost, thus missing the chance of moving closer to a post-season place. There are not many baseball games today, as Monday is quite commonly a rest day. But, as well as the Yankees' result, the evening sees the Mets lose, cutting their lead over Philadelphia to two, and San Diego lose, thus throwing away their lead in the National League wild card, where they are now level with the Phillies. Milwaukee manages to win though, so the Cubs are three ahead going into the last six games.

Maryland
Tuesday September 25

Phyllis is a gracious enough host to have given me her parking space in the underground garage. The downside of this is that we need to play hide and seek with her car, and move it before 9:00 this morning. So we set off relatively early and move it onto a friend's drive, return doing the peculiarly American thing of drinking Starbuck's coffee whilst walking, stroll to the local bagel shop, and sit by the fountain eating bagels and cream cheese by way of an al fresco breakfast.

The morning passes gently enough and, when Phyllis returns from her lunchtime meeting, we set off for Baltimore. Oriole Park at Camden Yards was the first of the new wave of ballparks, and is reputed to be one of the best, so I am excited about seeing it. But the first destination is a few blocks from the park, and is the Babe Ruth Museum, located in his birthplace. Ruth was born in this house, and in fact played first for Baltimore before being sold to Boston and then to the Yankees. The museum is a small terraced house, and contains a respectful tribute to the great man without going into too much detail.

Our ticket gives us entrance also to the Sporting Legends Museum, which is right next to the ground. This is a more extensive display, related directly to the teams and the athletes of Baltimore. The presentation of the stuff is quite innovative; an entire room is dedicated to Cal Ripken, Jr., one of the city's favourite sons, who holds the major league record for the most consecutive appearances— 2,632. This amounts to more than 16 seasons of playing 162 games a season, without missing a game.

We leave the museum and enter the ground. It is a beautiful, warm summer evening, and the sun is just setting over the stand. A visit to Boog Powell's is a must, a barbecue stand owned by a former local player and reputed to be one of the best. My barbecue beef sandwich is in the best American tradition, more filling than bread, and is delicious. We stand eating our sandwiches and watching batting practice and, at the appropriate juncture, grab a local brew and head for our seats. The park is indeed impressive, incorporating an old warehouse into its structure. Our seats have a first-class view, and it appears that all the reputations are well deserved.

Sadly the club does not have a team to match its stadium, and neither the Orioles nor the visiting Toronto Blue Jays have a chance of making the playoffs. So nothing is riding on the outcome. By the end of the third Toronto has a six-run lead, including a three-run homer from their famous slugger Frank Thomas, "the Big Hurt." In a more competitive game the pitcher may have been pulled at this point, but this one is allowed to struggle on. The game ends 11–4 to the Blue Jays.

The scoreboard does not bring much good news. A Cubs loss and a Milwaukee win reduce the lead in the NL Central to two games. The Yankees throw away a big lead, and thus fail to clinch their play off spot. The Mets and the Phillies both lose, so no change there; the only significant winner is San Diego, who once again edges in front in the wild card race.

Massachusetts
Wednesday September 26–Friday September 28

Phyllis, as usual, has commitments on Wednesday, so I take the opportunity of making an early start too. Once the early morning traffic starts to dissipate, the drive is not too bad; I'm becoming immune to I-95 and the New Jersey Turnpike, so I just pay the tolls and let it wash over me.

The weather is unseasonably hot, so it's not a bad day for driving in an air-conditioned car. Once I am past New York (after making exactly the same mistake as last time) the computer takes me along the Merritt Parkway, just as it did when I was driving into Connecticut three weeks ago. Autumn is that little bit further along, and the clumps of red amongst the green are becoming more pronounced.

The last bit of the journey takes me along the Mass Pike, which is the common vernacular for the Massachusetts Turnpike. It would appear that I am in a seriously sophisticated part of the country; the service stations on the Mass Pike have Lavazza and Ben and Jerry's, in New Jersey you get McDonald's!

My destination is Needham, a suburb of Boston, home of the Red Sox, my final major league visit on Friday. My hosts are Chip and Leca; Chip is a university friend of my neighbour Greg, and he and Leca live in a lovely house with Mark, the only one of their sons still at home. Leca is a teacher and Mark is a huge baseball fan, so there is never going to be a shortage of topics for conversation. The evening passes memorably in a huge downstairs den, with baseball on TV, dinner and drinks.

The Yankees manage a win, and so clinch the final playoff place for the American League; the niceties of who plays whom have still to be settled. The

National League is still no nearer resolution, with all teams seemingly trying hard to lose it. In the East the Mets again blow a lead, while Philadelphia wins— the gap is now just one game. In the Central the Cubs lose, but so does Milwaukee, so the gap remains at two. In the West Arizona loses, while third-place Colorado wins its tenth in a row, to severely test assumptions that it is a two-horse race. So it's still all to play for, with four days remaining.

I awake to a deserted house, and spend a relaxing morning taking advantage of yet more gracious hospitality, and responding to a few e-mails; I'm almost up to date now. Chip has arranged to take a few hours off work this afternoon and take me into Boston, and this is exactly what happens. Our first stop is at Fenway Park, home of the Boston Red Sox, where we are booked to see a game tomorrow. But today we are going to do the guided tour, and see behind the scenes. This is one of the great stadia of the world, and one of the shrines of baseball. It is now the oldest in the major leagues, but the thought of tearing it down and replacing it would be anathema to any Red Sox fan, so any extension is built upwards, and renovation is self-contained.

Until 2004, when they won the World Series after an 86-year gap, the Red Sox were the hard luck story of baseball. Similar to the Cubs, any number of bizarre events had taken place whenever they came close to winning, and the curse of the Bambino, which I have mentioned before, was blamed for everything. But in 2004 they won in spectacular fashion, and so the Red Sox Nation, as the fans style themselves, has little to complain about. They still hate the Yankees with a vengeance, but gloating is difficult even now they have won a World Series because, while they were waiting to do so, the Yankees won 26 of them.

The tour is interesting; our young guide is knowledgeable and enthusiastic. The ground is spectacularly idiosyncratic, and the left field wall features one of the most awesome sights in baseball, the Green Monster. This is a 37-foot wall, the sight of which greets opposing batters like a mountain, and which must be cleared in order to hit a home run on that side of the plate. Recently the club has placed seats on top of the Monster, the view from which is wonderful — at $140, it should be!

We see the press box and the executive lounges, and various parts of the outfield. As it's a game day, I guess that's about as far as it can go.

After a visit to the Bull and Finch, which proudly advertises itself as the bar on which the TV series "Cheers" was modelled, we head home for an evening of TV baseball, food and wine. The Cubs yet again fail to beat Florida, but fortunately San Diego beats Milwaukee to leave the Cubs still two games clear with three to play. The Mets lose and, due to Philadelphia's victory, have now managed to throw away the biggest lead in living memory. But no one is eliminated and, since Boston loses and the Yankees win, the American League match-ups are not yet decided either.

The main event of my time here is Friday evening's game at Fenway Park —

the Boston Red Sox against the Minnesota Twins. Chip, Mark and I drive into town just after five, and find a parking spot without too much trouble. As we approach the ground the atmosphere is tangible and traditional — there is nothing new or modern in sight. The Fenway Park of this evening is a different creature to the one I walked around yesterday. It's lit up, it's full to the brim, it's noisy and full of odours from the concession stands. The crowd is ready and waiting for the Red Sox to clinch the American League East.

The Boston pitcher is their expensive Japanese import, Daisuke Matsuzaka, Dice-K to the fans, and he pitches an excellent game, lasting eight innings. The Sox take an early lead, which gradually progresses to 4–0, and an easy win appears on the cards. But in the seventh a crushing Justin Morneau homer wakes up the Twins, and the lead is cut to 4–2. In the bottom of the eighth the crowd gets what it has been waiting for, a home run from its hero, "Big Papi" Ortiz. The closer, Papelbon, enters to the strains of "Wild Thing" and puts the game to bed, 5–2 to Boston.

Meanwhile the scoreboard tells us that the Yankees, Cubs and Brewers are all winning, so the respective races still have mileage in them. Returning home, we watch the scores come through. The Yankees lose their lead, and concede a winning run to Baltimore in the bottom of the tenth; Boston wins the American League East, Yankees take the wild card slot. The Brewers also give up their lead, and lose 6–3 to San Diego. That leaves the National League Central to the Chicago Cubs. The Mets lose again, the Phillies win again, so the Phillies are one up with two to play. In the West, Arizona has clinched a place, but San Diego and Colorado are still alive.

The Cubbies are in the playoffs, so after Hawaii I'll be Chicago bound. An e-mail from Channel 5 earlier today was to tell me they have found me a ticket for one of the playoff games in Chicago. Does it get any better?

Hawaii

Saturday September 29–Wednesday October 3

The household is awake and active early, so I seize the opportunity, and am on the road before 8:30. The journey south is largely familiar although, on this occasion, the computer uses a section of the I-95 I have not previously encountered. It is actually quite pleasant, taking me down the Connecticut coast. I even catch a glimpse of the Bridgeport Bluefish ground, scene of Sal's greatest triumph.

My destination is Philadelphia, in readiness for my big journey tomorrow. I have booked a room and parking deal with one of the airport hotels. By mid-afternoon I am safely ensconced in my room and, with the exception of a trip out for dinner, this is largely where I stay. I need to repack, to avoid taking my large suitcase on the plane, so there is the usual palaver of see-through bags for medicines and suchlike.

This also gives me the opportunity to keep track of the baseball developments. The televised game is only a few miles from where I sit, as Philadelphia attempts to consolidate its new lead over the Mets. The Mets started earlier, and won resoundingly to end their atrocious run. The Phillies, in front of a packed house, blow it completely, losing 4–2 after an error-ridden performance. So in the National League East the two teams are level with one game left.

In the National League West the Arizona Diamondbacks clinch the division before taking the field, thanks to San Diego's defeat. Arizona then loses to Colorado, who still has a chance of a wild card place. The wild card race is so close that there could be a four-way tie; this would be such a complicated situation that I'm not going to try and explain what would happen unless it actually does.

Earlier in this story, I wrote that my trip had reached the height of its mania, because I was taking a flight to Alaska — 1,700 miles for two nights. This time it's 4,500 miles for three nights, so the mania must really have taken hold. I have repacked my bags so that I don't have to check any luggage, so I am travelling with one small hold-all and a laptop. For the first time in ages my accent gets me into trouble; I ask to be dropped at Terminal E and end up at Terminal A. No problem, a shuttle bus appears and puts me in the right place, and I'm on my way.

The first leg is a relatively short hop to Atlanta, for which the plane is crowded. But everything happens on time, and we have those little screens in the seats so I can keep track of what's happening in those four crucial baseball games. When I leave the plane, Philadelphia is winning, the Mets are losing, and San Diego is winning, which would remove the need for any complex tie-breaking arrangements.

The second flight is also on time, but this time the in-flight entertainment is not quite so contemporary. For the first part of the flight there is no cloud cover, and it is fascinating to see first the desert and then the mountains from above. It looks vast and desolate when you're driving through it, from the air it looks like the moon! Once we get over the Pacific, the next major sight is the sunset. When you're travelling west the sunset lasts for a long time, and this one is particularly beautiful. It eventually goes dark around midnight Eastern Time, but by now my watch is reset to 6:00 P.M. Hawaii time.

We arrive on schedule. I have paid a little extra for transport to and from the hotel, and this includes a traditional greeting; so I am welcomed by a very short local lady who places a garland around my neck and kisses my cheek, which she only just achieves without the aid of a step ladder. She points me to my transport, and my plan of not checking in baggage appears to have worked perfectly until I realise that I have to sit and wait for the luggage of the people sharing my transport. Thirty minutes later I am at the Hawaiian Monarch Hotel, in a 14th-floor room with an amazing view of the Waikiki lights. It's 9:30 in the evening, but 3:30 A.M. tomorrow where I was this morning. So I decide to leave the sightseeing for now.

I put on the TV to get the final results, and the Mets and the Phillies have remained the same. So Philadelphia wins the National League East, and the Mets win a place in the record books for losing a seven-game lead with 17 to play. In the wild card race there has been a turnaround, and San Diego has lost. Colorado wins their game, and we have a tie. This means that tomorrow will see a one-game playoff between the two teams. After 162 games each, they still need one more to decide the winner.

Unsurprisingly, I wake early, but since I have an 8:30 pickup that's no bad thing. My lift is to a complementary breakfast hosted by the company that organises the transport package I bought. I know there's no such thing as a free breakfast, and I know they will try and sell me trips and tours, but since I might want to buy one, I'll take a chance. Breakfast is interesting; I sit opposite a nice couple from Seattle and chat away, drinking the pineapple juice and coffee that is offered. Soon in front of me is placed the Hawaiian take on an American breakfast: sausages, scrambled eggs, a potato cake, a slice of fresh pineapple, a chocolate muffin and a gardenia — all on the same plate. I manage it all except the gardenia.

We get some traditional Hawaiian music and dancing, and then a gentle-man tells us what he has on offer, stressing the fact that we must not waste a second of our time on Hawaii, and taking an inordinately long time to do so. Eventually we are asked to decide, and I spend $50 on a tour of the island tomorrow. This seems a sensible way of seeing a bit of the place in the short time I have here, and ends at 4:00, giving me time to get to the game in the evening.

Or so I think. I walk back to my hotel and ask the desk clerk how I might get to the stadium. He says a bus is my best bet, although it will take an hour and a half each way. But then he discovers there are none returning late in the evening. A taxi, he informs me, will cost $100 each way. He suggests I rent a car! I call Hawaii Winter Baseball to see if they have any suggestions—like giving me a lift — but they don't rise to the challenge. They do, however, give me their corporate account number for Enterprise, so that I can get their rate when I rent my car.

I walk a couple of hundred metres to the Enterprise office, and arrange a car hire. They quote me $30, which is a slight improvement. Back to the hotel, and I e-mail Hawaii Winter Baseball's publicist, and the local paper, in case they are interested in me. The publicist calls back within the hour, is very inter-ested, and offers me a lift to the game tomorrow!! Enterprise is very under-standing when I cancel the car rental.

Meanwhile the playoff game has started on TV, so I settle down to watch.

Colorado appears to have the momentum from their recent successful run, and takes an early two-run lead. In the second a Torrealba home run makes it three. Then, from out of nowhere, San Diego loads the bases in the third, and Gonzalez hits a grand slam to put his team ahead. They add one more later in the inning to make it 5–3. The stadium in Denver, being a mile above sea level, has a reputation as a hitters' park, as the thin air helps the ball travel further. This theory is borne out in the bottom of the third, when Helton hits the third home run of the game to cut the deficit to one. Colorado squares it in the fifth with a couple of good hits.

In the bottom of the sixth a relatively unknown pinch-hitter called Seth Smith hits a towering triple, and a sacrifice fly brings him home. Tulowitzki hits a second triple, but can't get home, so it stays at 6–5. In the top of the eighth, a misplay in the outfield leads to a San Diego run, and the game is tied at six. As sudden death playoffs go, this is getting quite exciting. And it stays that way, nailbiting with no further score. This is getting worse; they can't decide who's best after 162 games, so they have a playoff, and they can't decide that within the normal frame.

When it gets to the 11th, I decide to give up, or else I won't get to see Waikiki at all. So I stroll along the beach, have a beer at a beach bar, and then turn into town. It's a bit like Oxford Street, only with a beach running parallel; lots of big designer shops, interspersed with cheap gift shops, and people thrusting leaflets at you for restaurants, trips and massage parlours. There's a lot that's tacky and stereotypical, and it's a little disappointing. I head out of the crowd and nearer to my hotel before eating. I have spotted a Thai place with seats outside, and it proves a wise choice.

Back at the hotel, I check the result, and it seems I was wise to leave when I did. There was no more score until the 13th, when another homer gave San Diego a two-run lead. But the Rockies came back with two doubles and a triple to tie the game, and a sacrifice fly drove in the winning run; Colorado wins, 9–8.

So the lineup for the Divisional Series is complete; in the American League it's Anaheim against Boston and the Yankees against Cleveland; in the National League the Cubs play Arizona and Colorado plays Philadelphia. Each is a best-of-five series, with the second-named team having home advantage. This means they host the first two games, travel to the next two, and come home again for the fifth. Once one team has won three the series ends.

At 7:15 the next morning I find myself waiting outside the hotel, almost awake, ready for my tour of the island. Our driver introduces himself as cousin Dave. Hawaiians have these euphemisms which they feel delight tourists. Every other Hawaiian is referred to as "cousin" (it's a polite way of describing inbreeding); the rain, which appears briefly each morning, is known as "blessings." But I wish they didn't find it necessary to explain this to you on every occasion.

As we wait to leave my phone rings. It's Erik from Channel 5; it seems there is still some doubt over my Cubs ticket for the weekend, so we can only wait and see.

So off we set around the island, with a non-stop commentary from cousin Dave. We are taken to a blow hole, where the waves are forced through a hole in the volcanic rock to create a water spout. The stops seem to alternate between scenes of natural beauty, and opportunities for us to buy local stuff. The first of the latter is a coral shop, so keen for us to come in that they offer free drinks, and use of their rest rooms, just to get us in the shop.

So, after the Pali lookout, which gives us a wonderful view of Honolulu, and nearly blows our heads off, we stop for lunch at a pineapple plantation, where it's possible to buy all things pineapple. Next we have the macadamia nut centre. You might be detecting a theme now. We finish the tour with a visit to a Buddhist temple, tucked away behind a cemetery, and cousin Dave ensures I am back at my hotel in good time for my lift.

My evening is totally unexpected in many aspects. Dave Rolf is an American living in Hawaii, who has his own advertising agency. One of his clients is Hawaii Winter Baseball, which is why his name is on their website, and why he has responded to my e-mail. He picks me up outside my hotel, and is immediately enthusiastic about my adventure. Before we have gone a mile, he receives a call from the president of HWB, who needs a press release putting out for tomorrow's game. So we double back to Dave's office, and I sit and enjoy a stunning view of Honolulu while he deals with the press release.

Jumping back in the car, he tells me he wants to show me something on the way to the game, and we stop at the cemetery. Here lies Alexander Joy Cartwright, an American who, before moving to Hawaii, put together the game of baseball as we know it today. I know that, while I was in Cooperstown, I gave you the legend of Abner Doubleday, and said that its veracity was in doubt. Well, Cartwright's is the version of which most historians now approve.

We then move on to the stadium, where Dave has arranged for us to be met by a local TV reporter, who just happens to have been born near Sevenoaks. So I spend the first half of the game sitting in the stand, pretending not to notice being filmed, and answering some very interesting questions. I then proceed to the press box, where a guy who used to work in the major leagues is doing a ball-by-ball commentary for local radio. That's a skill you just have to admire. We finish the evening in what Dave calls the "sky box." Imagine a small cricket pavilion with an open front, about 15 feet up a hill to the side of the pitch, with a completely uninterrupted view; add a hamburger, a root beer, and a beautiful Hawaiian evening, and you will appreciate that my parting memory of Hawaii is a very fond one.

And in case you're interested, West Oahu Cane Fires beat Waikiki Beach Boys, 14–4.

I sleep soundly after such a full schedule. Because of the time difference, the playoffs are starting at 9:00 A.M., the first game between Colorado and Philadelphia. But I have a couple of things I want to do in town, so I set off just as the game is starting. I want to post a couple of cards, get some breakfast and buy a book on Hawaiian birds. All of this is accomplished fairly quickly, and I return to the hotel to find Colorado with a 3–0 lead. I need to sort myself out and pack, as my shuttle arrives at 12:00. While I'm doing this, Philadelphia hits two home runs to close the gap but, just as I am leaving, Colorado scores again to make it 4–2. As I leave it's the end of the eighth.

There are two schools of thought when it comes to flying through multiple time zones. The first is that you don't change your watch until you arrive, the second that you change it as you board the plane, to sooner get used to where you are going. In the first instance, I arrive in Atlanta at midnight, and it's just getting light; in the second instance, I leave Hawaii at 9:30 in the evening, in broad daylight. Whichever way you look at it, I miss out on a night's sleep.

Divisional Series, Chicago
Thursday October 4–Saturday October 6

Arriving in Atlanta, everything goes relatively smoothly. I board my flight for Philadelphia, there is a 30-minute delay, but that's all. The shuttle takes me to the hotel where I have left my car. I head west in the general direction of Chicago. Two things prevent me from getting to Chicago tonight; first, it's almost 800 miles, second, I want to go to sleep! I manage the first hundred miles with little difficulty, then stop for lunch. A short while later, I am very attracted to a rest stop somewhere on the I-80; I push the seat back and close my eyes.

When I suddenly wake up, it's three o'clock. I have no idea what time I went to sleep. I know that all I have to do is go west on the I-80 until I get tired. The radio is just starting to broadcast Game 2 of the Rockies at the Phillies. It turns out there was no further score yesterday; today the Rockies dominate again, winning, 10–5. So they lead the series 2–0 without having yet played a home game.

In yesterday's other games Arizona beat the Cubs 3–1, after the Cubs manager pulled the starting pitcher to save him for Sunday. I hope he's worked out that if they don't win today or Saturday, there won't be a game on Sunday. Boston beat Anaheim, 4–0, with pitcher Josh Beckett throwing a complete game.

By 5:30 I have had enough, so I pull off and find a motel. I catch the end of the Philadelphia game, and then the Cleveland game starts. The first round of the playoffs has been given to a different TV company, and they have obviously negotiated start times with the clubs to provide wall-to-wall baseball. The Yankees take a first-inning lead, and I go out to dinner.

By the time I return to my room Cleveland leads, 6–3, and this quickly becomes 11–3. It finishes 12–3. Next it's the Cubs' turn; they take a 2–0 lead in the second on a Soto homer, but a three-run homer from Young puts Arizona ahead. A Byrnes triple makes it 4–2, and then Arizona piles it on, 8–2. In the sixth a Ward pinch-hit brings it back to 8–4, but that's how it ends.

I'm getting tired now; six months of stuff like this is enough for anyone. When I first arrived I convinced myself it wasn't worth missing home, because I knew it was so far away. But now it's less than four weeks, and it's becoming a tangible. But first it's back to Wrigley Field, to pray for the impossible.

The missing night's sleep catches up with me, and I don't wake until after 8:00: so by the time I hit the road, it's 9:30. The drive is long, but not unpleasant and, since 95 percent of it is I-80, there are no complicated directions to think about. Pennsylvania is a lovely state, and heavily wooded. So at this time of the year the colours of the trees are changing daily. Ohio follows, then Indiana, and finally Illinois.

The first interruption of the day is a phone call from Erik. He tells me the bad news; tickets for the weekend games were impossible to get hold of. I am not surprised, but then comes the bombshell, "...so I got you a press pass instead!" I am speechless!

My mind flashes back to a conversation I had with Sally several years back, which in many ways was the genesis of what is now happening. She asked me what job I would choose if I could start my career again. I said I would like to be a sports journalist. Now I'm going to be sitting in the press box of one of the world's great stadia, as special correspondent for a national TV company! I pull over and take a break while I shed tears of joy and incredulity.

The drive goes well, and by 5:00 I have done 475 miles. Unfortunately, the remaining 20 miles takes another three hours, through Chicago traffic and roadworks. The radio is broadcasting Game 2 of the Yankees at Cleveland. The Yankees score early, and then the pitchers take over. The score remains the same until Lake Shore Drive, at which point I lose reception.

As I check in to my hotel, the desk clerk is watching on TV, and it is now 1–1. By the time I have settled into my room, the game is in the tenth. When I arrive at the restaurant, it is the 11th, and many of the customers cheer as Cleveland pieces together the winning run to go two ahead in the series. The captions have been showing a 2–0 Boston lead in the other game. No one is surprised as they are hot favourites. But when the TV switches to this game, Anaheim has gone ahead, 3–2.

Back to my room, and Boston brings the game level. Another close one, but Boston eventually wins it in the bottom of the ninth with a Manny Ramirez walk-off homer. That means each of the four series stands at 2–0, so the next two days could be decisive.

I awaken on Saturday to an e-mail from Erik; smart casual, it appears, is how one dresses for a press box; and one does not cheer. I had planned to appear in a grubby mac with a trilby hat into which I could tuck my press pass; but perhaps not. Chicago post-season baseball has a secret weapon, the weather. Get the southern softies into Wrigley Field, with sub-zero temperatures and a driving wind, and all will be well. Today the temperature is in the high 80s, with excessive humidity, so I wonder what plan B is.

First pitch is at 5:00, but I am in Wrigleyville before 1:00, determined to savour the atmosphere. I take a leisurely lunch, and then wander around the outside of the stadium, watching the crowd gradually assemble. The gates are due to open at 3:00, but at 2:30 I notice that there are people going in through the gate where I have been told to collect my pass, so in I go.

The people on the gate are quite excited at my arrival, a British "reporter" at a Cubs game being quite a novelty. I am given my pass and directed to the interview room, a concrete bunker under the stands, where my fellow hacks are assembled, waiting for their next victim. This turns out to be Ryan Theriot, the Cubs' shortstop. He is asked the usual questions and provides the usual answers; nothing earth-shattering there. There is a protracted gap before the next person arrives, so I wander off to the playing area, to which my pass gives me access.

Seeing some others with passes like mine, I follow them through the gate, and stand just behind home plate, watching the players start to warm up and wondering what to do. I see a suited gentleman whom I recognise as Jim Hendry, the Cubs' general manager, holding court with a small group. I eavesdrop, and it appears to be a social conversation about anything other than baseball. When a suitable gap occurs, I introduce myself. He looks impressed that I am here, and we chat about Scotland, golf and drinking.

Next I spot a woman whose name I recognise, Carrie Muskat. I read her stuff daily on the Cubs' website, and it's good to say hallo and thank her. I then witness the arrival of Ernie Banks, "Mr. Cub," a playing legend from the 50s and 60s. He is here to throw out the first pitch. Only a couple of weeks back, I was looking at his plaque in the Hall of Fame, now I'm looking at him.

It does not seem the done thing to talk to the players, so I stand and observe. Just then, a member of the club's staff nearby is beckoned by a steward, who informs him that the Reverend Jesse Jackson is here, and would like to come on the field for some photos. He agrees, and the Reverend and his minders emerge through the gate by which I am standing. As I am the first person he sees, he shakes my hand and I introduce myself. He smiles winningly but says nothing, presumably thinking that I know who he is. Maybe he is also quick-thinking enough to realise that someone from England does not have a vote, because the exchange ends there.

It's now an hour to game time, so I go in search of my seat. The press box is in the highest part of the stand, and it's a long way up. Eventually getting there, I find a chart which tells me that I am in the auxiliary seating, out in left field. The view is amazing; I am looking down on the whole field, from quite

Divisional Series — Wrigley Field from the press box, looking down on Cubs fans inside and outside the park, with my Channel 5 press pass ensuring that my ambition to be a sport journalist is fulfilled.

a height admittedly, and I can see the Cubs fans without tickets milling around in the streets, and the whole Chicago skyline.

It is the first post-season game at Wrigley this year, so we get the full works, with all the players and staff being introduced to the crowd. The fans are boisterous, full of expectation, but the very first pitch to Young, the Diamondbacks' leadoff hitter, is slugged for a home run. They score again later in the inning, and the writing is on the wall. The Cubs do little right; both teams score in the fourth, but the fifth proves crucial. After a series of mind games between pitcher and hitter, a walk loads the bases for the Cubs with only one out. But DeRosa hits into a double play, one of four in the game, and the chance is gone. The final score is 5–1 to Arizona, and they take the series, 3–0.

This is my third visit to Wrigley Field, but my first at night. It is a sight that will long live with me, particularly when the crowd desperately tries to lift the team at key moments. Why nobody on either team realises that they are spoiling a wonderful ending to a potentially best-selling book is beyond me. This has probably cost me thousands of sales in the Chicago area and, in this litigious society, I am giving serious thought to suing the Diamondbacks for loss of earnings.

Back at the hotel, I tell them I'll be checking out in the morning; the strange thing is that, for the first time in six months, I don't know where I'll be going. The TV shows Colorado one up against Philadelphia. The Phillies tie it up, but in the eighth a pinch hit single gives the Rockies a 2–1 lead, which they hang on to. So both National League series have ended in 3–0 sweeps.

Divisional Series, Cleveland

Sunday October 7–Monday October 8

There is no time for mourning; despite the Cubbies' demise there are still playoff games happening. Anaheim and New York are both too distant for a one-day drive, so I decide to drive to Cleveland and watch the Indians vs. Yankees game in a bar near the ground. It is a six-hour drive, and I am going to lose an hour en route, so I get an early start. The weather is again unseasonably warm and humid. As I drive south on Lake Shore Drive, I notice certain turnoffs closed due to the Chicago Marathon and, sure enough, I soon see a huge body of runners going past me in the opposite direction.

I toy with the idea of doing a u-turn, to see if anyone wants a lift, but decide to keep going. I know there are enthusiasts out there but, for me, a marathon holds no attraction either as a participation or spectator sport. Marathons did at one time attract my enthusiasm, but then they changed the name to Snickers and the moment was lost. Incidentally, later in the day I hear that the marathon has been cut short due to the weather, and that several people have been hospitalized. Why wouldn't they listen to me?

The drive to Cleveland is without incident. As I near my destination the radio tells me that Boston has a two-run lead in the third game against Anaheim. After settling into my room I watch the remainder of the game, and it's not really a contest. Boston wins, 9–1, and so three series have finished in a sweep. It's all down to the Yankees.

I head for Local Heroes, the bar opposite the ground last visited in August. On my way there a scalper asks me if I need tickets, which I find curious as the game is in New York. When I get to the bar I find that the game is being shown in the ballpark on a giant screen, which is what the tickets were for; the club had given out the tickets free, so the scalper was chancing his arm somewhat.

As a result the bar is not as crowded as I had assumed, but the few people in there are enthusiastic. Cleveland scores in each of the first three innings, and the fans are cheerful. The guy next to me keeps predicting things just before they happen. I ask him for next week's lottery numbers. He laughs and says, "Gimme some butter — I'm on a roll!"

The Yankees pitcher, Roger Clemens, has elbow and hamstring trouble, and exits in the third. We witness possibly the end of an extraordinary career. New York pulls a run back, and then a hideous error from Cleveland's Nixon turns a one-run hit into three. The Yankees go on to win, 8–4, and we have a Game 4 tomorrow.

Just before the end, a crowd of Indians fans comes in, and I get chatting to a guy named Pedro. He tells me he has a spare ticket for the big screen tomorrow, and says I can have it. So I return to my hotel and book in for another night.

Nothing on my schedule until Monday evening, so I take the first opportunity for a week or so to take it easy; sleep late, shave, do laundry. I don't actually leave my hotel until 1:00, and stroll to the warehouse district, an area of Cleveland that has been revitalised and has lots of apartment blocks and restaurants. There is a visible excitement in the city; a win in New York this evening will take the Indians to the Championship Series, and to do so against the Yankees would be icing on the cake. Even the buses have "Beat the Yanks" where their destination should be.

Around 4:00 I get a call from Pedro, who has got me a ticket for the big screen showing of tonight's game. So around 6:30 I meet him in the same bar as last night, have a quick beer, and off we go. Pedro is a diehard Indians fan, and turns out with his face painted red, white and blue, and wearing a feathered headdress. There are around 10,000 fans in the ground, and there is a festival atmosphere.

Cleveland starts well, with a home run in the first at-bat. By the second, they lead, 4–0, and the Yankees' starter has left the game. By the fourth inning it is 6–1, and the crowd is loud and confident. The Yankees get a run back in the sixth, and another in the seventh. The crowd is standing going into the ninth with a three-run lead, but the Yankees get another homer to make it 6–4. Posada then hits another blast, but it is foul by inches. Victory to Cleveland, and the streets of the city are immediately full of cars with horns honking, and passengers screaming from the windows.

I am quietly envious that I didn't get to be part of this in Chicago, but delighted to be part of it at all. Cleveland now faces Boston in a best-of-seven series for the American League, while Arizona and Colorado do likewise for the National League. Since 2000, no team has won the World Series more than once; a Cleveland-Colorado World Series would ensure that this record is maintained, so that's what I'll be hoping for, with apologies to Boston and Arizona fans.

Championship Series

Tuesday October 9–Sunday October 21

Cleveland's victory last night left Wednesday's Game 5 unnecessary. My chances of travelling to Arizona or Colorado are slim, therefore my next baseball commitment is Friday night back in Cleveland.

First time around, I was unable to visit Nashville, without which no musical tour of the States is complete. So I am taking advantage of this four-day break to remedy the omission. It's 530 miles from Cleveland, and I plan to do the majority on Tuesday, so I should get almost a full day in the city.

First thing this morning, I walked back to the Indians' stadium, to see if there were any big screen tickets being given away yet. No sign of life there, so I leave a message on Pedro's phone and I'm on my way. The drive is very straightforward, I-71 most of the way. Kentucky in particular is beautiful at this time of year, and the route goes past Churchill Downs, the venue of the Kentucky Derby.

On Wednesday morning, the final hundred miles of my journey south are completed quite quickly, and by 10:30 I'm having breakfast in Nashville. Nashville is the capital of country music, and its cathedral is the Grand Ole Opry. So I spend the morning there, inspect the museum and wander round the delightful plaza where the theatre is located.

From there I drive into Nashville itself and find a place to park near my next destination, the Country Music Hall of Fame. This is a stunningly elegant building. After buying your ticket, you take a lift to the third floor and take winding walkways downwards.

The museum is beautifully done, and the Hall of Fame itself is simple and beautiful, similar to its baseball counterpart in Cooperstown. I spend a peaceful couple of hours taking it in, then move on to my downtown hotel, and write until late afternoon, when I decide to go and discover Nashville. Basic research tells me that most of the live music is to be found on Broadway, which is just a couple of blocks from where I am staying.

After a leisurely dinner, I return along Broadway, and decide I should see some live music while in Nashville. I dive into a club at random, and it proves to be an inspired choice. Playing is the Don Kelley Band, three scruffy middle-aged guys, with a 22-year-old guitarist who has just stepped out of the 70s, with black shirt and frock coat to match. They play a fine selection of country tunes, some of which I recognise: "Crazy Arms," "Together Again," "Sixteen Tons," "You Win Again." But the highlight of the show is an instrumental version of "Ghost Riders in the Sky," in which the young guitarist goes through his full repertoire, playing with his teeth, behind his head, all with dazzling skill. If Hendrix had lived long enough to record a country album, it might have sounded something like this.

I now have two days to do a journey I could almost do in one. So I decide to go where the spirit takes me, and head off in a general northerly direction. One of the things I have largely been unable to do so far is to spend time looking at the countryside; I usually see it from the interstate as I wing from one destination to another.

I decide to take lunch and ponder the rest of the day. It occurs to me that I will soon be leaving Kentucky, and thus the south, for possibly the last time. I had not realised before this trip how strong the dividing line between the north and south still is; they might have sorted out the trivial stuff like civil rights, but I believe it is still a federal offence to cook candied yams or collard greens north of the Mason-Dixon Line. So I find a Shoney's (also illegal in the north), and I am in luck — the buffet has fried chicken and candied yams. I eat my fill, and wonder if I can learn how to make this stuff at home.

I remember one of my rules for travelling: always head for somewhere, even if you don't get there. So I consult my map and head for a Wildlife Conservation Centre; within half an hour I am sitting in the reception area of the Heaven Hill Bourbon Heritage Centre. See, the theory works! After an interesting tour, we finish, of course, with a tasting of the 12-year-old and the 18-year-old. Our guide gives us an interesting lesson on how to taste and what to look for, and splendid it is too.

I drive for another hour or so, and then find a motel in Carrollton. I change back to Eastern Time, so an hour disappears. The National League Championship Series starts tonight so, having had a good lunch, I pop out for some takeaway and settle into my room; Game 1—Arizona Diamondbacks vs. Colorado Rockies. The Championship Series are best of seven. Arizona has home field advantage, and so hosts the first two games. Arizona scores in the first,

Colorado draws level in the second, and then breaks the game open with three in the third. The game finishes 5–1 to Colorado, thus giving them a 1–0 lead in the series.

On Friday I return again to Cleveland, in preparation for the American League Championship Series. On my journey, I decide to check out some sports talk radio. In last night's game there was a controversial incident in the seventh inning. In baseball, when a double play looks likely, it is acceptable for the runner going to second to slide at the baseman, in order to disrupt his throw to first. It is generally deemed fair if the runner is within reach of the base when he attempts to hit the fielder.

On this occasion, the runner, whilst getting back to his feet, threw himself at the fielder. The umpire gave interference, which meant that the runner was out, the runner at first was also out, and the runner going to third had to return to second. All this occurred at a point when Arizona was threatening to get back into the game, so the decision was not taken kindly by the home fans, who started to throw stuff on the field. The game was delayed for eight minutes, and there were several arrests. For the record, the vast majority of sports commentators this morning were saying the umpire's decision was correct, and the Arizona fans were out of order.

Back to Friday, and back to Cleveland, and back to my usual hotel in good time for a rest before the game. At 6:30, I head for the bar and find no sign of anyone I know. So, without a ticket for the big screen I decide to stay and watch the game. Friday is no different here than anywhere else, and the bar is full and loud.

Each team is starting with its top pitcher, Beckett for Boston and Sabathia for Cleveland, two of the season's best performers. Beckett starts as expected and strikes out the first two batters, but then Travis Hafner hits him into the crowd to put Cleveland ahead. Boston pieces together a run in the bottom of the first, and from then on takes control of the game. Sabathia fails to rise to the occasion, twice walking in runs with the bases loaded. He leaves the game with his team trailing, 7–1.

At this point most of the bar has lost interest, so I head back to the hotel to see the game end 10–3 to Boston, while Game 2 of Colorado vs. Arizona has kicked off on a different channel. Colorado has taken an early lead. In the third the Arizona pitcher comes up to bat, and surprises everyone by hitting the ball into the outfield and driving in the equalising run. This game is much more of a contest than the earlier one, and the game remains tight. In the fifth a sacrifice fly from the veteran Helton puts Colorado ahead again.

It looks like staying this way, but in the bottom of the ninth Arizona scratches out a run to take the game into extra innings. Bear in mind that, because of the time difference, the game started at 10:00 P.M. here, so, as the tenth comes and goes, it is nearing 2:00 A.M. My eyes tell me I have gone an inning too far.

They were right — it's 9:30 when I wake next morning. Once I am able to focus, I put on the TV, which informs me that the game didn't last much longer than I did last night. Colorado scored in the top of the 11th on a bases-loaded walk, and held on to take the game. That means they take a two-game lead back to their own stadium. Today is a rest day for them, and I'm staying in Cleveland for Game 2 of the Indians-Boston series.

The problem with staying in Cleveland for evening games is that you have to find something to do during the day. I wander off in search of breakfast but, before leaving, check the list that I made before leaving on my trip. This reminds me that Cleveland is the birthplace of rock and roll, and I have the address of the building where it allegedly started. Coincidentally, it is in the same street as my hotel, so I check it out on my way to breakfast.

Back in the 50s, 1375 Euclid Avenue was the headquarters of WJW radio, and Alan Freed was working as a disc jockey for them when he supposedly became the first person to use the phrase "rock 'n' roll." The building has been completely re-styled in the last few years, but it is still owned by an entertainment concern, and is holding theatre workshops as I pass.

On my way back from breakfast, I call in at the Indians' club shop, and manage to acquire a couple of tickets for the big screen showing of tonight's game. They are free, so it gives me the choice of watching outside or inside depending on the weather.

I spend the afternoon listening on the internet to England beat France in the semi-final of the Rugby Union World Cup. I also try to book a hotel for my return to Cleveland next week, but find that my usual hotel is full, as are all the other city centre hotels. It seems Boston is moving to Cleveland en masse. I settle for a hotel by the airport, which will mean having to drive in and find somewhere to park.

Around 6:30 I wander into the centre for some dinner, and then head for the ballpark. I arrive in good time for the 8:20 start. The game is a good one, with much ebb and flow. Cleveland goes ahead in the first with a Martinez double, but in the third Ramirez draws a bases-loaded walk, again, and a Lowell hit scores two to put the Sox ahead, 3–1. Next inning, though, Cleveland puts two on base, and a home run from Jhonny (yes, that's how you spell it!) Peralta gives them a 4–3 lead. The lead is extended with a Sizemore homer in the fifth, but back-to-back homers give Boston a 6–5 lead. Cleveland scrambles an equalising run in the sixth, and then the bullpens take some sort of control.

Although exciting, the game is one of the slowest I have witnessed and by the time it reaches the end of the ninth it is 12:45. The temperature has dropped, and I decide to hurry back to the hotel to watch the extra innings. In the top of the 11th Cleveland puts in Trot Nixon as a pinch-hitter. Nixon is a former Boston player, and he breaks the tie with a hit to right. This opens the floodgates, and the Boston bullpen falls apart. A couple more hits make it 10–6, and then a three-run homer by Guttierez seals Boston's fate. Cleveland wins

13–6, and the series returns to Cleveland level. After 5 hours and 14 minutes, those who stayed in the stadium deserve medals.

Sunday is a rest day, so I drive the 140 miles to Pittsburgh to spend the day with my old friends Steve and Liz. While answering some e-mails, I read an article, sent to me by a friend in England, about the Colorado Rockies. Apparently, their owner, general manager and team manager, along with some of the players, are born-again Christians. The club actively recruits Christian players, who are encouraged to attend chapel on Sunday and prayer meetings on Tuesday. The odd thing is that Major League Baseball does not appear very keen on that, because whenever it is mentioned in an interview, it does not appear on any of the highlight shows. Say what you will, the Rockies have now won 19 of their last 20 games.

Tonight's only game is indeed in Colorado. The stadium in Denver has a reputation as a "hitters' park"; at high altitude, the ball has a tendency to fly further, and statistics for pitchers playing there tend to have a negative skew. In the bottom of the first, Matt Holliday homers to give Colorado the lead. In the top of the fourth, Mark Reynolds does the same for Arizona, and the game is tied. In the sixth Colorado puts two men on base, and Yorvit Torrealba (yes, that's his real name) homers to put the Rockies 4–1 ahead. That's how it stays, Colorado has a 3–0 series lead, and Arizona is looking down the barrel. Colorado has now won 20 of its last 21 games.

I stay in Pittsburgh until late next morning, and take a leisurely drive back towards Cleveland. I detour on a couple of occasions to see some of the Ohio countryside, and get to Cleveland around 3:00. When I say Cleveland, I actually mean a hotel somewhere near the airport, around eight miles from the centre.

I plan to watch the game in the bar opposite the ground, so I deliberately wait as late as possible, so that those attending will have gone in, and the congestion will have died down. I am a little concerned about parking, but last week, while walking from my hotel to the ground, I would walk past several car parks charging between $5 and $10. I discover, to my horror, that these same car parks are tonight charging from $25 to $30. So I drive a little further away from the ground, and park on a meter, free after 6:00. An extra five minutes' walk has saved me $30.

I arrive at the bar shortly after the first pitch, and settle onto a bar stool. My face is becoming known now, and I receive a friendly welcome from the bar staff. In the second inning, Kenny Lofton, a veteran player who began his career here and has recently returned, hooks a ball just over the fence to give Cleveland a two-run lead. The bar suddenly becomes louder and less tense. Cleveland adds two more in the fifth, putting Boston's starter, the mysterious Matsuzaka, out of the game. Cleveland's Jake Westbrook, who was definitely the less touted of the two starters, is meanwhile pitching a blinder. He holds Boston scoreless until the seventh, when Varitek hits a two-run homer to give Boston hope and put Westbrook out of the game. The bar suddenly becomes a very nervy place, but Cleveland's bullpen holds on, giving the Indians a 4–2 win and a 2–1 lead in the series.

I get back to the hotel to find Arizona with a 1–0 lead in Game 4 of the other series, but Colorado is obviously just waiting for me to arrive. In the bottom of the fourth a double, a single and a three-run homer give them a 6–1 lead. Arizona comes back into it late on, but the game finishes 6–4 to Colorado, giving them a series sweep and putting them in the World Series for the first time in their relatively short history.

On Tuesday I kill time at the zoo, then return to my hotel for food and rest. I set off for the city, again find a free parking meter, and head for the bar. The first good news of the evening is that Great Lakes, the local brewery, has released its Christmas Ale, so I settle down over a pint (heavy on the nutmeg!) and watch the game. Nothing much happens in the top of the first, and I am drinking deliberately slowly, as I have to drive home. Then one of the bar staff asks me if I want a ticket. He has a $70 ticket which he has been unable to get rid of, and I can have it for $25. I consider his proposition carefully for a tenth of a second before biting his hand off. I'm in!

The only remaining problem is nine-tenths of a pint, which is quite cold and fizzy, but I manage it and set off across the road. I find my seat, just by the first base-side foul pole, and settle in. The club has issued everyone coming in with a white bar towel, with the words "It's Tribe time" inscribed in red, and at crucial points in the game the entire crowd rises, screams, and waves these things around. It's an amazing sight.

By the time the fifth starts, my bladder is reminding me that I drank a cold pint very quickly, and my stomach is reminding me of my plans to eat at the bar, so in the middle of the inning I set off to rectify both problems. The queue for the toilet is six deep, but the atmosphere is very jocular. A roar from outside tells us we have missed something, and a guy runs in and shouts, "Casey Blake! Home run!" He is shouted down as a wind-up merchant by the assembled cast. Emerging from the men's room, I notice from the overhead TV that Cleveland is one up. I ask someone in the burger queue what happened, and he says, "Casey Blake! Home run!" Hmm!

Meanwhile I see from the TV that Gutierrez has singled and Shoppach, the catcher, has been hit by a pitch ("taken one for the team"). Sizemore hits into a fielder's choice, which puts runners at first and third. So when Cabrera hits a dribbler off the pitcher for an infield hit, another run scores. Hafner is out swinging, two out, and it seems the bleeding has been staunched, but when Martinez grounds to left another run scores, and an end is called for Boston's starter.

I take this as a chance to get back to my seat, and find my neighbours somewhat elated. Boston's new pitcher, Delcarmen, sees his fourth pitch to Peralta deposited into the crowd, and Cleveland leads by six. Kenny Lofton comes in and singles, then steals second, so a single from Casey Blake (remember him from the start of the inning?) drives in Lofton for a seventh run.

Boston is stunned, so much so that their first batter, Youkilis, smacks a homer; so does Ortiz. That signals the end of the evening for the Cleveland pitcher, Byrd, who receives a standing ovation. His replacement starts by giving up yet another home run to Ramirez; 7–3. The game then settles down. Both sides threaten, the crowd roars Cleveland on, we stand up a lot, sit down a lot, wave our towels a lot; and at the end of it all there are no more runs and Cleveland has a 3–1 lead in the series.

The city is buzzing as I head back to the car. Horns sounding, people dancing around, a city celebrating. The traffic is appalling, but no one really cares. It takes me an hour to get out of the city and back to the motel. But what an evening!

No baseball on Wednesday, so I take a quiet drive over to Williamsport, Pennsylvania, the headquarters of Little League Baseball. I'll have a look at the museum tomorrow and drive back to Cleveland in time for the game.

I drive along I-80, while the radio talks of nothing but Cleveland's impressive display last night. But, oddly, the main topic of conversation is Manny Ramirez, who hit the third of Boston's three home runs. Manny is Boston's star, and a former Cleveland player to boot. When he hits a game-winning home run, his habit is to pause at the plate and raise his arms to the heavens before slowly circling the bases. This he did last night, seemingly oblivious to the fact that his team was still four runs behind.

He also glared at the pitcher and exchanged insults with his former teammates, both of which are definitely outside of baseball's unwritten code of etiquette. The usual reprisal for such behaviour is to have your pitcher throw at him, but as this was in the middle of a must-win game, it didn't happen. People were actually phoning in, expressing opinions as to whether they should throw at him tomorrow, or wait for a less important game next season. I didn't know whether to laugh or cry.

Thursday is my introduction to the world of Little League. Little League is organised baseball for kids, and it started in 1939 here in Williamsport. Since then, the three Pennsylvania teams have turned into thousands of teams worldwide, and Little League is big business. But its headquarters have remained right here.

The museum documents the changes in Little League structure over that time, with other countries starting to join in the 50s, girls being allowed to play in 1974, and so on. Perhaps the most interesting part of this rather small building is the Hall of Fame. This honours former Little Leaguers who have gone on to successful careers, not just in baseball, but also in other areas of society. Thus George W. Bush has been inducted, the first former Little Leaguer to achieve the presidency.

Other familiar faces include Kevin Kostner, whose support of baseball, and leading roles in films such as *Bull Durham* and *Field of Dreams*, is well documented. More surprisingly, Bruce Springsteen has been honoured; he is not widely known as a baseball supporter, although his song "Glory Days," which begins with a description of a baseball-playing friend from high school, is often played at ball games.

Behind the museum the valley opens up, and sitting snugly down the hill is a small baseball stadium, which is where the Little League World Series is played every year, regardless of the teams involved.

On the drive back to Cleveland, two stories are emerging. Manny Ramirez, subject of one controversy yesterday, is at it again. When interviewed last night about the possibility of losing tonight and being eliminated, he replied, "It wouldn't be the end of the world, there's always next year!" Now English is not Manny's first language, and something may have been lost in translation, but Boston fans are in an uproar. I fully expect the Cleveland fans to have something to say about it, and there may be some well-phrased banners around this evening.

The second big story is that Joe Torre, the Yankees' manager and a revered figure in baseball, was offered a one-year contract on a reduced salary, and turned it down. The feeling is that the offer was a dud, which they knew he would decline. No further negotiation took place, so he has effectively been dumped.

So to the evening, and I return to Local Heroes, the bar opposite the ballpark. Even on the way there, there is something different about the evening. The ticket touts are trying to buy tickets! The bar is heaving, and I manage to find a stool a couple of metres back from the bar. The crowd is loud, enthusiastic, and getting drunk quickly. Folks are desperate for a Cleveland win, to clinch the series without having to go back to Boston.

The pitching matchup is the same as for Game 1— Beckett for Boston, Sabathia for Cleveland. In Game 1 Sabathia was knocked about badly, and Boston won, 10–3. This evening Sabathia is much better, but Beckett is still almost unhittable. There is always the feeling that Boston is about to have a big inning, and Cleveland does well to hold the score to 2–1 until the sixth. In the seventh and eighth Boston slowly eases away, and the score finishes at 7–1. My plans to head to Virginia Beach for a few days' rest are scuppered, and I shall now need to be back in Cleveland for Saturday night, and perhaps Sunday.

So on Friday, instead of heading east, I'm looking for a way to fill a day. A glance at a map indicates that there is an area of water to the north, named Lake Erie. It's only the fourth largest of the Great Lakes and at 9,940 square miles, is only 1,700 times the size of Lake Windermere, but it might be worth a glance.

But before that, I have a job to do in Cleveland. I walk round to Jacobs Field, to collect tickets for Saturday's big screen viewing and, if necessary, Sunday's, then it's time to hit the road.

It's a very pleasing drive, and effectively fills a day before I spend the night in Toledo. I retrace my steps on Saturday, return to my now familiar Cleveland hotel, listen to an internet broadcast of the Rugby Union World Cup Final, and then fall asleep. By the time I wake, there is little time to do anything other than get ready for my evening.

I meet up with Pedro and a couple of his mates in Local Heroes, and we wander over to the ballpark, being interviewed for some documentary or other as we enter. Both teams have their number two pitchers starting, Schilling for Boston and Carmona for Cleveland. When they met in Game 2 of the series, neither got the win, as you may remember the game finished with that seven-run 11th inning.

Tonight Carmona doesn't look as good. In the bottom of the first, he loads the bases with nobody out. The crowd roars its support as he dismisses the next two batters, but then Drew connects with his next pitch for a grand slam — 4–0 Boston! A Martinez homer immediately pulls a run back, but the third is a disaster. Carmona is pulled and Cleveland gives up six, to give Boston a 10–1 lead.

The crowd quietens, but remains enthusiastic, joining in with the cheering and singing. I am intrigued by the fact that "Hang On Sloopy" by the McCoys, which those of you old enough to remember 1965 may recall, always receives a good response when played. It appears that it is the official rock song of Ohio, confirmed by a resolution of the Ohio General Assembly in 1985. Ohio is the only state with its own official rock song. If you recall the song, at the end of the chorus "*Hang on Sloopy! Sloopy hang on!*" the word "Yeah" is repeated four times. At this point the Ohians raise their hands above their heads, and shout "O-H-I-O" while forming the letters with their hands, similar to the "YMCA" dance.

They may enjoy that bit, but the final result is 12–2 to Boston, so we go to a Game 7 tomorrow. The game will be in Boston, but I will be watching with the Cleveland faithful on the big screen.

Cleveland is beginning to have a certain familiarity about it, which is comforting. Fortunately my room is available for another night, so there is no moving to be done today. I can't really plan tomorrow either, as I don't know whether I'll be staying around here or heading towards Boston. So I spend a relaxing morning on the usual maintenance, have a little drive around the university area, and go out to Starbuck's for coffee.

And so to the game; as I walk towards the bar, Pedro hails me from his car, and I wait while he parks. We walk to the bar together and he is visibly nervous. As we enter the ground he gets selected to take part in a "craziest fan" contest, and ends up winning $50!

The game gets underway, and Boston gets on top. Instead of a rush of runs, like last night, it is gradual. A run in each of the first three innings puts them comfortably ahead. Cleveland hangs in, scoring in the fourth and fifth to close to 3–2. The next couple of innings are unbearably tense, with a couple of bad coaching calls and umpiring decisions preventing Cleveland from levelling. In the seventh Boston scores two more, and the game is over as a contest. A rush of runs in the eighth makes the final score 11–2, and Boston advances to the World Series.

The crowd tries to feign cheerfulness; there are lots of handshakes and hopes for next season. Pedro walks me back to my car, full of regret for all the things we could have done next week. We exchange hugs and addresses, with him promising to visit England.

So, Boston advances to the World Series, and I advance to Boston.

The World Series
Monday October 22–Sunday October 28

Baldwinsville, New York, has, in my book, one thing going for it. It is 300 miles closer to Boston than Cleveland is. I freely admit that my assessment is based on one after-dark tour on Monday evening, but suffice to say that the restaurant at the top of the food chain is Pizza Hut.

The upcoming World Series will be between the Boston Red Sox and the Colorado Rockies. Rules are the same as for the Championship Series; two games in Boston, three in Denver, then two more in Boston. The first to win four games takes it. Boston is one of the oldest and wealthiest clubs in the league, with a team composed largely of experienced, well-paid players. Colorado is one of the most recent additions to the league, has one of the smallest payrolls, and has many young players. So the press is making the most of the contrasts; old vs. new, rich vs. poor, east vs. west, Sox vs. Rox!

My first peep through my bedroom window on Tuesday morning finds steady rain. I haven't experienced too much rain during this trip, so I suppose I shouldn't complain. Today is the last free day before the start of the World Series, so I decide to see a little more of Vermont. It will get me nearer to Boston, and give me another glimpse of this beautiful state. So I consult my magazine of hotel discounts, find a well-discounted hotel in what seems a nice area, and off I set.

The first 100 miles or so is I-90, and it's dire. If there's one thing worse than a crowded interstate, it's a crowded interstate in the rain. After a few more miles I leave the interstate and the sun peeps promisingly through the clouds, but it proves to be a false dawn; soon it's raining again. Vermont manages to be beautiful despite the rain. It's only a pity that I am unable to stop and enjoy some of the views.

Eventually I arrive in Ludlow. The next town is named Shrewsbury, so it's not difficult to work out which part of England the early settlers of these parts left behind. The hotel proves a little difficult to locate, probably because the name on the sign is not the same as the one in the magazine. But locate it I do and it is a fine country hotel, which will become a ski centre in a couple of months' time. My room is beautifully furnished, with a leather recliner and a flat screen TV; and my coupon lets me have it for $59. The one drawback is that I can't access the internet from my room, so I have to sit in the lobby. This is fine, except when I'm using Skype, and the other guests look at me as if I'm talking to myself.

After dinner, I return to my hotel in the rain, and settle down to watch my flat screen TV in my leather recliner. Before retiring, I check the curtains. It's stopped raining!

Wednesday starts gradually until I stroll to the lobby to pick up my e-mails. There's one from Erik asking me to call him so that we can meet up in Boston. So I'd better get to Boston! I quickly pack up my things and hit the road. The drive is very interesting, but not very quick, as the route keeps me away from the interstate. The road signs are like an American history book; Concord, Lexington, Harvard, Princeton, and eventually Boston.

As usual it's impossible to park, so I drive until I recognise Boston Common, and pull over to make my call. It transpires that Erik is too busy with permits and suchlike to meet up now, so we arrange to try that evening. I have arranged to spend the night with Chip, as I did when in this area before, so I decide to head for the house. A door has been left open for me, so I put my feet up for an hour or so until Chip returns from work.

He has taken advice from his sons, and we are to watch the game at the Baseball Tavern, near Fenway Park. An early arrival is advised, so that we can get ourselves a seat. So that's what we do, and find ourselves seated with plenty of time to spare. We have chosen upstairs, which is slightly less noisy than downstairs, and conversation is just possible. The place is full of Boston fans, who obviously feel this is the next best thing to being in the stadium. So they cheer the national anthem, and they cheer the fly-past, and they cheer the names of the Boston players as they are announced.

Just as the game is about to start, Erik arrives. He is accompanied by David Lengel, who was one of the Channel 5 presenters for a couple of years. It transpires that the bar won't allow the camera crew to come in, so I am dragged out into a cold and damp Boston street for an interview. It's all very informal and comfortable, and over in no time. They decry the fact that I am unable to get tickets, and we arrange to talk tomorrow.

I return to my seat to find that Boston has started well. Beckett, their pitcher, has struck out the side in the first. Their lead-off man, Pedroia, then hits the second pitch he sees over the Green Monster, and Boston has the lead. Two more runs score in the first, and Boston looks comfortable.

Just then my phone rings, with a text from Erik. He has got me a ticket for tomorrow's game! I am greeted with backslaps and high fives from all my companions, who I would have thought had every right to be extremely jealous.

Back to the game, and Colorado pulls a run back in the second, which is immediately cancelled out by a fourth for Boston, which adds two more in its fourth inning. The Boston fifth is almost embarrassing. Colorado is woeful; as well as regular hits, there are two pitching changes, two runs are walked in, and the game becomes a rout. Boston leads, 13–1. We stick it out until the seventh, when we decide we have had enough beer, baseball and banter for the night. It transpires there was no further scoring, and Boston leads the series, 1–0.

By Thursday, exhaustion is setting in fast. I sleep late, sit around a bit, take a nap, and sit around a bit more. I speak to Erik and arrange to meet him at gate B at seven o'clock to collect my ticket. So at around four o'clock I drive into Boston, miss my turn, drive down a couple of dead ends, and eventually find myself in a traffic jam pointing in the wrong direction. Risking the wrath of the law I perform an illegal left turn, get myself pointed in the right direction, and find the area I am looking for. On the third circuit, all in heavy traffic, I find a vacant parking meter, feed it enough change to take it to six o'clock, and set out for Fenway Park.

It's about a mile away, but in a straight line, so easy to find. Erik is waiting at gate B as promised, and hands over the ticket. It contains two surprising pieces of information: the price, $225, and the word "roof." So I enter, find the stairs, and climb, and climb, and climb! The seat is in right field, level with the foul pole, and right at the back: behind me just a long drop into the street. I wander around, admiring the Boston skyline. The Prudential Insurance building obviously has a very enterprising caretaker; the top 20 floors have the lights of carefully selected offices turned on, to spell the words "Go Sox."

So here I am, at a World Series game. One way and another, it turns out to be quite a musical evening. As part of the warm up, the p.a. plays "Sergeant Pepper," while the scoreboard somehow links the lyrics of each track to the Red Sox, a bit contrived but an entertaining way of passing 45 minutes. The organist is also on splendid form, treating us to a variety of pieces, some expected, some not. Have you ever heard "Bohemian Rhapsody" played on an organ?

Eventually, it comes time for the national anthem, and tonight's chosen artiste is none other than James Taylor. So now I can boast of seeing James Taylor live, even if the gig only lasts 90 seconds.

The game is all about pitching — Jimenez for Colorado, Schilling, veteran of two World Series wins, for Boston. Colorado gets off the mark quickly; Taveras is hit by a pitch, and a single from Holliday and a groundout from Helton score him. The pitchers take control until the fourth, when a sacrifice fly from Varitek levels the score. A double from Lowell in the fifth gives Boston the edge, 2–1. With one man out in the sixth, and two men on base, Schilling exits the game to a standing ovation. His replacement is Hideki Okajima, the less celebrated of Boston's Japanese imports, thought to be a possible weak link. He excels himself, dismissing the next seven batters without giving up a hit before leaving to his own standing ovation.

That leaves the closer, Papelbon to finish off. He gives up a hit to the first man he faces, Holliday, but then, for the first time in his Boston career, picks him off at first to get out of the inning.

Some baseball parks have a relationship with a particular piece of music, with the link not always being obvious. In Fenway, at the end of the eighth, they play Neil Diamond's "Sweet Caroline." After the words "Sweet Caroline" the p.a. is killed for the three brass notes, and the crowd fills in with "Oh, oh, oh!" The song follows with "Good times never felt so good," and the crowd echoes "So good, so good, so good." The crowd loves it, particularly when a tense finish is at hand.

Papelbon, roared on by the crowd, dismisses three straight in the ninth, the third on a 99 m.p.h., fastball. The crowd goes home smiling, and Boston goes to Denver with a 2–0 lead.

So that the West Coast can view at a reasonable time, these games are starting ridiculously late. This one finishes at 12:15. So, after walking back to the car and driving back to Needham, it is 1:15 by the time I creep into the home of my hosts, who have thoughtfully left the back door open and a couple of lights on. As I tiptoe upstairs I feel just like a naughty teenager ... but where would I find one at this time of the morning?

I have no further promise of tickets, so I have decided that to fly to Denver on the off chance would not be sensible. If I am to watch the games in a bar, it might as well be a bar here as a bar there. The Red Sox are not just Boston's team, they are New England's team. So I plan to watch the remaining games in different New England towns, which will give me the chance to see a bit more of the area. When I was travelling in August, Portland struck me as a town I would like to see a bit more of, and I know it's full of Red Sox fans, so that is Friday's destination.

It is a comparatively short drive, and I limit my speed to enjoy it more. I stop a couple of times, to savour the morning, and enjoy a leisurely coffee. I find my hotel, which is of a good standard, and relax for a couple of hours before setting out for dinner. At the mall earlier I had been recommended to the Sebago Brewing Company as a possible place to watch the game tomorrow, so I head for there. I'm not sure it's the right place to watch the game, but I dine handsomely on seafood chowder and fish and chips.

After Friday's fine day, Saturday has it pouring down. When it eases somewhat, I decide to go and explore Portland. I'd like to work out where I'm going tonight, while there's still some light. Not that there's much now; it's a thoroughly miserable day, the sort of day where you decide it's not raining, and before you've gone a few yards you can't see through your glasses. Giving up on walking, I return to the car, determined to find the part of town Alan and I discovered during the last visit. I get thoroughly lost, twice, but eventually find what I am looking for. I work my way back to the hotel, remembering the route, so that hopefully I can find my way back later.

Game time comes, and I find my way back to my target easily. The weather is still damp, but much clearer. I investigate a brew pub called Gritty McDuffs, and find a cellar bar with some space, and a dozen or so Sox fans. I wedge myself into a corner of the bar, and we're away. They have a good range of beer, but I'm driving, so I have to be very restrained. The barman is clad in a Red Sox cap and a judo suit, and can control the volume of the TV and stereo from behind the bar. Thus, for the introduction of the Sox players, the volume is pumped up; when it comes to the Rockies, the volume is killed, and we are treated to "Mana, Mana" by the Muppets.

You may remember me explaining the difference between the American League and the National League, namely, the designated hitter batting for the pitcher. In the World Series, they play home team rules. So tonight, the first game in Denver, Boston has to lose their designated hitter, and their pitcher, Matsuzaka, will have to take his turn at bat.

The game starts cagily, with both teams putting men on base without managing to drive them home. Then in the third, hits from Ortiz and Lowell give Boston a three-run lead. After two outs, the pitcher Matsuzaka steps up, and it is assumed the inning is over. But he slaps a single to score two more runs and help his own cause immensely. Another run gives Boston a 6–0 lead. It remains that way until the sixth, when a tiring Matsuzaka walks the first two batters. His replacement, Lopez, concedes two hits to reduce the deficit to 6–2. He is relieved by Timlin, and a stunning catch from shortstop Lugo gets Boston out of the inning.

In the seventh the first two Colorado batters get on base, and Boston looks to Thursday's hero, Okajima. His first pitch is hammered by Holliday to deep centre, and the score is 6–5. There is much muttering of expletives amongst the locals, but Okajima regains his composure, and gets the next three outs. In the top of the eighth, Boston comes back strongly. Three runs score, and another in the ninth sees them to a comfortable, 10–5 victory. They are now one win away from the title.

There's a chance that Sunday will be the last game of the Series, of the season, and of my trip, so it seems sensible to move south, to make my ultimate journey a little shorter. As I was so unimpressed by my last visit, I decide to give Rhode Island another chance. There must be more to it than Pawtucket! Yesterday's weather must have been a blip. This morning we have returned to the glorious autumn sunshine of Friday, and driving is an absolute pleasure. The route takes me through forests and past waterfronts, and the drive flies by.

The hotel I have aimed for is a delight. It is full of character, unlike most of the symmetrical boxes in which I have stayed. It also overlooks a long stretch of sandy beach. After settling in, I drive the couple of miles into town, and take a look at Newport. It is a boating and fishing centre, with a large harbour and a fish market. There is also a glut of restaurants, coffee shops and boutiques, all designed to cater for the obvious wealth strolling around the town on what one shop advertises as "the last day of the season."

Back at the hotel, the receptionist informs me that there is a sports bar just around the corner, so that will be my target for tonight. Before that, though, a nap is in order; these one o'clock finishes are beginning to take their toll! Tickets is the name of the restaurant and sports bar I have targeted for Game 4. When I walk in with minutes to go to the first pitch, I am devastated to find that it is deserted. I explain to the waitress what I want, and she tells me to try the sports bar upstairs. This is better!

I find a place at the bar, and the game starts. The starting matchup is interesting. Both pitchers have made comebacks from serious illness; Jon Lester for the Sox has fought blood cancer; Aaron Cook for the Rox has suffered blood clots in the lungs. Two fourth-string pitchers against two big-hitting line ups in the thin air of Denver threatens a glut of runs. In the first inning, Ellsbury doubles, advances on a groundout, and is singled home to give Boston an early lead.

But the pitchers perform well and take control. There is no more score until the fifth, when Lowell doubles, and is brought home by Varitek. Lowell, who is later named Most Valuable Player of the Series, homers in the seventh to give Boston a comfortable 3–0 lead. I am starting to think about home when Hawpe homers for Colorado to reduce the deficit. Enter Bobby Kielty, Boston bench player, called upon to pinch-hit for the pitcher in the eighth. He faces one pitch, smacks it into the crowd, and Boston leads, 4–1. The Rockies will not quit; in the eighth Atkins belts a two-run homer to produce a tense finale, but Papelbon pitches out the ninth to give Boston a 4–3 victory and their second World Series in the last four years.

The bar staff buys us all a drink, something strong and bitter with a lot of pineapple juice, and I walk down to the sea on my way back to the hotel. I stand looking in the general direction of home and shed unashamed tears of joy. It's all over! I've achieved what I set out to do; had a fantastic, if sometimes bumpy, ride; seen some fabulous sights, met some wonderful people; now I'm going home!

A day later I arrive at cousin Pam's house in Virginia Beach, thus completing the circle. I drove down the drive of this house on the morning of April 5, and I drive back up it on October 29 after a couple of hundred days and 45,000 miles.

Two days later, I depart the USA, and arrive back at Heathrow surprisingly on time. My welcome party is double what I am expecting, and I am met by one wife, two daughters and a granddaughter, who is placed in my arms before

I have even crossed the barrier. After hugs and kisses all round, we find some-where that sells an English breakfast, and I eat bacon with meaty bits on the end, just like it should be!

An Interlude

When my eye had gone haywire in Albuquerque, and it became apparent that I would not fully achieve my objectives that summer, Sally was insistent that the trip should be completed at the earliest possible opportunity. So my mind was already planning something of this nature for April, 2008.

But first there was the triumphal celebration of my homecoming. Nine days after my return, my family threw me a "welcome home" party, to be attended by around 30 people from various parts of my past and present. I was permitted to help with the food preparation. As the food was to have a ballpark theme, my expertise in such matters was essential.

A splendid time was had by all, and we managed to produce hot dogs, chili, bratwurst, tacos with cheesy dip (not quite as yellow as the genuine arti-cle), pulled pork sandwiches, and even made a reasonable stab at a Philly cheesesteak. Sal had managed to find a diagram, on the web, of Philadelphia's famous "Schmitter," and partygoers were invited to transform their cheesesteak into this unique, and incredibly messy, ballpark sandwich. Thankfully, no one suggested we should drink American beer.

As is usual with our Saturday parties, there were still people around on Sun-day, so the party effectively lasted until Sunday afternoon. The following Tuesday I visited my doctor. There was nothing wrong, I just wanted to bring him up to date with stuff, and tell him about my detached retina. I had heard he had been off work himself and, when I enquired as to the state of his health, it turned out he had suffered two detached retinas (retinae?). We chatted happily for a while and, as I left, I informed him that the specialist in San Francisco who had checked me over had announced that my right eye did not have any problems.

Me and my big mouth! The following morning, as I was stepping into the shower, I noticed a small bubble in the corner of my right eye, oddly reminis-cent of the one I had seen in my left eye back in May. Strangely calm, I phoned my doctor for another appointment, and called Sal to bring her home from work (she only works next door, so it's a reasonable journey).

In we strolled, and the doctor couldn't force back a grin. He said he wouldn't bother to examine me, as he was sure I knew what I was talking about; and anyway, he still couldn't see very well!

Eight hours later, I am in the operating theatre. Once again I am given a local anaesthetic, and the alien abduction scene begins. Whereas in the States I was surrounded by quietly spoken American accents, here I have Dr. Patel, of Asian descent but with an impeccable middle class accent, Dave the Aussie, and Panos the Greek. There is also a suction sound, which causes a light show in my eye so spectacular that I would like to know exactly what drugs they were pumping into me, and can you get them on E-bay.

Approaching 9:00, the deed is done. These guys have been working since early morning, and I am amazed at their stamina. Towards the end of the operation Dr. Patel tells Dave that the hard work is done, and that he may go home. Dave replies (and you have to read this bit in an Australian accent to get the full effect), "No, mate, we arrive as a team, we leave as a team!" No wonder their sports teams win everything.

Mercifully, the lying-on-my-front phase only lasts for one night, and I am returned home the following day to cope with the tribulations of more retinal recovery. Have you ever tried telling your boss that, immediately after seven months' special leave, you're going on the sick? Although this detachment is less severe, recovery is in many ways more difficult. Remember that the left lens of my spectacles has still not been corrected following the first operation, so my left eye is rubbish, and my right eye is covered.

By the time I am signed off by the hospital it will be February, and then I will have to wait a few weeks for my eyes to settle until I can have my spectacles made. So it looks as if the April trip will have to be postponed, and I reschedule for September. I go through the slow process of recovery, February arrives, I am signed off by the hospital with the warning that retinal surgery can sometimes cause cataracts, and a few weeks later I have spectacles and am functioning fairly normally.

After a very few weeks of this "normality," my eyes start to become cloudy. I try to ignore it, as I am so tired of not being able to function adequately, but eventually the optician has to be consulted. His diagnosis is cataracts—OK, I was warned, but I was thinking maybe a couple of years! So, it's back to the hospital, the diagnosis is confirmed and, this not being nearly so urgent as a detached retina, I'm placed on a waiting list.

By now it's March, so I wait patiently for an appointment to arrive in the mail. When it arrives, it's for July 31. This turns out to be for one eye only, and I am warned that it may be ten weeks before the second one is arranged. This precludes my being able to travel in September, so the completion of the trip is again postponed, this time until April 2009.

I should, at this point, pay tribute to my planned hosts for this leg of the journey, and the officials of the baseball clubs in Anaheim and Denver, who have provided me with free tickets twice, tolerated my two postponements, and are now agreeing to entertain me again in April 2009.

Both operations come and go successfully, the second in October. Such is the progress of cataract surgery that the procedure now involves removing the lens and replacing it with a new one. The result is that my vision is better than it has been since I was eight years old! It's an ill wind, as they say.

Spring Training, 2009
Sunday March 29–Thursday April 2

I sleep through my five o'clock alarm, but still manage to leave the house at six for the brief drive to Birmingham Airport. No hugely traumatic farewells this time — compared to the massive sojourn of two years ago this is a drop in the ocean.

So here I go again. In case you have lost count, to achieve my objective I still need to see games in Arizona and Colorado, which will be covered by the Diamondbacks and the Rockies, plus games at the Padres, Dodgers and Angels.

My first destination is Newark, so I reset my watch in yet another pathetic attempt to influence my body clock. Just 3,347 miles later, we land at Newark, not too late. I fill in a form which assures Customs I am not carrying any soil, and I hold my breath as I go through immigration. One awkward question as to why I have a six-month visa for a five-week trip, and I'm in.

Five hours later, I board my connection to Phoenix. It is 5:30 in Newark and a five and a half hour flight, but the miracle of time zones means we are due in at eight. My neighbour is very chatty. By 1815 miles later, I know that Alice Cooper has a bar in Phoenix, and that the area has a senior citizens' baseball league.

We disembark (I still refuse to "deplane"!), I find my car, and manage to find my way through the lights of Phoenix to the Tempe Econolodge, which is to be my home for five nights. It's ten o'clock in Tempe, one a.m. in Newark, and six a.m. back home — exactly the time I left home this morning, or yesterday. My head's on another planet, and sleep doesn't come easily.

I sleep fitfully, with too much going on in my head. When I picked up my rental car last night, they gave me an upgrade to a premium car from an intermediate, for which I had already paid. As I was going to collect it, I said, "Everything is paid for!" He replied, "Yes, I've just added the upgrade!" When I got to my hotel and checked my receipt, the upgrade had been charged at $550! My fitful sleep, therefore, was probably about rehearsing the conversation I was to have with the rental company this morning!

As it turns out, they are extremely helpful and put things right, but it does involve an early morning drive to the airport to exchange cars. I now have a slightly smaller car, a Chrysler Sebring for those who care, and a much larger bank balance. While I am retracing last night's route, I notice that someone has snuck out in the night and scattered mountains around the city.

Soon it's time to leave for the first game of the year. The season itself does not start until the coming weekend, but I have booked to see the last four games of spring training. Each major league team has a pre-season headquarters, either in Arizona or Florida. When spring training begins, those in each state play a series of friendly matches against each other. Teams as a rule invite around 60 players to spring training and, over the course of six weeks or so, these are whittled down to the eventual 25 that the club will take into the season. You could probably name 20 of the players before it all begins, so it's really just fine tuning and practice for the season. By this time in late March the roster is around 30, so most of the players on view are big leaguers.

For these four days I am following the Cubs, and today they are on the road in a town called Surprise, against the Kansas City Royals. Surprise is around 40 miles from here, along I-60, a dull road with loads of car dealerships and hardly any diners. I eventually find a Denny's for my first breakfast of the trip, and arrive at the park with 45 minutes to spare. The stadium is a beautiful new structure, which is not surprising as Surprise itself was only founded in 1960. The crowd is quiet and friendly, with a significantly higher age profile than most, equally unsurprising as we are just a few miles from Sun City, one of the largest retirement communities in the country.

Add to the mix the fact that the Cubs are one of the best-supported teams outside their own area, and the atmosphere is a good one. The game is a good one too with the Cubs never ahead. In the eighth, with the score 5–5, the Cubs centre fielder, Fukudome, drops a fly ball, and the Cubs go behind, 8–5. At this point many of the supporters leave, but in the top of the ninth Fukudome makes amends with a home run, and the Cubs pull back to 8–8. There is no more score and, with the convention being that, in spring training, extra innings only go to the tenth, we end with that most un–American of results, a draw.

Tuesday's game is in Mesa, which is only six miles away, and houses the Cubs' home facility, HoHoKam Park; not quite as homely as yesterday's venue, more big-time and no free parking. But still beautiful surroundings, and a splendid day to watch baseball. Before finding my seat, I treat myself to a pork tenderloin sandwich, a cut above the average hot dog.

The line-ups are again strong, with the Cubs fielding eight potential starters. The pitcher, Sean Marshall, has recently been given a starting job, but he does his cause no good in the fourth, when the Angels send 12 men to the plate, seven of whom score. That ends the game as a contest, although the Cubs continue to scramble and it finishes 8–4. The bizarre highlight of the day comes during the seventh-inning stretch, when "Take Me Out to the Ball Game" is performed by a tap dancing troupe on top of the home team dugout.

My friends Steve and Liz, from Pittsburgh, arrive in town today for a vacation, and, as I'm on my way back from the game, Steve calls. We meet up in Mill Street, the happening part of town, and catch up over an excellent dinner.

Wednesday starts with a drive across town to Liz and Steve's hotel. My laptop has a terminal illness, and Steve has one that works, and an internet link. So we get on to Skype and I am able to talk to folks at home for the first time since early Sunday. I discuss my laptop predicament and my wife immediately tells me to go out and buy a new one, which is the response I was hoping for, as I had reached the same conclusion. Then more good news, Sal has received a small windfall!

"How much?" I enquire.

"A new laptop for you and a new sewing machine for me!" comes the reply.

Soon it's time to leave for the game. Today the Cubs are visiting the Oakland Athletics, at Phoenix Municipal Stadium, a few blocks east of the hotel. This is another beautiful Arizona spring day — temperature in the 80s, cloudless sky, gentle breeze — and we sit with our snacks and drinks just enjoying being there. The Cubs are pitching their opening day starter, Carlos Zambrano, and he acquits himself well before being withdrawn early in preparation for the real thing. The game is the reverse of yesterday. The Cubs score a run at the start of the third, and then load the bases. Johnson is hit by a pitch, to force in a second run, and then Soto hits a grand slam. Cubs lead, 6–0.

Almost all of the starting players are withdrawn, and the Athletics chip away at the lead, so much so that it ends 8–8. Oakland is leaving for the coast straight after the game, so the teams decide against extra innings. I have just witnessed my second 8–8 tie in three days— what odds could I have got against that on Monday morning? This is the Athletics' final game in Arizona this year, so the announcer sends them on their way with good wishes for a successful season, and signs off with the epic "Happy Trails To You," by Roy Rogers and Dale Evans.

We head straight for Tempe Mall, and within minutes I have purchased a new laptop which works perfectly. We continue to Scottsdale, and head for Don and Charlie's, a sports bar packed to the roof with sports memorabilia. We dine well in a splendidly convivial atmosphere, and head off into the Arizona night. I spend the rest of the evening setting up my new toy, feeling much more comfortable now that I'm in touch with the rest of the world again.

Thursday I awake a much more settled bunny. The jet lag is gone, I have a car I can afford and a laptop that works. I even get Skype up and running, complete with my inbuilt camera, so I can see what others are seeing of me all at the same time. It's a bit scary really.

The first piece of news in my e-mails is sad, at least if you're a baseball fan. It appears that Channel 5 in England has dropped its twice-weekly coverage of major league baseball, which was the only place it could be found on British free-to-air television. You may remember they gave me a fair amount of coverage two years ago. I add my electronic voice to the internet protest.

Today's game starts at noon, early because it's the last game of spring training, and the Cubs are flying off tonight to New York, where they will play two exhibition games against the Yankees, to inaugurate their new stadium. The Cubs enter to the sounds of the Blues Brothers, and the announcer amuses the crowd with a comparative weather bulletin — 78 degrees here in Mesa, 44 in Chicago!

Again there is a big inning early in the game. In the first the teams exchange home runs, then in the second a series of walks and hits gives the Cubs six runs. When they score a single run in the fourth to extend their lead to 8–3, alarm bells ring. Surely Cleveland will now score five runs and the game will end 8–8, which seems to be mandatory in spring training. Sure enough, they get three in the sixth, one in the seventh and one in the ninth to tie the game, leaving the Cubs just the bottom of the ninth to explode this myth. They bring in Reed Johnson, a first-team regular who singles to get on base and goes to second on a ground out. A single from the reserve shortstop brings him home, the Cubs win, 9–8, and the majority of the crowd goes home happy.

Arizona

Friday April 3–Tuesday April 7

With all the driving I did two years ago, this week has seemed as if the trip has yet to start. Five nights in the same motel have spoilt me, so it's with a sense of excitement that I start my journey on Friday morning. I rise early, and am on the road before eight. It's 62 degrees and sunny, and the rush hour traffic into Phoenix is heavy. Fortunately I'm going the other way, and as soon as I find my way to I-10 the speed limit increases to 75, so I make good time.

My destination is Tombstone, "the town too tough to die," scene of the gunfight at the OK Corral. It is immediately apparent that they are going to be milking it, but that is to be expected. I don't mind the truth being stretched to accommodate a good story, but it grates a little when every establishment has Western references. I'm pretty sure that Wyatt Earp didn't spend his off-duty hours at the Mad Miner's Crazy Golf, for example.

I park the car and head to the Longhorn Restaurant for my cowboy breakfast, but I have missed it by 20 minutes. It seems that owning guns is fine, gay marriage is totally acceptable, but selling someone a breakfast after 11:00 is a step too far for most Americans. So I make do with a couple of mugs of coffee and a barbecue beef sandwich, and head off to sample the delights of Tombstone.

Walking around the place quickly becomes tedious, as it is largely a one-trick pony. But eventually the appointed hour arrives, so I head back to the OK Corral for the re-enactment of the famous gunfight. It transpires that, although we are in the actual OK Corral, this is not exactly where the deed took place. I guess "Gunfight just up the street from the OK Corral" doesn't have quite the same ring, does it?

I am curious as to how the re-enactment will be dealt with, as presumably it only lasted a few seconds, and it turns out to be a curious combination. First we get a couple of the Earp brothers doing a bit of stand-up to get the audience onside, then we get a melodrama showing how the stepdaughter of one of the Earps had a crush on one of the cowboys, Billy Clanton. Then we get the actual confrontation, which is all over in a moment, and leaves three of the cowboys dead. Who started it all is left deliberately vague and, to their credit, the cowboys remain dead until the crowd disperses. I don't think I could have coped if they had got up and taken a bow.

I return to the car and head towards Sierra Vista. I am looking for the street which contains my motel when I go a couple of blocks too far and, going through some lights, find myself heading irreversibly for a military installation. So I am security checked into Fort Huachuca, have the traffic held up while I perform a U-turn, and am security checked out of Fort Huachuca!

The only reason I came to Sierra Vista is because the hotels in Tombstone are stupidly expensive, but it turns out to be the birdwatching capital of the country. I have to at least make a token gesture, so on Saturday I set off for San Pedro House, seven miles east of town. When I get seven miles west of town, I realise my mistake and, 14 miles later, there it is. It's a small building in an ecologically sound garden.

At one side of the garden, I see what I really came for, the hummingbird feeders. If you have never seen a hummingbird, it is about two inches long. If you see one out of the corner of your eye and you're not expecting it, you might think it was a dragonfly. The feeders are just inverted two-litre plastic bottles full of sugar water. When the hummingbird hovers, its wings are invisible, and it appears to be hanging in mid-air. I stand entranced with my binoculars focused on the feeder, even though I'm less than six feet away, while two or three different varieties come and feed.

A short drive brings me to Tucson, and a very comfortable hotel with a lovely pool. After a relaxing afternoon, I walk into Tucson to try to discover the music scene of which I have read. I eventually arrive at the centre, and find myself outside the hotel at which I asked directions earlier. I remember seeing a bar there, and, seeing signs to a tap room, find a good range of drafts. After a few moments I find myself deep in conversation with Bradford, a local man whose father was born in England. A second beer is necessary, as the talking continues.

He eventually leaves, and I set out on my search. I am sadly disappointed. I guess I was expecting an area such as is found in Memphis or Nashville, but, apart from the odd cafe with a desultory guitarist, there is nothing. Eating places are few and far between too, so I return to the hotel.

Sunday brings me back to the task in hand, and I quickly negotiate the 120 miles back to Phoenix, and find the home of my hosts relatively easily. Lissie is the daughter of some friends of my mother back home in Byfield, and you may remember her and her husband John coming to my assistance when I suffered my detached retina in Albuquerque two years ago. I immediately receive warm greetings and a cold marguerita, and we sit in the garden exchanging news, and letting Louie, their pet bulldog, get to know me. Then it's off to a local establishment for lunch, and on to the guided tour of downtown Phoenix, which goes past the main reason for my visit, the ballpark. We drive around the scenic areas of the city, and there are lots, before stopping at a Mexican bar for a refreshing beer. Today is the opening day of the baseball season, and the television is preparing people for the game that is imminent.

Back to the house, and we watch the first few innings of the Philadelphia Phillies, last year's World Series winners, against the Atlanta Braves. The Braves are no respecters of reputation, and take a four-run lead before we have to move on to higher things, such as dinner. We want to meet up with my friends Steve and Liz, as it is their last night in Phoenix, so, having made contact and established the whereabouts of their hotel, we decide to rendezvous at the Four Peaks brewpub.

It's a good choice of venue, as regards both food and beer. Thoroughly sated, we bid farewell to Steve and Liz and drive home. The television is showing the Pretenders, one of my favourite bands, playing at Cornbury, only a few miles from where I live back home. It's a small world!

Lissie and John both have to work for a couple of hours first thing Monday, but they soon return, and we get ready for Opening Day, Arizona's first home game of the 2009 baseball season. Phoenix has recently built a light rail system, so we take advantage of this to go straight to the ground without anyone having to drive and with no extortionate parking fees. The ride is pleasant — Phoenix is a bright, open city, with lots of space and many attractive buildings.

We soon arrive at Chase Stadium, named after the team's latest corporate sponsor. It was previously known as Bank One Ballpark, which gave the stadium its catchy nickname, "the BOB." I think many of the fans will ignore the change and continue to go with this. The park is modern and well-designed, with a retractable roof, which is closed when we enter. We are given free T-shirts as we go in and, they do think of everything, follow the sign which lets me exchange mine for one that fits me.

John's short trip into work has proven to be worthwhile. His receptionist has given him the cell phone number for her husband, who runs the executive restaurant in the ballpark. So, a quick phone call later, we are in a lift leading to said restaurant, and are greeted by the chef, offered a taste of his wares, and ushered to a table overlooking the playing area. There we are told we are on the chef's account, and advised to help ourselves from the buffet. This includes grilled smoked salmon, Italian tenderloin wrapped in pancetta, ribs of beef, and a wonderful selection of salads, sauces and vegetables. All this is followed by poached bananas, fresh fruit and a summer fruit cobbler. Sure beats hot dog and Coke!

While this is happening, the roof is opened, the teams are introduced, it being Opening Day, and we get a fly-past of planes from a nearby air base. As first pitch approaches, we rush down to our seats on third base side, and arrive just in time.

The game is bizarre. Both teams have their best pitcher out, and a pitching duel is predicted. Instead, we get a record number of home runs, eight in all. Two of the Arizona players, Tony Clark and Felipe Lopez, each hit two home runs. Both are switch-hitters, which means they can bat right- or left-handed, and both hit a home run from each side of the plate — the first time this has been achieved on Opening Day. Colorado plays its part, with three homers of its own, and it is not until late in the game that the home team gets its final homer to edge the game, 9–8.

During the game, the announcer introduces any famous guests who happen to be present. First is the governor of Arizona, who smiles sweetly and elicits a polite round of applause; next up is a guaranteed standing ovation — Muhammed Ali, no less, looking frail but still the greatest!

Thoroughly entertained, we head off for refreshment. Two years ago, you may remember me in Cleveland, looking for a bar called Cooperstown, owned by Alice Cooper. It had changed hands, and now I know why. Alice had moved to Phoenix, so it is to Cooperstown we go, and a splendid place it is too, a cavernous bar with much rock and baseball memorabilia, waitresses with Alice Cooper eye make-up, and a fair selection of draughts. I slake my thirst with a Sam Adams cherry wheat, before moving on to a Bare Knuckle stout.

While all this is happening, we watch the Yankees lose to Baltimore, and the Cubs take a good lead over Houston. When enough has been had, we head home on the light rail, and Lissie heads off to prepare some food while John shows me the local record shop, Stinkweeds. This is an excellent place to waste half an hour, although the change in the exchange rate makes buying lots not such an attractive proposition as it was two years ago. I content myself with a Pogues retrospective, which will keep me awake on the long desert drives ahead.

We return home to a great steak dinner, more baseball on TV, and an Elvis Costello concert as we lapse into exhaustion. I bid my hosts fond farewell, as they will be gone when I rise tomorrow. What an excellent day!

I have been in and around Phoenix for most of the time since arriving in this country ten days ago, but on Tuesday I'm really leaving. I gather my stuff together, make sure my hosts' house is securely locked, and I'm away by 10:00, headed for Yuma.

I find my hotel with no difficulty, sort myself out and take a swim. The brochures talk about the delights of Old Town Yuma, so off I set to sample them. Sadly, they don't exist! I arrive in Old Town around 4:40. Most of the shops say they are open until 5:00, but are already closed. The cinema is open, but the brew pub is closed — permanently! I find a coffee shop open, so decide to find some postcards, and sit outside the coffee shop writing them. Sadly, nowhere is open that sells postcards, and by the time I return to the coffee shop, that's closed too. There is a second-hand bookshop fighting the trend, so I spend a little while in there, buy a couple of baseball books and, as the temperature is now in the 90s, head back to the hotel.

California (Part Three)
Wednesday April 8–Saturday April 11

On Wednesday morning, no sooner do I hit I-8 and start heading west than I'm in California. Almost immediately the traffic starts to slow down, and I suddenly remember from my last visit that California has its own border controls. The fruit police flag me down, a very serious young woman asks where I'm coming from and, when I tell her, beams and waves me through. They are obviously on the lookout for people who didn't spend last night in Yuma. I am about as far south as I can be in mainland USA, and every exit is for a different border crossing into Mexico. There is a strong visible presence of border police, and twice the traffic is stopped for a check. On both occasions I am flagged through, so my pallid complexion obviously constitutes no threat.

Eventually I turn onto my old friend I-10, but only utilise it for a few miles before hitting SR-62, the 29 Palms Highway, just as the whole landscape is taken over by a huge wind farm, a quite stunning sight. The highway rises steeply through the mountains, with lots of tourist traps, until I reach my destination, the Joshua Tree Inn, "the cosmic American motel."

A cool, slow-speaking dude in a cowboy hat checks me in and shows me to my room. I have booked room 8, the Gram Parsons room, where the eponymous musician spent his last night on this earth in September 1973. Parsons was considered by some to be the founder of country rock in the 60s, and played with the Byrds, the Flying Burrito Brothers and the Fallen Angels.

The building is old and quaint, with local artefacts and rock music memorabilia everywhere. The rooms open off an outside corridor, which contains armchairs and tables, and which borders a rectangle containing a large swimming pool. The edge of the corridor is full of a beautiful purple plant. Outside my room there is a small shrine to Parsons, and the room itself contains much of his memorabilia. They have also thoughtfully provided a CD player and some of his music. Unless you're a true fan, or on a whimsical trip such as mine, I doubt whether the contents of the room justify the extra charge. But it's a nice place to be nonetheless.

As I walk back to my room after dinner, there is a full moon, a clear sky and a view that stretches for miles; the palms and Joshua trees are silhouetted against the night, and the purple stuff around the corridor is releasing an amazing perfume. Maybe it is worth the extra for a bit of cosmic, after all!

On Thursday I arrive at breakfast at 8:00, as an early start is the order of the day. It's the usual cold carbohydrates, but at least the bread looks like it comes from a bakery rather than a factory, the jam isn't in little packets, and the coffee is quite excellent.

Soon I'm under way, and I don't have far to go. Just around the corner from the hotel is my first destination, the Joshua Tree National Park, so-called because it's full of Joshua trees. For the uninitiated, these look like a cross between a palm tree and a cactus, and have strong branches reaching upwards. Allegedly, a group of Mormons in the middle of the nineteenth century, while crossing this area, were reminded of the extract from the Bible in which Joshua reaches up his arms to heaven, and thus the tree received its name.

In 1987, U2 named their album *The Joshua Tree*, and that probably did more for the publicity of the park than the Mormons. Neither is my reason for visiting the park. It is more to do with Gram Parsons, as the park contains a slightly odd memorial to him. I enquire at the park office, and am told where to find the memorial, although the ranger informs me that the mementos left by fans are quickly removed, as they are not good for the environment. He says that if I wish to leave anything, perhaps just a thought would suffice!

I drive slowly through the park, and eventually reach the place I am looking for, Cap Rock. Since the somewhat bizarre death of Gram Parsons, the spot has become a shrine to those who choose to see it as such. Following the ranger's directions, I eventually find the spot. True to their word, the rangers have removed everything they can. All that remains is the graffiti carved into the rock by the afficionados, much of it based around the title of one of his albums, *Safe at Home*, which also happens to be a baseball phrase. You can't say this stuff doesn't have a certain symmetry.

Curiosity sated, I return to the car, and head for the exits. I have decided to spend the night in Palm Springs, holiday home of the rich and famous. Entering the town, every other road is named after a household name, Bob Hope, Kirk Douglas, Frank Sinatra, Gerald Ford. My hotel is the Caliente Tropics Resort, which is basically a large motel with Pacific Island designs spread around a big swimming pool. Unfortunately the part of the resort in which I might have been interested, the bar and restaurant, has closed down so, come the eating hour, I have to venture out.

You may not have to be famous to live in Palm Springs, but being rich certainly helps. The first two restaurants I pass don't have a steak for less than $30, twice what I've paid elsewhere. Eventually I come across an Italian place which, while not cheap, at least presents the opportunity of a meal without a mortgage. The waitress, however, 75 dressed as 35, is very Palm Springs!

On Friday I head in the general direction of the coast. Almost instantly I am out of town and into the mountains, and yet another huge wind farm looms into view. This morning we have the wind to go with it, too. After a couple of instances of seeing somewhere to eat just after driving past the exit that would take me there, I see Ruby's Diner, and pull off.

I eventually find the car park, and emerge to fifty degrees and thin mountain mist. It is 11:20, just past the breakfast hour, so I am prepared for the worst. Instead, I am asked whether I want breakfast or lunch. When, in hushed tones, I opt for the former, I expect to be ushered into a back room, and asked if I want to buy some nuclear fuel or a Mexican immigrant or two while I'm at it. But no — this is California — anytime is breakfast time!

Eventually I reach I-5, negotiate my way through dense traffic, find my turnoff, and arrive in Cardiff. There's lovely, isn't it? This Cardiff is a beach community to the north of San Diego. I am greeted by Debbie, my host, whom I have not met before. Debbie is a good friend of Gail, with whom I stayed in Cincinnati two years ago. Gail is the sister of Steve, whom I was with in Phoenix last week. Are you keeping up?

On Saturday we drive into San Diego, past beaches and boatyards and surfers, until we reach Coronado, which I have asked to visit. Coronado is an island in the bay off San Diego, connected only by a small isthmus of sand and, these days, a spectacular six-lane bridge.

The reason for my visit is the Hotel del Coronado, a spectacular edifice of a hotel built in 1888 to attract tourism to the area. One of my favourite movies, *Some Like It Hot*, was largely filmed here, which is why I wanted so much to see the place. If you are vaguely familiar with the film, you will know that the characters, including Marilyn Monroe, Tony Curtis and Jack Lemmon, have supposedly fled to Florida, but it was actually shot here in California.

Moving on, we pay a visit to the museum area of town. There are lots of them, but we choose the sports one in keeping with my theme. Interesting it is, too, with big displays around the American football team, the Chargers, and the baseball team, the Padres, more of whom later. Ever onward, we progress to Old Town, scene of the original San Diego, a cluster of adobe buildings, most of which appear to be Mexican restaurants, coffee shops or boutiques. We leave the car around here, and use the light rail to get to Petco Park, a lovely little stadium in the heart of the city. Debbie's partner Chris was one of the architects who worked on the design of the stadium, so I get an insider's view of the building.

Outside the park we meet up with Sallie and Rod, last encountered in the August, 2007, stage of my odyssey. Sallie is the sister of my neighbour Greg, and was part of the family holiday which I invaded two years ago. Now fully assembled, we enter the stadium. It is Mexican night, so we get an extra national anthem, and a free T-shirt honouring the Padres' Adrian Gonzalez.

The game starts slowly, with the two pitchers throwing extremely efficiently. But in the bottom of the third, Padres back-up catcher Henry Blanco hits a home run. The San Francisco Giants reply with a run in the fourth, but in the bottom of the fifth Blanco makes a hero of himself by repeating his home run feat. The Giants pitcher is now struggling, and walks the bases loaded before tonight's honouree, Adrian Gonzalez, clears them with a double to put the home team ahead, 5–1. A third homer, this time from Chase Headley, puts the game out of reach and, although the Giants pull a couple back, the Padres' starter, Jake Peavy, pitches into the ninth to record a well-earned victory.

By now the stadium is a beautiful sight, having come to life as darkness descended, and the crowd disperses into the night with remarkably little congestion.

California (Part Four)
Sunday April 12–Thursday April 16

Sunday is my 30th wedding anniversary. In fact, it's a double celebration, since it's my wife's 30th wedding anniversary also, which is something of a coincidence. Fortunately, with the wonders of science and my new laptop, we are able not only to converse but to see each other too, which is something of a consolation.

The baseball season is now a week old and, quite refreshingly, none of the big names have started too well. My Cubbies have won four and lost two which, considering that their first six games have all been on the road, is a decent start. The most notable event of the first week has been a tragedy. A 23-year-old pitcher, Nick Adenhart of the Anaheim Angels, pitched his first game in the major leagues on Wednesday, threw six innings without conceding a run, and was later killed in a hit-and-run accident. Such a tragedy so early in the season has shocked the baseball community, which has reacted in its usual quiet, supportive manner.

Just for the record, today is Easter Day, a day of family and friends, and Debbie has invited me to a party at the house of her business partner. I volunteer to drive, as the party is in Orange County, so that Chris can carry on to his Los Angeles house ready for work tomorrow. The party is excellent, with lots to eat and drink, young kids running around, and good conversation.

On Monday, after a breakfast of very spicy chicken andouille sausages, I leave Debbie to deal with her week and set off on an extensive trek to Sallie and

Rod's house. It's all of 22 miles, and I'm there in half an hour. It is a delightful house, in an elevated position, with a very colourful garden. This Sallie, like my Sally, is an obvious enthusiast for all things feathered, and the garden has many feeders. Within minutes of arriving I spot a hummingbird.

Sallie has to go to the hospital and donate platelets, so I am given the wireless code, the TV remotes, and left to my own devices. I sit in the California sunshine and look at how the Cubs are doing in their lunchtime game, only to find that the start has been delayed. Chicago is 39 degrees and raining! When the game eventually starts, I find it is being televised, so relax in front of a huge TV and watch the players struggle with the cold and damp. Cubs pitcher Ted Lilly takes a no-hitter into the seventh and the Cubs win, 4–0 — good stuff.

Following this, nothing remains but to sit on the porch, writing postcards and identifying the birds using the feeders. I get a ruby-throated hummingbird, different kinds of goldfinch, house finches, purple finches and pine siskins. Hiding peanuts elsewhere in the garden is a pair of western scrub-jays, and overhead flies a heron, although exactly which type I'm not sure.

Tuesday and Wednesday I do little more than play the guest and the tourist — the Wild Animal Park, dinner at the Stone Brewery Bistro, Queen Califia's Magical Circle, Del Mar racetrack, Torrey Pines, and the USS *Midway*. Thursday is my final day at Sallie and Rod's so, as they make their preparations, I enjoy a last half-hour on the porch, watching the hummingbirds. Today is another game day, so my hosts have begged a lift with me to Los Angeles. The journey is longer than I thought, just over 100 miles, and the traffic ranges from busy to congested all the way.

After a brief stop in Santa Anita, to pay homage at the family home where Sallie and my neighbour Greg grew up, we head into Los Angeles, and the home of Karen, one of Sallie and Rod's daughters. There we are joined by Ben, Greg's eldest son and, therefore, Sallie's nephew. Ben grew up in England, so I know him very well, but he has lived in Los Angeles for 12 years now.

The five of us head off for Dodger Stadium, scene of tonight's game between the Los Angeles Dodgers and the San Francisco Giants. It is a pleasant, cool evening, and, as we wait for proceedings to get under way, I watch the palm trees either side of the scoreboard waving gently and feel as if home is a long way away. Despite his long-term residency, this is only Ben's second baseball game, and I feel strangely gratified by being able to field all his questions.

The game is decided on errors; the Dodgers play well while the Giants continually mess up. So, although San Francisco gets the most hits, the game finishes 7–2 to the home team. At an appropriate juncture, we partake of the mythical "Dodger dog," which, LA residents will tell you, is superior to any other dog in baseball. It's certainly tasty, but a decision as to whether the claim is completely justified will have to wait pending further research.

The most challenging part of the day is yet ahead. Ben has his own car, so I have to drive through LA traffic to his place. Attempts to follow him prove futile, so I have written instructions as a back-up. I almost make it, getting just a few miles from the coast before the incessant, 70 mile per hour, nose-to-tail traffic forces me into an exit I don't want. I'm almost in the airport, so I find a place to do a U-turn, pull over and phone Ben for directions. Unfortunately, as the police officer informs me, I have pulled over in a right hand turn lane, so I continue until I am completely lost. This time Ben's directions match the names on the street signs, and I eventually arrive at my destination in a somewhat frazzled state.

California (Part Five)
Friday April 17–Tuesday April 21

I wrote at the beginning of this odyssey about the way in which American place names are evocative of music and film. Now I am in Los Angeles, Hollywood is but a traffic jam away, and the evocative place names come at you thick and fast.

Ben and I spend Friday on and around Venice Beach. We toy with the idea of driving into Hollywood, but the traffic, never easy in this city, is in Friday afternoon mode, so we head back for some down time. The combination of the walk, the sea air and the splendid lunch takes its toll, and I collapse in a gentle heap for a nap.

Just before I arrived here, Ben e-mailed me with a choice of three restaurants for my Friday night farewell treat. Not knowing much about any of them, but knowing I have a predilection for Greek food, I opted for Taverna Tony. This turns out to be in Malibu, and has to be reached by driving up the Pacific coast as the sun sets over the mountains. This is the culinary highlight of the trip to date, and will take some beating.

We drive home with the lights of the coast flickering over us, and don't stay up very long. This is my final night of hospitality, tomorrow I'm back on the road. It sure was the icing on the cake.

On Saturday morning, I take the coast road south. I'm beginning to realise that greater Los Angeles is one big movie location, and I have been tipped off that the oil refinery I duly pass was used to film the science fiction films *Logan's Run* and *Soylent Green*.

The town of Torrance is my first destination, to see the location of the climax of my favourite gangster movie, *White Heat*, made in 1949. From there I drive on to Hawthorne, a working class suburb of LA in which the Beach Boys grew up, for breakfast at a Foster's Freeze which is mentioned in one of their songs.

My third stop is the sports stadium of UCLA. I am here to see a statue of Jackie Robinson, which is inside the stadium. I explain my purpose to the car park attendant, he checks with his boss, and tells me I have to pay $5 to park, as there is a game today. The game starts at 2:00; it is now 12:05. I figure that $5 is a fair price to see the statue, so I give up the argument and pay up. When I get to the stadium the ticket clerks tell me I have to pay another $7 for a game ticket. The statue is visible at the top of the staircase in front of which they are sitting, maybe 15 metres away. I explain how far I have come, what I am doing, but it is no good, so I return to my car. Had it not been for the fact that I have other things planned for today I may have stayed for the game, but $12 for five minutes in front of a statue is silly. I explain to the parking attendant as I leave, and he shakes my hand and returns my $5. I like to think that, had Jackie himself been here, he would have let me in!

I spend the night in a motel in Sylmar, in the shadow of the interstate, and wake at 6:45. The traffic noise is such that I may as well be trying to sleep on the central reservation, so I concede defeat and get up. The early morning sports news is focussing on last night's result from Yankee Stadium, where the Yankees lost to Cleveland. They conceded 14 runs in the second inning, thus equalling a major league record, and the final score was 22–4.

I have selected my Janis Joplin T-shirt for today, as my intention is to visit the hotel where she died, and then eat breakfast at a restaurant she frequented. So at around 9:00 I start to load up the car. Isn't it strange how long it sometimes takes to notice the painfully obvious? As I put my dirty laundry in the appropriate place, my trunk looks unusually grey. It's a grey trunk, so what's the problem? The problem is that it's normally full of a large maroon suitcase, now notable for its absence. Also missing is the broken laptop, although my trainers, fleece jacket and dirty laundry remain. I appear to have been robbed!

Once I manage to close my mouth, I report the loss to the hotel, and the manager arranges to call the police. I return to my room, call home, and appraise the situation. It's not actually as bad as it would seem. The laptop was redundant, I have all the important stuff on a stick at home, and the suitcase contained just clothes, which can largely be replaced. The show can go on. At least I still have my Janis Joplin T-shirt!

The manager calls to say that the police would like me to go to the station, so I drive the couple of miles to Mission Hills police station and wait my turn. I am eventually interviewed by a large, exceedingly bored police officer, who asks why I want to file a report. I explain what has happened, and that I have been asked to come down here, and he asks why I want to file a report. I take this to mean that he isn't going to do anything and that the chance of recovering my property is less than zero. He says I can file a report if I wish, and we agree that if I wish to claim anything on my insurance it might be worthwhile.

So Officer Castellanos, for that is his name, asks several pointless questions, rubs out each answer that doesn't fit neatly into his American form, such as my postcode and, on completion, utters the ubiquitous, "Have a nice day."

"What? You mean starting from now?" I reply, and I could swear I detect a trace of a smile at the corners of his mouth.

I try to piece together the remnants of my day. I decide to postpone the morning visit to Hollywood, and head straight for my afternoon schedule, a minor league game in Rancho Cucamonga. If you have been keeping count, you will realise that I don't need this game to complete my set. But when I read about the place, I couldn't resist. Some of you will be old enough to remember the American comedian Jack Benny. On his old radio show, there was a station announcer who repeatedly referred to the "train now leaving for Anaheim, Azusa and Cu ... camonga." Having been thus put on the map, the township built a statue to Benny, placed it outside the minor league stadium, and named the road after him. It's got to be worth a visit.

When I arrive the temperature is up to 89, the sky is blue with wisps of cloud, and the mountains line the horizon. The stadium is delightful, and surrounded by sports facilities. While waiting for the gates to open, I stand and watch a local softball game. My seat is directly behind the plate and two rows back. I manage seven innings before fleeing into the shade. The game is one for the purists, a pitching duel. The score is 1–0 to the visitors, who have the rather sinister name of the Inland Empire 66ers. Towards the end the hometown Quakes commit several bad errors, and go down, 4–0.

It's good to be back in the minor leagues; the dinosaur mascots, Tremor and Aftershock, cavort and dance the YMCA; little kids race around; the anthem is sung tunelessly by a school choir; the beer is a locally produced microbrew, Ramrod Orange Wheat; all's right with the world.

A text from home asks about my prescription drugs, and I am reminded that there was something more than just clothes in my suitcase. Don't panic, I'm not ill, but I do take a couple of things which make my life more comfortable. One of them I will now be without in four days, so it's something I need to sort.

I find my hotel easily for once, looking forward to relaxing and watching the Cubs on ESPN. It's rained off! It's been that sort of day!

I wake at the usual time on Monday, and look from the window of my room to check that my car is still there. It is, so things haven't got any worse in the night. My first task this morning is to make sure I have the necessary prescription drugs, and it doesn't prove as much of a challenge as I had feared. I call Sallie, and she is pretty sure that Rod, who is a doctor, will be able to help me.

I am on the road by 9:00, and have to deal with the usual freeway chaos for a few miles before turning off onto a more sedate route. My first destination is the leafy suburb of Riverside, and a small wooded area called Low Park. I find it without too much trouble, and stroll around for a while looking for what I am after. In 1914 several members of the Chicago White Sox planted a tree here during spring training, and it still stands, with a plaque to attest to its origins. I find myself wondering whether the famous Joe Jackson was with the Sox by then, and if so whether he was involved in the ceremony.

I move on to Pasadena, and find a parking space easily outside the very elegant city hall building. Opposite is what I have come to see, two huge statues of the heads of Jackie Robinson and his elder brother Mack, who finished second to Jesse Owens in the 1936 Olympics. This monument is very impressive, each head standing nine feet tall — and no one tries to make me pay admission!

Once more to the freeway, and it dawns on me that this is probably my final encounter with the living hell that is LA traffic. It is so hectic and intolerant that a traffic jam comes as a blessed relief. I find my hotel easily, and set off for a nearby Target to restock my wardrobe. Anaheim is the home of Disney, and my hotel is just up the road from Disneyland. The tone of the hotels and restaurants nearby bears this out. Target proves a relative success, and I return to the hotel to blood my new swimming shorts.

I have promised my old mate Sue that I will call her brother during my visit, as he lives locally. I remember Brian from the odd night out in the 70s, and it is a pleasure to hear his voice again. We arrange to meet for lunch tomorrow.

Just as I am finishing dinner Rod phones to put the final touches to my prescription, and the drugs should be waiting for me tomorrow morning at the local Walgreens. That gives a nicely symmetrical conclusion to my day.

Tuesday, my last day in California, is again sunny and warm, and I get up full of good intentions. I go straight to Walgreens, and the pharmacist listens carefully to my request. She checks her fully computerised system which has been completed by Rod's phone call of last evening, and confirms my name, date of birth and home address. Unfortunately the system does not tell her the name of the drug. So, after phone messages to Sallie and calls to Rod's hospital, she eventually manages to speak to Rod and confirm the prescription.

The pharmacist, a charming and helpful young woman who is doing everything within her power to expedite the situation, duly prints out the script, finds a box of the appropriate medication, and checks her catalogue. "Mr. Taylor," she enquires, "Do you have any idea of the cost of this medication?"

"None whatsoever!" I reply innocently.

She looks somewhat embarrassed. "It's 324 dollars and 99 cents!"

"Well, I have to have it, so let's hope the insurance company is sympathetic."

"How much would it cost you at home?" she asks.

"It's a prescription drug," I explain, "About 10 dollars!"

If they raise prescription charges again, think of me before you start whining!

Brian arrives at 2:00 with his partner Lisa, to take me to lunch, and at this point I get my first real exposure to Disney. I am taken to Downtown Disney or, as Brian puts it, "Disney for grown-ups!" It's a large open-air mall full of restaurants, and shops selling the kind of thing they imagine you want to take home from here. We find a restaurant to our taste, and catch up on lost years while ordering lunch.

And so to my real reason for being in Anaheim, a baseball game. I have booked a hotel which I had thought was within walking distance of the ground, but I am advised to the contrary. As it is quite a warm afternoon I don't feel like proving anyone wrong. Anaheim, being really just a suburb of Disneyland, has something called the resort transit, which goes around the city, and which costs only $4. So at 5:00 I buy my ticket, and am told to take a number 6, which goes past my hotel, and change at the park. The number 6 takes me round several hotels before coming to the park, which I now realise is the local term for Disneyland. I could have walked there from my hotel in slightly less time than the bus. I then have to wait 25 minutes for a number 15, which goes to the stadium. The stadium comes into view, and the driver tells me not to get off yet. He circles the park, waiting outside the odd hotel or two, until he eventually deposits me in the car park at around 6:30. I could have driven in about ten minutes. Entry to the car park would have cost $30!!

The club has kindly given me a complementary ticket, which I gratefully collect. The signs to my section keep sending me up and, although I am not one to look a gift horse in the mouth, I start to think they have placed me in one of the cheaper sections. How wrong I am. My seat is next to the press box, one level up, overlooks home plate and has waiter service! It'll have to do, I suppose.

The arena is an attractive one, and the first thing I notice is the retired shirt numbers. Number 26 is retired in honour of Gene Autry, screen cowboy and first owner of the major league Angels. It's unusual to honour an owner in such fashion, but there he is, with a statue at the entrance to ice the cake.

The game is a close one. The leadoff hitter of the visiting Detroit Tigers, Curtis Granderson, starts proceedings with a home run, and the Tigers double their lead in the second. Anaheim pulls one back before Granderson repeats his trick. Again the Angels pull a run back and equalise in the fifth. One of the traits of the Anaheim faithful is that they wave cuddly toys, known as rally monkeys. The scoreboard shows a video of a real monkey performing tricks, and the crowd responds vociferously. A load of nonsense maybe, but immediately the Angels score the winning run, and the monkey goes home feeling, no doubt, fulfilled.

Colorado
Wednesday April 22–Saturday April 25

Denver is my final park of this tour, and it's a long way from Anaheim, so I have allowed three days for the drive. Wednesday takes me 520 miles to Winslow, Arizona, for no better reason than the Eagles wrote a song about it.

On Thursday I move on to Santa Fe. The drive goes well until I pass Albuquerque, at which point my eye starts to hurt and I have to suppress an urge to lie face down. Soon I reach Santa Fe. I was thinking that Joel, who you may remember came to my rescue two years ago, might drive over with his mom for a beer, but I hadn't realised quite how far it was. So we have a good chat on the phone and defer our reunion until they come to England later this year.

I pass a splendid evening in Santa Fe, and would have liked to linger longer, but I have almost 400 miles ahead of me again Friday, so a reasonably early start is called for, and I'm on the road a little after eight o'clock. I eventually cross the border into Colorado. This is the last of the 50 states in which I have set foot, so I am already experiencing a sense of completion. The scenery is rugged and mountainous to start, but soon opens out as I drive the remaining 200 miles.

As I reach Denver, I note a voicemail coming through to my cell phone, so I pull off when I see a Target, to buy some credit so that I can hear the message. I am expecting it to be my host for this evening, but instead am greeted by the voice of John Woolard. John is a radio presenter in Los Angeles, who was given my contact details by Ben's wife Donna, and he wants me to phone him regarding tonight's show.

I find my destination easily, and am reunited with Denise, my host for the next couple of days. We last met at a youth camp in 1975, and have only heard of each other since through a mutual friend. But 34 years simply drop away, and Denise is the same vivacious, chatty person that I remember. We do the catching up and photographs of family bit, and then Denise has to visit a friend, so I take the chance to phone John Woolard. He is very enthusiastic about my trip and wants to interview me on tonight's show. Unfortunately, 11:00 in LA is midnight here, but hey! The price of fame!

We spend a fun evening at a birthday party, where almost everyone is of Greek descent. Arriving home, while my host goes off to bed, I have to hang around for the promised radio interview. The show starts at midnight Mountain Time, and they don't want me to call until ten past. But I manage to keep myself awake, and the host is good to his promise. There are two guys in the studio, so it's more of a conversation than an interview. As well as the usual questions, they ask more fun stuff, like where the best snacks are.

On Saturday, after an excellent morning of book and record shops, we leave to pick up Denise's friend, Alan Gottlieb. He is a huge baseball fan and has written a book about the Colorado Rockies' first-ever season, "In the Shadow of the Rockies." We drive downtown to Denise's husband's office, where he has a parking space which is walking distance from the ground, and I am taken for an early dinner at the Wynkoop brewery, just a couple of blocks from the ground.

It is a short walk to the park, where I collect three complementary tickets.

At this point, I must pay tribute to Scott Donaldson, who is responsible for ticketing at the Rockies. He has now given me tickets three times, been extremely patient when I have twice had to cancel, and even called me to enquire after my health when I had eye surgery in Albuquerque. He wishes me luck on my travels, and we discover that the tickets are on the third base side, only two rows back. As promised, I call Patrick Saunders from the *Denver Post,* and he comes down from the press box to meet me and have a chat. It appears that the story will be in the paper on Monday morning.

The game starts badly for the Rockies, and their starter concedes four runs in the first. The Dodgers' starter lasts a little longer before falling apart, and concedes three in the third, but the Dodgers score two of their own in the fourth. The Rockies immediately pull two back again, but that's the end of the scoring. The night is cold and damp, and there remains only one job to be done. I have read somewhere that the best ballpark snack is to be had here, Rocky Mountain Oysters so, against the advice of my companions, I try some. These are, allegedly, sliced, deep-fried bulls' testicles and are, to be honest, quite palatable if a little bland.

The game ends 6–5 to the visitors, and that's it. As the masked man once said, "My work here is done." Thirty major league ballparks and 50 states. Maybe it took a little longer than it should have, but I've done it. I receive congratulations and handshakes, and head off into the night with a smug grin. Denise's husband, Kevin, is back from investigating colleges with their son, and we meet up with him in yet another brew pub. A couple of glasses of fine barley wine, and we head home.

I pause only to greet son Charlie before retreating to my room, to sleep the sleep of the incredibly self-satisfied.

Conclusion

The trip didn't end there. From Denver I moved on to Dodge City, Wichita, Kansas City (where I saw one final game) and St. Louis, whence I returned to the bosom of my family, but the real journey ended on that cold April night in Denver.

What started as a pipe dream in the Indian restaurant all those years ago has been achieved, and a lot more besides. These days I have to be careful with the wording of my boast. I can't say I have seen a game in every major league ballpark, because the Yankees, the Mets, Washington and Minnesota all have new parks—and more are in the pipeline. So I have to say I have seen each major league team play a home game, and that I have seen a baseball game in each of the 50 states.

The former achievement is commonplace amongst baseball fans; the latter may well be unique, and there is a small part of me that would like the feat to be acknowledged. I remember standing in the Hall of Fame in Cooperstown, reading a section about fans and, if I'm honest, none of their accomplishments was quite as extensive as mine.

But the acknowledgement about which I really care has been received; from those who met me along the way, from those who read my daily e-mails and lived that summer vicariously through me and, above all, from my wonderful family who knew just what it meant and were with me in heart and spirit every mile of the way.

Index